China: Transition to a Market Economy

Studies on Contemporary China

The Contemporary China Institute at the School of Oriental and African Studies (University of London) has, since its establishment in 1968, been an international centre for research and publications on twentieth-century China. *Studies on Contemporary China*, which is sponsored by the Institute, seeks to maintain and extend that tradition by making available the best work of scholars and China specialists throughout the world. It embraces a wide variety of subjects relating to Nationalist and Communist China, including social, political, and economic change, intellectual and cultural developments, foreign relations, and national security.

Volumes in the Series:

Art and Ideology in Revolutionary China, *David Holm*
Demographic Transition in China, *Peng Xizhe*
Economic Trends in Chinese Agriculture, *Y. Y. Kueh and R. F. Ash*
In Praise of Maoist Economic Planning, *Chris Bramall*
Chinese Foreign Policy: Theory and Practice, *edited by Thomas W. Robinson and David Shambaugh*
Economic Reform and State-Owned Enterprises in China 1979–1987, *Donald A. Hay, Derek J. Morris, Guy Liu, and Shujie Yao*
Rural China in Transition, *Samuel P. S. Ho*
Agricultural Instability in China 1931–1990, *Y. Y. Kueh*
Deng Xiaoping: Portrait of a Chinese Statesman, *edited by David Shambaugh*
Propaganda and Culture in Mao's China, *Timothy Cheek*
Greater China: The Next Superpower?, *edited by David Shambaugh*
The Chinese Economy under Deng Xiaoping, *edited by R. F. Ash and Y. Y. Kueh*
China and Japan, *edited by Christopher Howe*
The Individual and the State in China, *edited by Brian Hook*

China

Transition to a Market Economy

JOSEPH C. H. CHAI

CLARENDON PRESS · OXFORD

1997

Oxford University Press, Great Clarendon Street, Oxford OX2 6DP

Oxford New York
Athens Auckland Bangkok Bogota Bombay
Buenos Aires Calcutta Cape Town Dar es Salaam Delhi
Florence Hong Kong Istanbul Karachi
Kuala Lumpur Madras Madrid Melbourne
Mexico City Nairobi Paris Singapore
Taipei Tokyo Toronto
and associated companies in
Berlin Ibadan

Oxford is a trade mark of Oxford University Press

Published in the United States
by Oxford University Press Inc., New York

British Library Cataloguing in Publication Data
Data available

Library of Congress Cataloging in Publication Data
Chai, C. H. China: Transition to a market economy / Joseph C. H. Chai.
—(Studies on contemporary China)
Includes bibliographical references (p.   ) and index.
1. China—Economic policy—1976– 2. China—Economic
conditions—1976– I. Title. II. Series: Studies on contemporary
China (Oxford, England)
HC427.92.C3126 1997 330.951'058—dc20 96–36785
ISBN 0–19–829067–5

1 3 5 7 9 10 8 6 4 2

Typeset by Alliance Phototypesetters
Printed in Great Britain
on acid-free paper by
Biddles Ltd., Guildford & King's Lynn

Acknowledgements

This book is dedicated to Professor Kenneth Walker, without whose encouragement and advice this volume would never have been completed. Kennneth Walker's pioneering work on Chinese agriculture is a major advancement in our knowledge of the Chinese economy. His tragic and premature death took from us a great teacher, an outstanding expert in Chinese agriculture, and a close friend. I am also deeply indebted to Robert Ash not only for his enthusiasm for, and constant encouragement of, this project but also for unknowingly providing inspiration for this book. I also owe Y. Y. Kueh a particular debt of gratitude for his support and valuable feedback on my work over the past few years and for pushing me towards the finishing line. During the production of this manuscript I have been fortunate to receive enormous help from friends and colleagues at the Economics Departments of the University of Hong Kong and the University of Queensland. In particular, I would like to thank Dr. Y. C. Jao and Professor Clem Tisdell who read and commented on parts of the manuscript. I would also like to express my gratitude to the University of Hong Kong and the University and Polytechnics Grants Committee of Hong Kong for the financial assistance received for research on parts of my manuscript. Special thanks are due to the Centre of Asian Studies, University of Hong Kong, *Hong Kong Economic Papers*, and *Communist Economies and Economic Transformation*, who have published earlier versions of some of the research findings and allowed me to make use of them in this volume.

Finally, I gratefully acknowledge the help of my wife, Karin, who typed the manuscript and did endless computing jobs with patience and efficiency. She also provided me with inspiration to persevere under sometimes difficult circumstances and was my best critic.

Contents

List of Tables

List of Figures

Abbreviations

ABC	Agricultural Bank of China
ADB	Agriculture Development Bank
BOC	Bank of China
BOCs	Bank of Communications
CASS	Chinese Academy of Social Sciences
CCP	Chinese Communist Party
CESRRI	China's Economic System Reform Research Institute
CITIB	China International Trust and Investment Bank
CRS	contract responsibility system
EBP	extra-branch production
EC	Economic Commission
EO	export oriented
EXIM	Exports and Imports Bank
FDI	foreign direct investment
FIE	foreign-invested enterprise
FTC	foreign trade corporation
GNP	gross national product
HRS	household responsibility system
IC	industrial corporation
ICA	industrial co-operation agreement
ICBC	Industrial and Commercial Bank of China
IE	individual enterprise
IOCR	incremental output-capital ratio
IRS	intra-enterprise responsibility system
IS	informal sector
JV	joint venture
MNC	multinational corporation
NBFI	non-bank financial institution
NMP	net material product

NRP	nominal rate of protection
PBC	People's Bank of China
PCBC	People's Construction Bank of China
PE	private enterprise
PPP	purchasing power parities
RCC	rural credit co-operative
SDB	State Development Bank
SEC	State Economic Commission
SEZ	Special Economic Zone
SOE	state-owned enterprise
SPC	State Planning Commission
TA	technologically advanced
TE	township enterprise
TFP	total factor productivity
TVE	township and village enterprise
UCC	urban credit co-operative
VAT	value added tax
VE	village enterprise
WOFE	wholly owned foreign enterprise

Throughout the book, $ denotes the US dollar.

1 Introduction

The experiences of the Central and the Eastern European countries show that the costs of transition from a planned to a market economy can be substantial. Most countries undergoing such a transition suffered a sharp drop in output and employment and increased social and political instability in the early phase of their transition (Siebert, 1991: 14–16). Some countries like the former Soviet Union and Czechoslovakia even disintegrated politically under the reform pressures. In contrast, the Chinese transition appears to be relatively smooth. With the exception of the Tiananmen Square tragedy in 1989 China has so far not incurred any serious political or social upheaval. Economically it not only experienced no drop in output and employment during the transition but actually saw an increase in output at an annual average rate of over 9 per cent over the last 15 years. Thus the Chinese reform model is very often considered superior to other transition models and extolled as *the* model for other socialist countries.

This study is a comprehensive assessment of Chinese economic reforms introduced during the last 15 years. Its purpose is to provide a firmer judgement on the key issues of whether the Chinese reform model is superior to those adopted by the Central and Eastern European countries and whether it provides a viable alternative transition strategy for other socialist countries. Specifically, this study addresses the following questions: What has been the progress of the reforms achieved so far in various sectors of the economy? Has China succeeded in establishing a functioning market mechanism in its economy? What has been the impact of the reforms on Chinese economic performance? What lessons can be learned for other socialist countries from the Chinese transition experience?

ORIGINS OF THE REFORMS

Prior to reforms China adopted a centralized planning system with Maoist ideology (Donnithorne, 1967; Howe, 1978; and Dernberger, 1982). The reforms were initiated in 1978. The origin of the reforms can be traced back to the pressures for change which had gradually been building up since 1957. Given the party leaders' emphasis on rapid economic growth and their intent to catch up with the world's most advanced economies as soon as possible, the most important cause of the reforms was the declining rate of growth of the economy since the first Five-Year-Plan period (1953–7). Economic growth in China in terms of net material products in comparable prices had been fairly rapid during the first Five-Year-Plan period, reaching on average almost 9 per cent a year (*ZGTJNJ 1992*: 33). But since 1957, economic growth had slowed down significantly and averaged only about 5 per cent per year during the years 1957–78 (*ZGTJNJ 1992*: 33).

This slowdown in growth seriously eroded the credibility of the Communist government in China. This is because, first of all, it widened the economic distance between China and other neighbouring Chinese societies which had adopted a different political and economic system. While in the 1960s and 1970s real GDP grew at an average annual compounded rate of 10 per cent in Taiwan, Hong Kong, and Singapore the comparable rate of growth in China was only half as high (James *et al.*, 1989: 6). As a result China's per capita income lagged further behind that of the other Chinese societies. In 1960, for example, China's per capita income was $74 which was about half of that of Taiwan and 22 per cent of that of Hong Kong (Garnaut, 1990: 41). At that time all three Chinese societies belonged to the group of low-income countries. Twenty years later in 1980, however, both Taiwan and Hong Kong had advanced to the ranks of the middle income countries with a per capita income of $2,341 and $5,441 respectively whereas China's per capita income was only $249. This was only 10 per cent of that of Taiwan and 5 per cent of that of Hong Kong (Garnaut, 1990: 41).[1]

Furthermore, the slowdown in growth increased the disparity between the living standard of China and those of other Chinese societies. In the 1960s and 1970s the annual average rate of increase of consumption per capita in Taiwan, Hong Kong, and Singapore varied between 6 and 9 per cent (World Bank, 1980: 117) whereas in China the corresponding rate was only 1 to 2 per cent (*ZGTJNJ 1990*: 291–2). Worse still, most of the growth of the consumption standard

---

[1] This comparison is based on exchange-rate-converted GNP. In terms of purchasing power parities (PPP)-adjusted GNP, China's income per capita was much higher at $1,619 (constant 1980 $). But even in terms of PPP-adjusted GNP per capita China was still falling behind Hong Kong and Taiwan in 1980 (Summer and Heston, 1988).

in China in this period was mainly due to the growth of public consumption whereas private consumption per capita actually declined. This is evident from the fall of both the real average wage of workers and the real average income of farmers during this period in China (Liu Guoguang, 1984: 379).

The main cause of China's stagnant consumption standard in the past was the increased inefficiency in the use of resources under the old economic system. An overall indicator of the efficient use of resources in an economy is the total factor productivity (TFP). During the period 1952–7 China experienced an average annual growth of TFP of 3 per cent (T. C. Liu, 1968: 137). Since 1957, however, the growth of TFP has turned negative (Yeh, 1984: 711). With a declining TFP the tempo of economic growth can only be maintained by expanding inputs, such as labour and capital. But since capital can be expanded only at the expense of current consumption and labour at the cost of declining leisure, economic growth in China during this period was sustained mainly at the cost of consumer welfare.

Given the country's emphasis on modernization and its ambition quickly to catch up with the technology of advanced countries, another very important pressure for economic reforms emanated from the worsening technological backwardness of Chinese industry. The technological gap between China and the advanced countries can be closed either by increasing the rate of China's own innovation or by a higher rate of technology transfer from abroad. However, the former was only marginally possible and the latter was limited by China's capacity to import and diffuse the imported technology.

Under the old economic system and trade policy China's capacity to import technology was severely limited. In the 1950s the source of China's imported technology was limited to the former Soviet Union and the Eastern European countries because of the economic boycott of China by the western countries and the subsequent 'lean-to-one-side' foreign trade policy adopted by China at that time. During the 'self-reliance' period in the 1960s and the early 1970s China's capacity to import foreign technology was constrained by its inability to increase its manufactured exports to earn foreign exchange, for under the old economic system enterprises were neither interested in, nor capable of, producing competitive exports for overseas markets because of widespread shortages and the prevalence of a seller's market. Furthermore, under the import substitution trade policy, there was a built-in incentive bias against export production.

China's ability to diffuse imported technology was also severely limited because the old economic system did not offer sufficient price and income incentives to enterprises which successfully adopted new technology. The upshot was that by the late 1970s Chinese industrial technology overall lagged 10 to 20 years behind world levels with a gap of 20 to 40 years in some fields (Ma and Sun, 1981: 617 and Harding, 1987: 33). This was confirmed by the observation of World Bank delegates sent to China in the early 1980s that industrial equipment produced in China tended to be 20 to 30 years out of date (World Bank, 1983: 158).

Another important cause for the reforms was the growing disequilibrium of the economy. Not only was the old economic system incapable of delivering long-term sustained growth but also it was incapable of maintaining an equilibrium in the economy. The use of plans to co-ordinate supply and demand proved to be very costly and ineffective because the cost of information gathering was very high and rose with the growing complexity of the economic structure. The problem was exacerbated by the imbalances generated by the Stalinist growth strategy adopted in the past. This gave preference to the development of heavy industry in general and the machinery industry in particular, to the neglect of agriculture and other complementary industrial branches. The weakness of the Chinese system of planning itself further contributed to the problem.

The Stalinist system of planning adopted by other centrally planned economies tended to give rise to bureaucratism and administrative over-centralization which were in direct contradiction to the Maoist idea of socialism. To counter these problems Mao introduced widespread administrative decentralization within the Chinese planning system. The basic idea was to establish relatively independent localities with discretion to allocate resources and distribute income according to broad criteria enunciated from the centre, but implemented in constant consultation with lower levels (the mass line) (Riskin, 1987: 80–4). Though this idea is commendable, it is difficult to put into practice. The upshot was a severe weakening of Chinese planning capacity to co-ordinate the economic activities.

The growing disequilibrium of the economy manifested itself in increasingly serious shortages of transport facilities, energy, and industrial and construction materials. In the late 1970s it was estimated that one-quarter of China's industrial production potential remained unutilized because of electricity shortages (Ma and Sun, 1981: 31). At the same time the transport system was able to satisfy only 50 to 70 per cent of the country's transportation needs (Xu Feiqing, 1988: 8). Similarly, the supplies of steel, cement, and timber fell short of their respective demand by 60 to 70 per cent in the late 1970s (Kojima, 1988a: 62–3).

Initial attempts to reform the economic system were undertaken in the early 1960s, immediately after the failure of the Great Leap Forward. However, the reform was short-lived and soon suppressed by the Communist Party due to the Maoist emphasis on ideology, on class struggle, and on the building of socialism at that time (Riskin, 1987: ch. 7). Following the death of Mao and the fall of the Gang of Four in 1976 and the subsequent rise of the reformers led by Deng Xiaoping in the party hierarchy, the emphasis shifted away from socialist ideology. Economic modernization was given priority over the building of socialism. Hence the stage was set for a complete overhaul of China's economic system in the late 1970s (Harding, 1987: ch. 3).

CHRONOLOGY OF THE CHINESE REFORMS

Analytically, China's economic reforms can be divided into three stages. In stage one (1979–84) only partial reforms were carried out. Though some aspects of a market mechanism were introduced during this period the planned economy was still considered the 'primary' mechanism which was only in part supplemented by the newly created market. Reforms during this period focused on institutional changes in the agricultural sector which were primarily directed at improving peasant incentives through the decentralization of property rights and the abolition of the commune system as well as the upward adjustment of agricultural purchase prices (Ash, 1993).

Reforms in the urban sector were very modest during this period. Measures taken were confined mainly to the administrative stream-lining of the industrial system and the state enterprise reforms. The latter were experimental in nature, and focused mainly on expanding enterprise autonomy and the restoration of enterprise financial incentives. Externally, the open door policy was initiated during this period with the intention to increase trade and attract foreign investments. But both foreign trade and the foreign investment regime were still heavily regulated.

In stage two (1985–91) the focus of the reforms shifted to the urban sector, and a comprehensive reform programme was launched. The official goal of the reforms in the second stage was to change China's economic system so that resource allocation would be done by markets and the government would exercise control only indirectly through the market. A package of reform measures was introduced simultaneously to establish a functioning market mechanism in cities and the countryside. They included the reduction in the scope of planning, the strengthening of enterprise autonomy and accountability, the liberalization of product and factor prices, the creation of both product and factor markets, and, finally, the further liberalization of foreign economic relations. At the same time, attempts were made to create tools and institutions for indirect macro-economic control through monetary and fiscal policies.

The comprehensive reforms in stage two were, however, briefly interrupted by the austerity programme and the Tiananmen Square tragedy in mid-1989 (Kojima, 1992: 315). The austerity programme was introduced to control the overheating economy. With the phasing out of the austerity programme, the reforms were resumed and continued at full speed in the early 1990s. The pace of the reforms accelerated dramatically after the southern tour of Deng Xiaoping in early 1992 and his subsequent call to open up China further to the West. The reforms entered the third stage in late 1992 when the 14th Party Congress finally cast aside the concept of the planned economy and proclaimed the establishment of a fully fledged market economy in China as the country's reform objective (*CD*, 13 Oct. 1992) the achievement of which is planned for the end of the 1990s (*SCMPIW*, 8–9 Oct. 1994).

MAJOR CHARACTERISTICS OF THE CHINESE REFORM MODEL

The Chinese reform model differs from that of the Central and Eastern European countries in several respects. First, there was no overall reform blueprint from the outset. The process of the reforms was described by Chinese officials as 'crossing the river while groping for the stone' which is similar to the metaphor of Vaclav Klaus, Minister of Finance of the Czech and Slovak Federal Republic, that reform is like playing chess, one needs to know the rules and have a sense of strategy but it is not possible to plan each specific move at the beginning (Klaus, 1990).

Second, China adopted an incremental approach. The reforms were first carried out in the sector where resistance was weakest (Byrd, 1991: 8) and then spread to those sectors where the reform measures were more complex and less popular. Thus economic reforms preceded political reform. Economic reforms in the rural sector preceded those in the urban sector and in the latter enterprise autonomy and incentive reforms were allowed to run ahead of price, ownership, and other market institutional reforms. Reforms were started only after extensive experimentation, and most changes were not introduced at once but slowly over a period of several years.

Third, China adopted a 'two steps forward, one step backward' strategy (Srinivasan, 1990). Reforms were allowed to be halted or even reversed whenever they gave rise to problems. A new wave of reforms, however, more radical than the previous one, was then introduced as soon as the problems were solved. This strategy generated a cyclical pattern of reforms in China (Sung and Chan, 1987: 8 and Harding, 1987: 71–4). Four such cycles can be identified between 1978 and 1992 (Cyril Lin, 1988: 9–12). The first cycle started in 1979 with the introduction of the household responsibility system (HRS) in the rural sector, experimentation with enterprise reform in the urban sector, and the initiation of the open door policy as well as the establishment of four Special Economic Zones (SEZs) in the external sector. The reform was initially so successful that the government decided to accelerate the pace of reforms in 1981 by launching a nationwide campaign urging the compulsory adoption of enterprise reform. However, China incurred a huge budget deficit of 17.1 and 12.8 billion *yuan* and a trade deficit of 2 and 1.9 billion dollars respectively in 1979 and 1980 (*ZGTJNJ 1993*: 215 and 633). At the same time open inflation surged to a record high of 6 per cent in 1980, the highest figure since 1961 (*ZGTJNJ 1993*: 237). The growing economic imbalance during these years was primarily caused by the drastic increase in farm procurement prices (Kueh, 1984). In the wake of the growing economic imbalance the government decided to stage a temporary retreat from the announced reforms with effect from 1981 (Chai, 1981: 50). Thus, the first reform cycle ended with the recentralization of finance and trade control in 1981–2.

After the restoration of both the internal and external balance the second cycle started in 1983, with a move to transplant the responsibility system from the agricultural to the industrial and financial sectors. In addition to the four SEZs, 14 coastal cities were opened to foreign trade and investment in 1984. In 1985 attempts were made to implement the comprehensive urban industrial reforms announced in late 1984. The accelerated pace of the reforms once again threw the Chinese economy into a serious imbalance in 1985. In that year China suffered the greatest trade deficit in its entire history—amounting to almost 15 billion dollars (*ZGTJNJ 1992*: 627). At the same time open inflation jumped to another record high of 9 per cent (*ZGTJNJ 1992*: 237). To restore the balance the government once again was forced to stage a temporary retreat from the reform programme by reasserting centralized control over bank loans, foreign exchange, and investment in 1985–6.

The third cycle began with the 13th Party Congress calling for political reforms and the establishment of a regulated market economy in 1987. In the following year a comprehensive retail price reform was announced and partly implemented. At the same time reform of the ownership of state enterprises was accelerated through the adoption of the contract responsibility system and the leasing of small state enterprises to private individuals. Experiments were also under way to transform large- and medium-sized state enterprises into joint stock companies.

In the external sector another 11 coastal provinces were opened for more foreign trade and investment and the responsibility system was extended to foreign trade enterprises as well. Increased economic liberalization resulted once again, however, in rampant inflation and massive trade deficits. The retail price index increased at a rate of 18 and 19 per cent respectively in 1988 and 1989, the highest in Chinese history. The trade deficit, which had fallen in 1986, also started to climb again in these years. The third cycle ended with the introduction of the three-year austerity programme and the Tiananmen Square tragedy in 1989. In the following three years monetary and fiscal controls were recentralized and the comprehensive price reform programme was shelved.

The fourth cycle began with the resumption of the reform of retail prices and foreign trade at the end of the three-year austerity program in 1991. The pace of the reforms picked up quickly after the southern tour of Deng Xiaoping in early 1992. In late 1992, as mentioned earlier, the 14th Party Congress finally endorsed the creation of a fully fledged market economy as the ultimate goal of the Chinese reforms.

The economy is once again overheated, with GDP growing at a rate of over 10 per cent since 1992, and inflation and the budget deficit hitting a record high. At the time of writing it is still too early to predict when this fourth cycle will end.

Fourth, China adopted the populist approach towards reform. Unlike reforms in other socialist countries those in China were initiated not from above but from below. The central authorities simply accepted what had happened in the provinces and at the local level. Examples of this populist approach abound. In the rural reforms the HRS was first introduced in Anhui and later diffused throughout the rest of China without official sanctioning (Chai, 1985: 76). Similarly, in the urban sector enterprise reform was first introduced in Szechuan and later spread to other provinces without official endorsement (Sung and Chan, 1987: 12). In both instances the reforms were legitimized by the central authorities long after they had been adopted at the local level.

OUTLINE OF THE STUDY

This study begins with an examination in Chapter 2 of the institutional changes in China's agricultural sector. This chapter traces the development of the HRS and analyses its impact on rural property rights arrangements and farm efficiency. This is followed by three chapters examining in some detail the changes in China's industrial system. Chapter 3 analyses the administrative streamlining of China's state industrial system adopted in the early stages of the reforms to reduce bureaucratic waste and improve industrial efficiency. It focuses on the attempts to simplify the industrial hierarchy, to delegate industrial enterprises to key cities, and to promote inter-enterprise lateral linkages in the period from 1979 to 1984.

Chapter 4 assesses the progress made under the reform by industrial enterprises in obtaining decision-making powers. It focuses on enterprises' powers in current input and output decisions as well as investment decisions. Chapter 5 reviews the evolution of China's new industrial incentive system. The discussion centres on the scheme of profit sharing between the state and the enterprise and the changes in incentives for workers and managers. Specifically, it attempts to ascertain how effective the new incentive system is in motivating state enterprise managers and workers to strive for greater industrial efficiency.

In Chapters 6 and 7 the analysis turns to the functional elements of the Chinese economic system, i.e. the price and financial system, the twin pillars of the resource-allocation mechanism in a market economy. Chapter 6 examines China's attempts to liberalize prices. It focuses on three sets of prices, namely industrial ex-factory price, agricultural purchase price, and consumer's retail price. It attempts to determine the progress which has been achieved so far and its major consequences.

Chapter 7 looks at the progress of the financial reforms in China. It focuses on the country's attempts to liberalize its financial system and to create new financial institutions to mobilize savings and increase investment efficiency. It also evaluates China's attempt to create a system of indirect monetary controls to ensure macro-stability. Chapters 8 and 9 look at the open door policy and focus on its two key elements: the liberalization of trade and the creation of an open foreign direct investment regime.

Chapter 10 investigates the progress made in the privatization of China's economy. Specifically it examines the growing importance of non-state enterprises, as well as their relations with and their impact upon state enterprises. Chapter 11 evaluates the results of the reforms in terms of growth, efficiency, stability, equity, and environmental conservation. It aims to ascertain the degree of success of the Chinese reform model and the lessons to be learned for other socialist economies in transition.

2 Institutional Changes in the Agricultural Sector

The discussion in this chapter focuses on the key element in China's agricultural reform, namely the introduction of the household responsibility system (HRS). It begins with a review of the development of the HRS and then turns to changes in (a) property rights arrangements, (b) the commune system, and (c) agricultural planning. The chapter ends with a discussion of the implications of the HRS for Chinese farm efficiency and the role of the new collectives.

EVOLUTION OF THE HRS

Among the various HRSs adopted in Chinese agriculture to improve farm efficiency in the late 1970s the most popular was *baogan daohu* (the system of contracting everything to the household). *Baogan* was first introduced in 1978 in Fengyang county in Anhui, the same province which pioneered the 'responsibility farm' in the early 1960s (*NYJJCK*, 1981, 3: 3). The spread of this new system from 1978 to the first half of 1981 was slow (see Table 2.1). However, it gathered momentum during the second half of 1981. Within less than a year the new system had swept through China's countryside and by June 1982 70 per cent of China's rural communes' basic accounting units reportedly had adopted the new system. Six months later, the new system had probably been adopted by 75 per cent of China's production teams and by the end of 1984 it had been adopted by almost all of them.

Tracing the development of the *baogan* system over time one can hardly fail to observe two distinctive trends. First, the system was apparently developed and diffused at the grass-roots level without official sanction. *Baogan* was introduced at a time when the party centre explicitly prohibited its twin system, *baochan daohu* (the responsibility system of contracting output to the household)—in an official policy document entitled 'Decisions on Some Questions Concerning the Acceleration of Agricultural Development (Draft)', which was adopted at the Third Plenum of the Party's 17th Central

TABLE 2.1. *Development of Various Types of Agricultural Responsibility System, 1980–1984*

Type of responsibility system	Share of commune basic accounting unit (%)						
	1980[a]		1981[a]		1982[b]	1983[c]	1984[c]
	Jan.	Dec.	June	Oct.	June	Feb.	
1. *Bu Lianchan zerenzhi* (resp. not linked to output)							
Dinge baogong (fixed quota labour contract)	55.7	39.0	27.2	16.5	9.0		
2. *Lianchan zeren zhi* (resp. linked to output)							
zhuanye chengbao (specialized task contract)		4.7	7.8	5.9			
baochan daozu (output contract to group)	24.9	23.6	13.8	10.8			
baochan daohu (output contract to household)	1.0	9.9	16.9	10.8	4.0		
baochan daolao (ouput contract to labour)	3.1	8.6	14.4	15.8			
3. *Baogan daohu* (contract everything to household)	0.02	5.0	11.3	38.0	70.0	78.7	99.0
Other incentive systems	15.3	9.2	8.6	2.2	1.0		
TOTAL	100.0	100.0	100.0	100.0	100.0	100.0	100.0

[a] *NYJJ,* 1981, 18: 70 and 1982, 7: 94.
[b] Derived from figures given in *NYJJWT,* 1982, 10: 12 and *JJYJ,* 1982, 12: 11.
[c] *RMRB,* 9 Feb. 1983.
[d] *SYC 1985*: 237.

Committee in December 1978 (Ash, 1993: 15). In the final draft of the 'Decision' adopted by the Fourth Plenum in September 1979, though *baochan daohu* was officially sanctioned for poor, remote, and hilly regions no mention was made of *baogan daohu* (*RMRB,* 6 Oct. 1979). As the responsibility system slowly spread from Fengyang county to other localities in Anhui and from there to other provinces, the party centre finally gave its official approval in a document entitled 'Certain Problems Concerning the Further Strengthening and Improvement of the Responsibility System for Agricultural Production' (also known as Document 75) issued by the Central Committee on 27 September 1980 (Ash, 1993: 16). As in the case of *baochan daohu* it was sanctioned only for poor, remote, and hilly regions as a temporary relief measure rather than as part of the permanent features of the agricultural responsibility system. However, Document 75 apparently failed to check the spontaneous diffusion of the *baogan* system from the poor and backward regions to the relatively rich and advanced regions in 1981. At the end of 1981, the party centre finally lifted all the restrictions on *baogan* and accepted it as a permanent feature of the agricultural responsibility system at an agricultural work conference. A party policy document entitled 'Summary of the National Rural Work Conference' was later issued in April 1982 (*NYJJ*, 1982, 7: 5–12).

Second, the development of the *baogan* system can be seen as an outcome of a movement in search of a better incentive system in the Chinese countryside in the late 1970s. A better incentive scheme is defined here very loosely as one which minimizes risks or uncertainties as well as transaction costs involved in the reward/penalty system (Cheung, 1969: 23–42). As shown in Table 2.1, the movement started with the reintroduction of the piece-rate system in the form of *dinge baogong* on a large scale. By early 1980 it became the major form of China's agricultural incentive system with well over half of the rural basic accounting units adopting the system.

A piece-rate provides a more accurate measurement method of the work-point entitlement of agricultural workers than the old fixed-rate-fixed-assessment method (*sifensiji*) or the fixed-rate-flexible-assessment method (*sifen huoping*) which both tended to award work points on a time basis (*ASDXB*, 1979, 1: 28–9). The piece-rate method which was founded on a complex system of labour norms and remuneration standards for all farm tasks (Crook and Crook, 1976: 264) was difficult to implement and involved a high transaction cost in a country where well over a quarter of farmers were reportedly illiterate and where there was a severe shortage of farm accountants and well-educated team leaders. Hence the search for a more efficient method of work measurement led to the substitution of the piece-rate system by the output and task contract system. Under the output and task contract system known as *lianchan zeren zhi* a task group or a house-hold or a labourer was assigned responsibility for cultivating a fixed area of land or for carrying out a specific farm task. The collective guaranteed them a certain number of work points for completing production and held out the promise that they could retain any output in excess of the production target.

As an incentive system the output and task contract system had two distinctive advantages over the piece-rate system. First, it reduced the transaction cost of the team in monitoring the work performance of its peasants. Second, it allowed the peasant to retain the excess output over the production quota and, hence, it established a more direct link between individual work effort and material reward.

The assignment of the contract in the initial stage of the development of the output and task contract system tended to be based on groups. However, the level of contracting was soon devolved to the lower units, namely the household and individual labour (see Table 2.1) due to the high transaction costs involved. For it proved difficult, if not impossible, to exclude free riders from groups and to design a suitable individual work assessment method which distributed work points and the excess output over the production target awarded to the group among its individual members.

The output and task contract system, though superior to the piece-rate system, had its own limitations. First, much accounting work was needed in formulating contracts and in assessing their fulfilment (*NYJJCK*, 1981, 5: 5). Second, the traditional method of income sharing based essentially on work points remained intact. The defect of the work-point system was that the relation between individual work effort and material reward tended to be rather tenuous and uncertain. One of the reasons for this was that the individual farmer could not retain the additional return to his additional efforts for himself and had to share it with his co-farmers through the work-point allocation. Another reason was that the practice of paying to individuals a share of the collective income partly in cash and partly in kind—with the payment in kind calculated partly according to labour and partly according to the number of people in the farm household—introduced an element of egalitarianism in the income distribution. This made the relationship between individual effort and material reward even more remote (*RMGSSCDCWGL*, 1981, ch. 8). Thus, the continuous search for a better incentive scheme finally led to the abandonment of the work-point system and its substitution by *baogan daohu*.

Under the *baogan* system a fixed amount of land together with farm animals and tools as well as specified quotas and taxes were assigned to the household. Once the specified quotas and taxes had been met, anything left over could be retained by the household itself (Ash, 1993: 16). The *baogan* system is a more efficient incentive system than the former work-point system for two reasons. First, all the transaction costs associated with the work-point measurement were eliminated. Secondly, the household effort-reward function was made more direct and certain as households are now allowed to retain the entire net income for themselves without having to share it with their co-farmers after fulfilment of all the obligatory deliveries to the state and collective as stipulated in the contract.[1]

REDISTRIBUTION OF COLLECTIVE PROPERTIES

The discussion below focuses on the changes in property rights arrangements brought about by the introduction of the *baogan* system in the Chinese countryside. For the purpose of this chapter, property rights are defined as a bundle of rights or a set of relations between people with regard to goods, services, or things (Pryor, 1973: 2). Among the many subcategories of property rights one of the most important is the right to appropriate returns from assets, which is known as income rights. Another important subcategory of property rights is the right to the use of assets, which is known as control rights. Still another important subcategory is the right to transfer all (e.g. sell) or some (e.g. rent) rights in that asset to others, which may conveniently be designated as transfer rights. The focus of the following discussion is on the first two categories of property rights. First, the ways in which such rights were transferred, held on to, or disposed of by the individual household under the *baogan* system are analysed. Second, an attempt is made to find out which subset of income and control rights was transferred to the household and to what extent.

Apart from large items of agricultural machinery, irrigation facilities, and public utilities, land and most of the other fixed capital

---

[1] The discussion here focuses on problems of monitoring work effort in a Chinese collective due to incomplete information and uncertainty. It is not intended to provide a theoretical assessment of the pros and cons of the collective versus the individual household farm. For an excellent exploration of these theoretical issues see Putterman 1985.

assets were transferred to the household in one form or another under the *baogan* system in the early 1980s.

Because of valuation problems it is not possible to arrive at a good estimate of the percentage of total fixed capital assets that was transferred. Land is the largest single item of all the fixed capital assets in agriculture. In 1923–5 Buck found in his survey of 2,866 farms that 75.5 per cent of total farm capital was land (Buck, 1930: 63). A more recent rough estimate by a Chinese economist puts the figure at 86 per cent in 1978 (see Table 2.2).

TABLE 2.2. *Distribution of Rural Productive Assets, 1978 and 1985 (in 100 million* yuan)

Types of assets	1978			1985		
	Collect.	Peasant	Total	Collect.	Peasant	Total
Land	12,000	900.5[a]	12,900.5		20,000[d]	20,000
Fixed capital assets	1,615	neg.[b]	1,615.0	1,146	1,554	2,700
Cash and reserves	56	69.4[c]	125.4	800	1,200	2,000
Others	329		329.0			
TOTAL	14,000 (93.5)	969.9 (6.5)	14,969.9 (100)	1,946 (7.9)	22,754 (92.1)	24,700 (100)

[a] Private plot.
[b] Negligible.
[c] Includes cash per capita of 32.09 *yuan* and grain per capita of 30 kg.
[d] Under contract.

Note: Figures in parentheses are percentage distributions.

Source: GGMLZDCX, 1988: 65–71.

Other fixed capital assets made up another 12 per cent. Since not only was 100 per cent of collective land contracted to households but most of the non-land fixed assets were also transferred to them in one form or another, Chinese farmers by 1985 owned practically 92 per cent of all rural productive assets as indicated in Table 2.2. In contrast they owned only 6.5 per cent in 1978.

Collective properties were transferred to the household through either assignment or exchange. Large pieces of property, such as land, draft animals, and medium-sized agricultural machinery and implements were transferred to the household through assignment. Other properties were transferred simply though exchange, e.g. either sale or rent. According to the policy guideline of the party centre, the mode of assignment of land to the household was partly based on egalitarian principles (i.e. according to the number of people) and partly according to the number of labourers in a household. Thus, if a represents the proportion of total land area Ld distributed according to the population, the total land area assigned to the household, ld, is given by

$$ld = Ld \{a\,(n/N) + (1 - a)\,(l/L)\},$$

where n and N represent the number of people in the household and collective; l and L the number of labourers per household and collective; and n/N and l/L the population and labour share of the individual household. If $a = 1$, then the assignment is egalitarian. If $a = 0$, then the assignment is strictly according to labour. Intermediate values of a represent a mixed system.

The average value of a for the whole country is not known. Government directives tended to play down the value of a. The reason for this was that the government wanted to ensure (a) that land was assigned to those households which had enough labour power to cultivate the land, and (b) that households with surplus labour power had enough land to cultivate. However, in practice there was a tendency to divide the land on an egalitarian basis. This can be seen from Table 2.3. Though these data are neither complete nor representative certain tentative conclusions can nevertheless be drawn from them. First, the value of a never approaches zero. This means that land was never distributed on a pure labour basis. Second, in most cases, the value of a tends to approach unity which suggests that a large proportion of land was distributed on an egalitarian basis.

There are at least two reasons why land in most places tended to be distributed on a per capita basis. First, the attachment to land is deep-rooted in Chinese peasant culture. The introduction of *baogan daohu* was equated with a second land reform by most peasants. Hence, individual households tended to press for an equal share of the land distributed. Some even insisted on having back the same piece of land that they had obtained during the land reform. Second, and most importantly, the scarcity of land tended to increase the value of a. The proportion of land distributed on a per capita basis was mainly aimed at providing sufficient food grain production to satisfy the fixed grain ration for each person in the collective. Given the fixed grain ration per person and grain yield of land, the value of a varies directly with the

TABLE 2.3. *Percentage of Land Distributed According to Population and Land–Man Ratio in Selected Areas, 1979–1982*

Units	Year	No. of teams	Value of '*a*'	Man–Land ratio (*mu*)
Guizhou				
Suiyang County, Shangping Commune, Diba Brigade[a]	1979	1	1.0	
Jiangxi				
Yongxin County, Tailing Commune, Changyuan Brigade[a]	1980	1	1.0	0.71
Hebei				
Shen County, Bingcao Commune, Guozhang Brigade[a]	1980	1	0.7	0.40
Guangdong				
Haifeng County, Chikeng Commune, Jiyu Brigade[a]	1980	10	1.0	0.91
Anhui				
Chuxian Prefecture[a]	1981	24,204	0.6	0.50
Jiangzhuang Brigade[a]	1980	11	1.0	0.83
Quangiao County, Kaji Commune, Kaji Brigade[b]	1979	2	1.0	0.77
Shandong				
Linqing County, Liuhai Zi Commune, Mazhuang Brigade[a]	1981		1.0	0.68
Lu County, Aiguo Brigade[c]	1979	1	0.5	0.66
Henan				
Wuyang County, Xinan Commune, Dongzhuan Brigade[d]		7	1.0	
Gansu				
Weiyuan County, Qijiamiao Commune[e]			1.0	
Guangxi				
Lingui County, Huixian Commune[f]	1981	417	$0 \le a \le 1$	
Hunan				
Huarong County[g]	1981		0.3	0.47
Yunnan				
Simao Prefecture[h]	1980/81		1 in most teams	0.46
Shanxi				
Zhangzhi County[h]	1982	598	1 in some teams $0 < a < 1$ in others	

[a] *NCRMGSSCZRZLB* 1981: 108-39.
[b] *NYJJCK*, 1982, 3: 41.
[c] *NCGZTX*, 1982, 12: 22.
[d] *NYJJ*, 1982, 7: 88.
[e] *NYJJ*, 1981, 11: 112; 1982, 4: 94.
[f] *NYJJCK*, 1981, 6: 20.
[g] *NYJJ*, 1982, 4: 94.
[h] *NYJJ*, 1982, 1: 70 and 85.

man-land ratio.[2] The available data on the man-land ratio presented in Table 2.3 support this hypothesis. They show that the value of a in most cases tends to follow that of the man-land ratio. The correlation coefficient between the two variables for those units, of which the absolute values are known, is 0.57, significant at the 5 per cent level. Since the man-land ratio is known to be relatively high in China's agriculture due to the scarcity of land it can be deduced that a large proportion of land must have been assigned on a per capita basis.

The assignment of draft animals and medium-sized items of agricultural machinery and farm tools to households followed that of land. The method used is known as *zhejia daohu*. It worked in the following way: the total number of draft animals, D, was first assessed in terms of their market value, Pd, to arrive at the total value of draft animals in the collective, PdD. The latter was then divided by the total area of land, Ld, to derive the average value of draft animals per unit of land assigned. The value of the draft animals to which each household was entitled, Qd, then depended on the amount of land it had been assigned, ld. Thus the following formula applies:

$$Qd = (PdD/Ld)\, ld.$$

The household was usually given an option to receive its draft animals either in kind or in money. In the latter case the household used the money to purchase the draft animal from the market. Since most of the land was distributed on an egalitarian basis and the distribution of draft animals, medium-sized items of agricultural machinery, and farm tools was tied to that of land it follows that a large proportion of collective properties was distributed mainly on an egalitarian basis.

Among the assets transferred from the collective to the household the most valuable ones were the household's own human labour and capital which hitherto were considered as collective properties subject to collective deployment. Since human labour is inalienable from its body, individual freedom in the Chinese countryside has been immensely enhanced under the *baogan daohu* system.

---

[2] Let n represent the number of persons in the collective, g/n the per capita grain ration, l_{fd} the land assigned for food grain production, and l_{fd}/g food grain-output ratio, then the proportion of land, ld, required for food grain production is given by

$$(g/n\ n\ l_{fd}/g)/ld,$$

which is equivalent to $g/n\ n/ld\ l_{fd}/g$.

Certain restrictions were placed on the holding and disposing of properties transferred to a household through assignment. First, there was a time limit on holding. Land, for example, was allowed to be held by the household for a specific period of time. Initially it ranged from three to five years. Later on, it was extended to 15 years for most contracts. Second, certain limits were placed on the use of land by a household. For instance, transferred land was to be used for cultivation only. Third, with respect to transferred draft animals, agricultural machinery, and farm tools the household had to maintain their book value if they were diminished by depreciation or other means (*baoben baozhi*). Fourth, the household had to fulfil certain obligatory deliveries stipulated in the contract. Finally, land assigned to a household was not allowed to be sold or rented and, hence, was initially inalienable. Later on, to encourage a more rational distribution of farm lands, the sub-letting of land assigned to a farmer was allowed. All these restrictions, however, were not strictly enforced in practice, as will be discussed later. Consequently, some collective properties transferred to the household through assignment became practically household private property.

REDISTRIBUTION OF INCOME RIGHTS

With the transfer of properties from the collective to the household, part of the right of ownership in the income derived from the properties was also transferred. Hence, a redistribution of income rights occurred in the Chinese countryside under *baogan daohu* among the state, collective, and household. During the first stage of the agricultural reform (1978–84) there was a significant decentralization of income rights in the Chinese countryside. The relative share of the household in net income increased from 81 to 88 per cent, whereas those for the state and collective shrank from 5 and 14 per cent to 4.5 and 7 per cent respectively (*ZGTJNJ 1981*: 196 and *1985*: 290). However, in the second stage of the agricultural reform (since 1985) the trend towards the decentralization of income rights was reversed. Consequently, the relative share of the household in net income fell again from 88 per cent in 1984 to 81 per cent in 1992, whereas the shares of the state and the collective rose again to 7 and 11 per cent respectively (*ZGTJNJ 1993*: 394).

To reveal the underlying source of change of the relative share of the household in rural net income derived from agricultural production under *baogan daohu* the latter can be decomposed as follows: net income, P, is defined as gross revenues, Y, minus cost, C, e.g.

$$P = Y - C.$$

The net income to which the household is entitled, Ph, can be expressed as

$$P_h = Y - C - T - R,$$

where T is the direct agricultural tax and R the reduction for collective accumulation and consumption. The share of household in net income, Yh, is then calculated as follows:

$$Yh = 1 - tYb/(Y - C) - r\,Yb/(Y - C)$$
$$= 1 - Ys - Yc,$$

where t is the rate of agricultural tax, r the rate of deduction for collective accumulation and consumption, and Yb the benchmark gross revenues which are usually determined on the basis of average output over the past three years plus a normal rate of growth ($NYSCZRZZXBF$, 1981: 22). Yb serves as the base for the calculation of agricultural tax and collective levies due for each household according to the amount of land contracted. Once fixed, the tax and collective levies remain unchanged for a period of time, usually for three years ($NYJJ$, 1982, 7: 88). Ys and Yc are the respective shares of the state and the collective in net income which are in fact the actual rates of agricultural tax and collective levies on the farm net income. Both Ys and Yc vary directly with the stipulated tax and deduction rate t and r and inversely with actual output and productivity.

In view of the above analysis, the decentralization of income rights during the first stage of the reform is attributable, in part, to two factors. First, since the commune was dismantled but no new collective had been established to replace it completely r was either reduced or abolished—with or without the consent of the higher authority. A sample survey of 100 villages throughout the whole country carried out by 155 agricultural economics students at the University of Beijing under contract from China's Rural Development Research Centre in the spring of 1982 reveals that in 55 per cent of the 100 villages surveyed the deduction for collective consumption and accumulation had either been slashed or become virtually non-existent (*NYJJCK*, 1982, 4: 4). Second, in the first stage of the reform there was a strong, positive response on the part of the farmers to the new incentive scheme which caused a huge increase in both farm output and productivity. Thus, for instance, a survey of 10,543 households in Anhui reveals that from 1976 to 1981 both land productivity and labour productivity had jumped by 225 and 172 per cent respectively (*NYJJ*, 1982, 2: 139).

The recentralization of income rights since 1985 can be partly explained by the reconstruction of communes into new collectives which not only resumed the collective consumption and accumulation functions but also reasserted their income rights through increased efforts to collect the collective dues from farmers. Furthermore, a significant shift in the composition of rural income occurred after 1985. Hitherto the main component of rural income had been income derived from the household farm. Since 1985, there was a tremendous surge in the output of rural collective enterprises, namely, the township and village enterprises (TVEs), and by 1988 the non-agricultural component of the rural output exceeded its agricultural counterpart for the first time. Consequently, the share of TVEs in total rural gross income jumped from 26 to 45 per cent between 1984 and 1992 (*SYC 1986*: 183 and *ZGTJNJ 1993*: 394). The method of distributing the income of TVEs differed significantly from that of the household farm. A significant proportion of TVEs' net income was deducted for state taxes and collective reserves. Thus, for example, in 1992, state taxes and collective reserves accounted for 19 and 31 per cent of the TVEs' net income respectively and only 49 per cent of the latter was distributed as personal earnings (*ZGTJNJ 1993*: 394).

Finally, farm household income was also hit by additional taxes and levies, some of them illegal, imposed by the local authorities to raise funds for building schools, roads, and other facilities.

REDISTRIBUTION OF CONTROL RIGHTS

The transfer of properties from the collective to the individual household not only meant a shift in income but also involved a transfer of control rights of properties. The following analysis tries to assess the impact of the redistribution of the control rights or decision-making power between households and collective under the *baogan daohu* system. It focuses on two major categories of decisions, namely those relating to current input and output. For decision-making power concerning both, it is important to know, first of all, to what extent the previous system of production planning survived. Under the previous system the farmer's decision-making power was severely limited by the mandatory targets issued by the government which determined the areas sown, yields, levels of input application, planting techniques, and so forth.

Available information indicates that initially the formal system of production planning remained intact and that output of major crops and the area of their cultivation were both specified in the contract in accordance with the state plan. Hence, farmers' output decisions were still limited and they only had freedom to decide on the output of minor crops and on crop rotation. However, in the early 1980s the scope of production planning was considerably reduced (Sicular, 1988: 677). The number of farm products subject to production planning was reduced from 21 before 1978 to 16 in 1981 and again to 13 in 1982. Similarly, the number of production targets issued was reduced from 31 before 1978 to 20 in 1981. By 1985, farmers' autonomy in output decisions appeared to have reached its peak as the central government announced the abolition of mandatory production planning for the agricultural sector.

Since the late 1980s, however, the poor performance of agricultural output in general and of staple crops in particular prompted the government to step up its control on farming once again. Thus, while mandatory production planning was not revived, administrative interventions in farm decisions by local governments increased (Sicular, 1988: 679).

Secondly, it is also important to know to what extent the previous system of compulsory procurement and central rationing of basic agricultural inputs survived. For these were in the past the main tools for the implementation of agricultural planning in China. On the output side, the procurement scheme limited the choice of farmers in the marketing of their products and the rationing of basic agricultural inputs limited the farmers' choice in the application of inputs.

Available information indicates that the system of procurement and central rationing of basic agricultural inputs continued initially. A procurement quota was assigned to the household under the *baogan daohu* system in accordance with the amount of land allocated. Basic inputs, such as fertilizer, seeds, and insecticides which the team received at subsidized prices from the authorities, were distributed in accordance with the area of land contracted to individual farm households. Hence, farmers' input and output decisions were limited.

However, from the early 1980s the scope of compulsory procurement and the central rationing of agricultural inputs were significantly reduced. For not only were the compulsory procurement quota levels for some products lowered but the number of products regulated by quota was also reduced from 43 to 18 in 1983 and again to 9 in 1984 (Kojima, 1988b: 721). In 1985 the government abolished the compulsory procurement system entirely. In its place a two-track system, a combination of contract and market purchase, was introduced. Under the contract-purchase system farmers signed an agreement with the state before the sowing season which obliged them to sell a proportion of their output to the state at a state-fixed contract price. Farmers were allowed to sell the remainder of their output on the market at market prices. Since the contract sale was supposed to be voluntary the farmers' marketing decisions were in theory significantly enhanced. With the end of the compulsory quota there was no longer any necessity for central rationing of farm inputs. In its place a two-track input supply system was installed under which a part of the inputs was still allocated at planned prices to those farmers who had signed a contract-purchase agreement with the state. But an increased proportion of agricultural inputs was only available through the market at higher market prices.

In the late 1980s, in response to the slowdown in agricultural production and subsequent difficulties for the government in ensuring contract-purchase fulfilment, the voluntary element in the contract procurement system was eliminated (Sicular, 1988: 700). At the same time, the two-track input-supply system caused a sharp increase in farm input prices. This occurred because the coexistence of two prices for a single product, of which the market price was significantly higher than the state-subsidized planned price, inadvertently created a potential non-exclusive rental income for the suppliers of farm inputs. Consequently, attempts on the part of the latter illegally to divert inputs destined for planned sale to market sale at the higher price were so widespread that most of the scarce farm inputs ended up being sold at the market price. As prices for farm inputs skyrocketed, the government was once again forced to reintroduce the state monopoly of basic farm input supply—which it did with effect from January 1989 (CP, 1989, 5: 40–2).

In the early 1990s, with the resumption of the market-oriented reforms, the scope of the compulsory element in the contract procurement system was significantly reduced and the state monopoly supply of basic farm inputs was lifted (*ZGJJTZGGNJ 1993*: 425 and 431). But the market prices of major agricultural inputs were still capped in 1993 (*CP*, 1993, 4: 43–5).

Last, it is also important to know whether the previous system of 'unified' management of farm work by the collective remained intact since a greater degree of 'unified' management of farm work by the collective allows less room for discretionary power on the part of the individual farmer. *Baogan* was initially designed to optimize not only incentives but also decentralization in the organization of farm work. The ideal arrangement is known as the two-tier responsibility system which was seen as combining 'unified' management with decentralization of farm work. All farm work involving economies of scale and externalities, such as irrigation, plant disease control, mechanized ploughing and sowing, the procurement of farm inputs, the marketing of farm outputs, and so forth was seen as requiring the 'unified' management system. The organization of all other farm work was to be decentralized to individual households. The implementation of *baogan* occurred simultaneously with institutional changes which saw the old communes replaced by newly established township- and village-governments. Since the latter were not immediately fully operational they were not able to take over the economic functions of the former communes and, hence, a 'unified' management of farm work was largely absent. For example, the 1982 sample survey of 100 villages in China mentioned earlier reveals that 80 per cent of the *baogan* contracts were without 'unified' management and only 20 per cent were under some form of 'unified' management (*NYJJCK*, 1982, 4: 18).

Later on, even though new collective institutions were established few of them were actually able to maintain a 'unified' management because they lacked finance (*GGMLZDCX*, 1988: 138). And in those few collectives which still implemented a 'unified' management approach its scope was severely reduced. A national sample survey of 1,200 villages by the Economic Policy Research Centre of China's Ministry of Agriculture in 1988 reveals that 'unified' management centred mainly on the following activities: mechanized ploughing, irrigation, and the procurement of basic agricultural inputs (*ZGNCZCYJBWL*, 1989: 280). In 1984, on average only 42 per cent of these activities were 'unified' across the nation. There were, of course, regional differences, with the more developed eastern regions showing a higher degree of 'unified' management than the less developed western regions of China. Furthermore, the survey showed that there was a general decline in the degree of 'unified' management between 1984 and 1987. However, in the late 1980s, in order to arrest the stagnant trend of agricultural output growth the authorities increasingly promoted the use of 'unified' management as a means to safeguard economies of scale. As a result, the degree of 'unified' management rose; and by 1990 50 per cent of mechanized ploughing, irrigation, procurement of farm inputs, and veterinary services were reportedly carried out by the new collectives (*ZGNYNJ 1992*: 99).

In summary, individual farm households gained increased control rights under the *baogan* system. The decentralization of control rights reached its climax in the mid-1980s with the abolition of mandatory production planning and the compulsory procurement system. However, the trend was reversed, towards more centralization, in the second half of the 1980s due to the combined effects of the slowdown in agricultural output and the government's growing loss of control over farm decisions. There was again an increase in administrative intervention by the local government in farmers' output decisions, and the government promoted the use of the 'unified' management approach to farm work by the new collectives.

EFFICIENCY IMPLICATIONS

The efficiency implications of the *baogan* system are mixed. On the one hand, both X- and allocative efficiency were significantly enhanced. X-efficiency increased under the *baogan* system because, as has been mentioned, the household effort-reward function was made more direct and certain as farmers were allowed to retain the entire output for themselves without having to share it with their co-farmers. Another factor which contributed to its rise was the decentralization of income rights under the *baogan* system. The assignment of income rights of collective assets to individual households made the latter more responsible for the profit and loss of those assets. It forced them to maximize their value, as non-maximal loss implies bearing a cost (Hall, 1984: 168). Allocative efficiency was also significantly enhanced as farmers gained increased control rights, over both the farm land and their labour, and were able to deploy them according to the principle of comparative advantage.

On the other hand, the egalitarian way of distributing farm land under the *baogan* system had serious repercussions for allocative efficiency. As mentioned earlier, to ensure that individual households could grow enough grain to satisfy their own needs, farm land was generally assigned to households according to the number of persons per household. Since households differ in terms of labour endowments, an equal man-land ratio implies inequality in the land-labour ratio across households. Some households found themselves short of labour whereas others were short of land. The upshot was a disparity in marginal products of land and labour across households and, hence, the violation of one of the marginal conditions of static efficiency of allocation of resources (Justin Lin, 1987: 3).

The egalitarian distribution of farm land also had serious implications for scale economies. Under the *baogan* system, farm land was distributed equally in terms of not only quantity but also quality. This was first achieved by grading the collective farm land according to its quality and then each person was allocated a piece of land from each grade. Consequently, as a national sample survey reveals, the scale of farm land averaged only 0.6 hectare per household in 1986 and the 0.6 hectare of land was on average fragmented into nine pieces (*ZGNYNJ 1988*: 89).

To counteract the irrational distribution of land and the limited scale economy, the government was subsequently forced to allow the sub-leasing of farm land among households. It opened a market for land-usage rights in the hope that this would lead to a concentration of farm land in the hands of specialized farmers (*zhuanye hu*). However, so far this policy has achieved very little in expanding the scale of farming. The limited market transaction of land-usage rights was mainly due to the lack of both demand and supply (*NCJJGGYFZ*, 1988: 185 and 193). On the supply side, though increased numbers of farmers found more profitable employment in rural industrial enterprises or moved to the cities, they were reluctant to part with their contracted land. Those who were working in rural industrial enterprises preferred to keep it as a kind of insurance for they did not regard employment in rural industrial enterprises as a stable source of income and employment. Those who moved to the cities were not acknowledged by urban authorities as permanent residents under the household registration system. Thus, to play safe they held on to their contracted land at home (*CD*, 17 May 1994). On the demand side, few farmers were willing to engage in large-scale specialized agricultural production because of (a) the relatively low prices and, hence, the low profitability of agricultural products compared to non-agricultural ones, and (b) the higher obligatory sales quota at the relatively lower state-fixed contract price imposed upon specialized farmers as compared to the non-specialized ones.

On balance, the net efficiency effect of HRS was positive. This is confirmed by a recent estimate of Chinese agricultural total factor productivity which shows that it grew at 6 and 3 per cent on average annually during the first and second stages of the reforms and accounted for most of the agricultural growth during these periods (Jefferson, Rawski, and Zheng, 1992).

However, *baogan* appears to have adversely affected the rate of investment in China's agriculture. With the transfer of income rights from the collective to individual households there was a shift of responsibility for saving from the government to farmers (Reynolds, 1989). Initially, the farmers' rate of saving rose but it declined significantly in stage two of the reforms (see Table 7.7).

More importantly, the incentive to invest in 'productive' investment was even weaker as most savings were spent in the construction of housing and the purchase of durable consumer goods (Walker, 1984: 800). The lack of incentive for farmers to invest in agriculture was at least partly due to the incomplete nature of property rights in land. Because farmers were not confident that they could keep their land even over the 15-year lease period, they were reluctant to invest in it (Perkins, 1994: 297).

Last the dismantling of the commune system made the mobilization of surplus labour for the construction of rural infrastructure, such as irrigation systems and water conservancy work, and farm land improvement increasingly difficult (Ash, 1992: 546 and Kueh, 1984). The incentive to maintain irrigation facilities as well as agricultural extension services was also weakened.

THE ROLE OF THE NEW COLLECTIVES

In the present context, the word collectives refers to collective entities set up at the village level to take over some of the economic functions of the former production brigades and teams. The names of those collective entities vary. In some localities they are known as agricultural co-operative associations or economic co-operatives, in other places they are called agricultural, industrial, and commercial complexes. And in still others the old names, production brigade and team, are simply retained.

With the introduction of the HRS the individual household became the rural basic economic unit. Both the economic functions of the commune and the justification for the commune's existence were drastically reduced. The reform of the communes began in 1982 and was completed in 1985 (Ash, 1993: 20). The commune was split into three entities, namely the township or town government, the party committee, and the collective. The town government was supposed to take over the government and the township party committee and the collective were to take over the party and the economic functions of the former commune respectively. By 1989 only about 40 per cent of townships had set up township collectives.

At the village level production brigades and teams were transformed into villagers' committees and small groups which took over the government functions of the former brigades and teams. The economic functions of the former brigades and teams were taken over by the village collectives. By 1991 about 1.8 million village collectives had been set up, comprising about 85 per cent of the former production teams (ZGNYNJ 1992: 100). However, most of these village collectives were housed in the same office as the villagers' committee or the small group. Only 10 per cent of the village collectives in 1987 had their own offices.

The economic functions of the new collectives are fourfold (Min and Li, 1988: 45–6). First, it is a provider of public utilities and agricultural production services. This includes mechanized ploughing, sowing, irrigation, plant protection, harvesting, procurement of basic agricultural inputs and marketing of agricultural outputs, technical training and consultancy, etc. Second, it performs a planning and control function. It organizes 'unified' management of certain agricultural work which can best be performed by the collective because of economies of scale and externality. It also serves as an agent of the government in issuing guidance on plan output and procurement targets to individual households.

Third, it manages the collective properties. Since most of these properties were contracted to individual households its main management function is centred on the formulation, monitoring, and enforcement of the contract so as to safeguard the property rights of the collective. Fourth, it also serves as a channel for the transfer of income. It channels part of the collective's dues from farmers to provide social welfare services, such as old age pensions, education, medical care, funeral expenses, subsidies, etc. for the agricultural households. It also uses tax revenues collected from rural industrial enterprises to subsidize agricultural production.

Finally, it also resumes its accumulation function. In 1988, in response to the lack of maintenance of irrigation facilities and a decline in the effective irrigated acreage under the *baogan* system, the labour accumulation system was reintroduced. In this system each farm worker is required to contribute 10 to 20 labour days each year to the collective for irrigation construction and maintenance (*ZGNYNJ 1989*: 569). Farm workers unable to contribute labour are allowed to contribute cash instead. Again, in 1989, in response to a lack of private productive investment in the agricultural sector, an agricultural development fund was set up at both the central and local government levels. At township and village levels the fund is mainly fed from obligatory contributions from rural collectives and enterprises and from part of the collective dues from farmers under the *baogan* system. The agricultural development fund is intended to be used for the development of the agricultural infrastructure, such as irrigation projects, land improvement, procurement of agricultural machinery, and strengthening of agricultural extension services (*ZGNYNJ 1990*: 143–5).

To what extent the new collectives are able to perform their functions well hinges on the financial strength of the collectives. As the survey of the Ministry of Agriculture, mentioned earlier, reveals, despite the re-establishment of the collectives, the percentage of collectives providing effective services and exercising 'unified' management declined between 1980 and 1987 (*ZGNCZCYJBWL*, 1989: 278). The major reason for this was not lack of demand for these services. On the contrary, the survey found that demand exceeded supply. The decline was apparently mainly the result of financial difficulties. The funding of collectives comes predominantly from two sources: (a) the collective dues from farmers under the *baogan* system and (b) the share of profits of rural enterprises. In the least industrialized regions the income from collective dues from farmers was only sufficient to finance public utilities and general administrative expenses. Only in the more industrialized regions, where the collectives own a significant number of rural industrial enterprises, were collectives able to obtain sufficient revenues under the scheme of 'using industry to subsidize agriculture'. These funds were used to finance social welfare and to subsidize unified cultivation activities such as mechanized ploughing, irrigation, and plant protection. This explains why collectives in the eastern region were able to maintain their 'unified' management function better than those in the western region. The reintroduction of the labour accumulation scheme and the establishment of an agricultural development fund, as well as the increased share of collectives in rural income in the late 1980s, further enhanced the financial strength of the collectives. By 1991 it was reported that the percentage share of rich collectives had risen to 60 per cent (*ZGNYNJ 1992*: 102).

Looking into the future, it is expected that the new collectives will play an increasingly important role in agricultural production in China. This, of course, does not mean a return to the former socialist collective system. The future Chinese agrarian system is set to look increasingly similar to that of Japan (Kojima, 1988*b*: 725). While private ownership of land-usage rights is likely to remain intact and individual farmers will continue to be responsible for the direct production process of agriculture the new collectives, like their Japanese counterparts, are likely to maintain control over farmers in respect of other aspects of the agricultural production process, such as the forward and backward linkages and finance. Since the new collectives are likely to retain control over a significant portion of income and control rights, property rights in the future rural China are likely to remain more attenuated and less well defined than in other comparable countries.

3 Changes in the Industrial System I: Administrative Reforms and Industrial Reorganization

Early attempts to reform the Chinese industrial system centred on administrative streamlining and industrial reorganization. The measures introduced included simplification of the industrial hierarchy, the delegation of industrial enterprises to key cities, and the promotion of inter-enterprise lateral linkages. Most of these reforms were implemented in the period from 1981 to 1985 (Xie and Luo, 1990: 218). This chapter examines the pressures that brought about these changes and analyses the nature, limit, and impact of these changes.

THE PRE-REFORM INDUSTRIAL HIERARCHY

The Chinese state industrial hierarchy on the eve of the reforms suffered from two major deficiencies. One was that enterprises were subordinated to too many administrative superiors. By the late 1970s China's state-owned industrial enterprises were placed under three systems of control: central, dual, and local (Ma, 1982: 158–9). Large and strategic enterprises were subject to the control of the central authorities. The number of centrally controlled enterprises fluctuated between 1,200 and 10,000 in the past (Liu Guoguang, 1980: 21–5). In 1978 their number was less than 2,000 or about 2 per cent of all state-owned industrial enterprises (*ZGTJNJ, 1983*: 213). Small and medium-sized enterprises of local significance were placed under the control of local authorities. Enterprises falling between these two categories were placed under dual control by both central and local authorities. Enterprises under dual control were further divided into two groups, namely the predominantly (a) centrally controlled enterprises, and (b) locally controlled enterprises.

Table 3.1 analyses the distribution of control rights over enterprise current input and output choices and investment decisions by the central and local authorities. It shows that the predominantly centrally controlled enterprises were mainly confined to the electricity generating industry whereas the predominantly locally controlled enterprises were mostly in light industry and textiles. Enterprises in metallurgy, electronics, machinery, coal, petroleum, and chemicals were subject to dual control. Table 3.1 also shows that the central authority was able to exert its authority over all enterprises as it controlled the allocation of their most important inputs, namely materials and investment capital.

TABLE 3.1. *Distribution of Control Rights over Current Input and Output Choices and Investment Decisions in China's Pre-Reform State Industrial System*

Industrial branches			Inputs		
	Output	Personnel	Working capital	Material	Investment
Metallurgy	L/M	L/M	L/M	M	M
Electric power	M	M	M	M	M
Coal	L/M	L/M	L/M	M	M
Petroleum	L/M	L/M	L/M	M	M
Chemicals	L/M	L/M	L/M	M	M
Machinery	L/M	L/M	L/M	M	M
Light industry	L	L	L	M	M
Textiles	L	L	L	M	M

Note: L and M denote local authority and ministry respectively.
Source: *GYJJ*, 1985, 3: 35.

Regardless of the systems of control, the structure of authority within each channel of command consisted of four levels. At the apex of the central hierarchy were the top economic organs which included the State Planning Commission (SPC), the State Economic Commission (SEC), and the functional bureaux of the State Council (Ma, 1982: 332). The SPC was primarily responsible for the drafting of both the short-term and long-term national plan, whereas the SEC's major task was to execute the plan as well as to co-ordinate the activities of the various ministries and regional authorities. The functional bureaux of the State Council, such as the State Price Bureau, the State Material Bureau, the Ministry of Labour and Personnel Affairs etc., were responsible for the co-ordination of activities in their more specialized areas (Ma, 1982: 332). Below the top economic organs were the ministries which were in charge of the administration of a branch of industry. Each industrial ministry had a subordinated industrial department or bureau, each of which in turn controlled a group of enterprises (World Bank, 1983, II: 133–4). The four-level organizational hierarchy was mirrored on a smaller scale at the level of the local authorities. Each local authority had its own planning and economic commission, functional bureaux, industrial bureaux, or general corporations, each in charge of a special branch of industry. Each local industrial bureau or general corporation often had its own specialized corporations in charge of a group of enterprises (*GYJJGLCK*, 1983, 4: 11). In some localities there were no specialized corporations and the organization was only three-tiered, with planning and economic commissions and functional bureaux at the top, industrial bureaux in the middle, and enterprises at the bottom (*GYJJGLCK*, 1983, 4: 11).

To add to the complexity of China's industrial hierarchy, an enterprise was very often subject to not only one but many immediate superiors. It often received targets not only from its parent bureau, that is, the respective industrial bureau or corporation, but also from specialized supporting functional bureaux, for example the finance bureau in charge of the finance of a group of enterprises. Enterprise initiatives in almost all areas often had to be cleared by both the industrial bureaux and the specialized functional bureaux.

With so many administrative superiors at both the intermediate and the highest level above the enterprise the line of command became blurred and problems of inconsistency, inflexibility, and evasion of responsibility in decision making appeared. Problems of inconsistency arose when input and output targets issued by various superior organs were not well co-ordinated before they were sent down to the enterprise.

Because of the highly hierarchical structure and parallel jurisdiction decision-making was often slow and inflexible. Enterprises were inhibited from responding quickly to changing market and technological conditions. Thus, for example, in 1978, Sichuan Chengdu Measuring and Cutting Tool Plant, then desperately in need of a special machine tool, went through more than 10 administrative bureaux with its request and wasted two years to no avail (Liu Guoguang, 1980: 59).

The steep hierarchy and parallel jurisdiction also led to the evasion of responsibility on the part of bureaucrats. Since decision making was preceded by a multi-stage itinerary process and needed clearance from various administrative bureaux too many organizations and persons were involved, and nobody was held accountable or responsible. If a wrong decision had been made individual bureaucrats and offices could easily evade responsibility by claiming that they were forced to compromise with other participants in the decision-making process.

Another major deficiency of China's industrial administrative structure on the eve of the economic reforms was the lack of co-operation and specialization between enterprises. The partitioning of enterprises and their subordination to different administrative units implied a transfer of parts of the property rights over the enterprises from the state to the supervising administrative units (Granick, 1990). Each of them acquired a part of the control rights over the enterprise by participating in its decision making. Each of them also acquired a part of the income rights over the enterprise as they shared in the revenues generated by the enterprise. Hence, each administrative unit tended to regard the enterprise under its authority as its own property. A favourable environment for the breeding of departmentalism, localism, and autarky was thus created.

Departmentalism or localism manifested itself in dysfunctional behaviour on the part of the administrative units which aimed at maximizing their own group interests at the expense of social interests. Thus, for example, to ensure the material supply of its own subordinate enterprises an administrative unit instructed its material-producing enterprise to transport its material to its own material-using enterprises several hundred kilometres away instead of shipping them to an enterprise under a different authority next door. Similarly, to protect the market of its own enterprises the supervising organ barred enterprises from other localities or administrative units from selling their products within its sphere of influence.

Autarky resulted from departmentalism or localism in combination with taut planning. Ambitious targets coupled with the shortage of materials and fuel made it risky for an organization to rely on external sources of supply and compelled administrative organs to aim for maximum self-sufficiency. It was also a result of the weakness of Chinese central planning which, as mentioned earlier, was under constant attacks by Maoist ideologists. Autarky resulted in duplicate investment and production. Thus, for example, 80 per cent of the 6,057 engineering factories in 1978 produced their own iron castings (Ma, 1982: 231). Most of the output was produced in small, inefficient shops in gross violation of the principle of comparative advantage and economies of scale. Similarly, in 1978 cars were produced by 130 factories under seven ministries and 26 provincial and municipal authorities (Ma and Sun, 1981: 709). Most of these factories produced them for use by their own administrative units. Thus, in terms of the number of car factories China ranked first in the world (Liu Guoguang, 1980: 3) yet the majority of factories had an annual output of several hundred cars only (Ji, 1980: 46). The deleterious effect of autarky on allocative efficiency is most evident in the comparative labour productivity of the most efficient bicycle plant in Shanghai which was more than five times that of the least efficient plant in Kunming (*RMRB*, 31 July 1983).

SIMPLIFICATION OF THE INDUSTRIAL HIERARCHY

In order to cut administrative costs and to accommodate the increased liberalization and marketization of the economy attempts were made in the early 1980s to simplify the industrial hierarchy through: (1) the reduction of the number of units at the bottom of the industrial hierarchy; (2) the formation of branch associations; (3) the reduction of the number of levels in the hierarchy; and (4) the transfer of the function of detailed supervision of enterprises from the top government economic organs to the branch administration. In the following sections the experience of implementation of these reform measures is briefly discussed.

Enterprise consolidation

Merging industrial enterprises into industrial corporations (ICs), where the component enterprises lose all autonomy and operate only as a part of the ICs, was designed to achieve two objectives simultaneously: (a) to minimize the number of units at the bottom of the industrial hierarchy which the top economic organs had to deal with, and (b) to increase the size of production enterprises in order to achieve economies of scale. Originally, it was envisaged that ICs would become the basic unit of the industrial hierarchy (Ma, 1982: 231).

The development of ICs was rather uneven. The number of ICs rose from 1,600 in 1979 to 2,300 in 1981, with 22,700 component enterprises (*GYJJ*, 1982, 2: 65). These accounted for about one-quarter of China's state-owned industrial enterprises. Since 1981, the merger movement has entered a consolidation phase which saw the number of ICs reduced to around 2,000 in 1984 (*GYJJ*, 1985, 7: 52). During the years 1984–6 existing ICs were further consolidated (*GYJJ*, 1987, 1: 91). Some ICs were abolished, others were re-formed into super-enterprises and still others were reduced to the status of an association of independent enterprises. The last group assumed different institutional forms, such as branch associations, economic unions, enterprise groups, etc.

An analysis of the ICs formed at the peak of the movement in 1981 reveals that the average IC contained about 10 enterprises. Most of them were regional or local ICs, that is, they included enterprises within the same region or locality. The number of nationwide ICs was small; there were only about 15 at the end of 1981 (Ma, 1982: 232). Most of the ICs were horizontally structured, that is, they combined enterprises producing the same goods. But some were vertically structured, that is, they combined enterprises which produced inputs for each other. Finally, many ICs were integrated only formally. Out of the 2,300 ICs established by the end of 1981, only 236, that is less than 10 per cent of the total, were business ICs whereas the rest were administrative ICs.

Administrative ICs were simply administrative units of the government. They had neither an independent accounting system nor independent managerial authority over the planning and management of the component enterprises. Their member enterprises maintained their own economic identity (*GYJJ*, 1982, 1: 62; 21: 52). Administrative ICs simply acted as a 'transmission belt' between the government and enterprises and thus they added another administrative layer to the industrial hierarchy (*GYJJ*, 1981, 10: 15).

Several factors are apparently responsible for the lack of real mergers among enterprises. First, there was strong opposition to mergers from vested interest groups. The IC was usually caught in the middle of the political playing field between the top and the bottom of the industrial hierarchy (*GYJJ*, 1981, 9: 5). On the one hand, the central ministries and local authorities at the top of the hierarchy were afraid of losing control of their own enterprises and were, therefore, very reluctant to devolve more power to the ICs (*GYJJ*, 1982, 2: 65; 22: 82). On the other hand, enterprises at the bottom of the hierarchy were also reluctant to transfer the expanded decision-making power which they had gained in the enterprise reform to the ICs (*GYJJ*, 1981, 21: 52).

Second, mergers were also hindered by the ministerial and local authority approach. Individual ministries and local authorities were relied on to draw up merger plans for their subordinate enterprises (Ma, 1982: 233). Ministerial or geographical boundaries were not supposed to prevent rational mergers in principle but in practice there were no well-established procedures for inter-ministry co-ordination or regional integration. Many ICs were, in fact, put together primarily from compact groups of enterprises belonging to the same administrative units for fear of being 'integrated' by other units. Hence, industrial departments within the central ministries and local industrial bureaux were simply renamed ICs; their formation merely amounted to 'changing the name on the door' with little consideration being given to the rationale behind the formation of ICs (*GYJJ*, 1981, 10: 16; 21: 52; 1982, 22: 82).

Third, conditions in some industries were not yet ripe for merger. Industries like machinery and consumer goods, which produce many different products and have a large number of producers spread throughout an area, each using a different kind of technology and serving different kinds of markets with complex and numerous ties to other branches, were not suitable for mergers, and the economies of scale resulting from their formation were very limited. A rigid application of the merger principle in these industries, coupled with the lack of management expertise and experience, very often resulted in greater inefficiency and costs. Thus, some highly centralized business ICs covering vast geographical areas soon found themselves in difficulties after a brief period of experimentation and had to be reduced to the status of an association of independent enterprises (*GYJJ*, 1981, 10: 16–17; 21: 52). Finally, the relatively large average size of a corporation makes monopolization easy in the case of eventual market competition. Thus, mergers appeared to contradict the general spirit of the reform, namely, the movement towards some form of a functional market mechanism.

Formation of branch associations

A branch association is conceived as a voluntary organization formed by independent enterprises in a special branch of industry. It has the dual role of acting as an agent of both the government and the enterprise (*DDZGDJJGL*, 1985: 543). In the first of these roles the branch association is supposed to assist the government in branch administration by (a) gathering information of branch enterprise activities on behalf of the government, (b) helping government to formulate and implement the branch development plan, (c) laying down branch technical standards, and (d) carrying out quality control of branch products. Acting as an agent of the enterprise the branch association is supposed to put forward requests and suggestions to the government on behalf of the member enterprises and to provide manpower training, technical assistance, management consultancy services, and marketing information to the member enterprises. As of 1986, some 78 national branch associations have been formed (*GYJJ*, 1987, 1: 74) of which only 64 appear to be genuine industrial branch associations. In addition to national branch associations there were also regional branch associations established in major cities.

Studies of the established branch associations reveal that most faced the following problems. First, they did not have their own facilities. Their offices were located either in the top government economic organs, e.g. in the local Economic Commissions or Industrial Bureaux or in the offices of key member enterprises (*GYJJ*, 1987, 3: 55). Moreover, the executive officials of branch associations were normally retired staff of these two units. The second problem of the branch associations was that their source of finance was neither independent nor stable. Most received the bulk of their funds from a mixture of fees and service charges from their constituent enterprises and from government subsidies (*GYJJ*, 1987, 1: 69–72). Third, they had little authority over their constituent enterprises. Most of them were administratively still under the jurisdiction of different central and local government authorities. The general shortage of materials, fuel, and funds and the underdevelopment of markets where enterprises could obtain these strategic inputs forced enterprises to be dependent on their administrative bureaux and to give heed to instructions from them rather than to those from the branch association (*GYJJ*, 1987, 1: 69–72).

Flattening of industrial hierarchies

To reduce the number of levels in the industrial hierarchy the reform blueprints envisaged the elimination of intermediate administrative units in the industrial hierarchy, namely of the industrial ministries or bureaux and their main departments. Enterprises were to be placed directly under the administration of a single body, namely the Economic

Commission (EC). Hence, the old four-level hierarchy (planning and economic commission–ministries–departments–enterprises) was to be reduced to two levels, namely the EC and enterprise (*GYJJ*, 1982, 18: 33). It was further envisaged that while a few large-scale and strategic industrial enterprises would continue to be administered directly by the central EC most industrial enterprises would be administered directly by the ECs of the cities where they were located (*GYJJ*, 1982, 18: 33).

By 1986 the implementation of this part of the reform was limited in scale and confined mainly to a relatively small number of counties and cities. The pace-setter was Qingyuan county in Guangdong province. In late 1978 the local authority in Qingyuan abolished its eight industrial and functional bureaux and placed its 17 state-owned industrial enterprises under the direct administration of the county EC (*GYJJ*, 1982, 5: 43). The Qingyuan model soon received support from the higher authority and a movement was launched to extend the Qingyuan experience to other parts of China. By the end of 1980, about 6 per cent of China's counties and cities had adopted the Qingyuan model and by 1982 this percentage share had increased to 17 (*ZGBKNJ 1982*: 313). The movement received a new impetus in 1986 when 16 medium-sized cities were drawn into the experiment with the Qingyuan model (*CSJJ*, 1987, 4: 36–8). The experiment with the Qingyuan model at the county and city level reveals that the achieved flattening of the industrial hierarchy structure was more apparent than real (*GYJJ*, 1981, 15: 18; 1987, 1: 91–5; *CSJJ*, 1987, 4: 36–8). In most cases, a significant number of intermediate administrative units were abolished and the local industrial hierarchy was reduced to two levels: the EC and enterprise. Yet within the local ECs, more or less the same number of so-called 'branch administrative offices' were re-created to handle their jobs. Thus, for instance, in Jiangmen city in Guangdong province, five industrial bureaux and five of their subordinate main departments, namely the specialized corporations, were abolished during the administrative reform in 1985. Yet seven new 'branch administrative offices' were re-established within the city EC to administer local industrial enterprises (*GYJJ*, 1987, 1: 61–3).

The lack of real progress in flattening the industrial hierarchy has been attributed to several factors. One of these was the resistance by the staff of the intermediate administrative units earmarked for dissolution, as they stood to lose both their influence and their jobs

(*ZGGYJJXB*, 1986, 4: 114–20). Another factor was the concern of the government that it might cause large-scale unemployment of bureaucrats without transferable skills. There was also concern about the internal inconsistency of the reform measures. For while industrial bureaux and their main departments had been abolished at the county or city level they continued to exist at the provincial and central government levels. However, according to the established channel of command the latter were required to deal directly with their local counterparts. Hence, many local intermediate administrative units which had been abolished had to be reinstated to prevent a breakdown in the channel of communication and command. Thus, for example, in Qianxi county in Hebei province, a mining bureau was abolished and became a mining administrative office in the county EC. However, according to the established channel of command, materials needed by the local mining enterprises were allocated by the central mining ministry through the local mining bureau. Since the local mining bureau had been liquidated the central mining ministry stubbornly refused to supply materials to the county EC as this was regarded as inappropriate. Consequently the county authority was forced to reinstate the mining bureau in order to secure the material supply for its mining enterprises (*GYJJ*, 1981, 15: 18).

By far the most important reason for the limited progress in simplifying the structure of the industrial hierarchy was the fact that in the absence of complementary changes in other areas of the economic system it was easy to liquidate intermediate administrative units but difficult to eliminate their functions. An analysis of the job responsibilities of the intermediate administrative organs shows that they performed four important functions in the past (*CSJJ*, 1987, 4: 36–8). First, they performed enterprise supervisory functions, which included the appointment and firing of enterprise directors as well as the formulation and implementation of enterprise plans. Second, they performed enterprise management functions, which involved the allocation of materials and loans to enterprises and participation in their marketing, technical renovation, and employment management. Third, they performed branch administrative functions in the form of co-ordinating the activities of all enterprises within the same industrial branch, mapping out branch development policies, establishing and ensuring branch technical and quality standards, etc. Finally, they also provided certain communal services to the enterprises. Originally, the designers of the administrative reforms hoped that the enterprise supervisory and management functions of the intermediate administrative units would become superfluous as enterprises were given increased leverage in decision-making powers and were guided by the market mechanism. It was also thought that the newly established branch associations could take over some of the branch administrative functions and that the provision of communal services could be delegated to either the corresponding departments of the communal government or the newly established specialized service corporations. With most of the important functions of the intermediate administrative units gone the designers of reforms hoped that after their abolition local ECs would be left with only the functions of branch administration.

However, the underdevelopment of some of the new institutions which were supposed to take over certain functions of the existing intermediate administrative units meant that few of these expectations were fulfilled. For example, since, as the discussion in the next chapter reveals, some form of mandatory planning was still in force and the markets for important materials and capital remained underdeveloped, the local ECs, after the abolition of the intermediate administrative units, still had to allocate materials and funds to enterprises and to supervise the implementation of their plan. Consequently, they were unable to hand over as many of the enterprise supervisory and the management functions as they had expected. Similarly, since branch associations were not yet fully developed and their role was still rather limited, they could not take over some of the branch administration functions from the local ECs either. At the same time, with the abolition of the intermediate administrative levels, the local ECs had to deal with a large number of subordinate enterprises directly and their span of control increased sharply. Overloaded with work, they were forced to reinstate the intermediate administrative units under a new name within the administration so that they could take over some of their administrative duties.

Inter-enterprise lateral linkages

In order to eliminate yet another source of inefficiency in China's industrial hierarchy, namely the lack of co-operation and specialization among enterprises across administrative boundaries, enterprises were urged to enter into a variety of industrial co-operation agreements (ICAs) with each other. ICAs among domestic enterprises were organized along similar lines to those concluded between domestic and foreign firms. The agreement normally involves two or more enterprises associated contractually with each other in the mutual pursuit of complementary objectives for a specific time without losing their own economic and legal identities. The collaboration may assume either a looser form, such as licensing, technical assistance, compensation trade, and subcontracting, or a closer form, such as co-operation in material procurement, production, and sales, or joint venture. A wide variety of confusing terms for domestic ICAs was coined by Chinese economists. Institutionalized co-operation agreements were known as economic union (*Jingji lianheti*). Unions in a closer form of co-operation were known as either enterprise masses or groups. Enterprise mass (*qiye qunti*) usually refers to a group of co-operating enterprises engaged in the production of a single product whereas those engaged in the production of a series of products are known as enterprise groups (*qiye jituan*). Hence, an enterprise group may consist of several enterprise masses (*GYJJGLCK*, 1988, 1: 76).

The number of co-operation agreements concluded increased from 3,400 in 1980 to 50,000 in 1986 (Liu Guogang, 1980: 5; *ZGBKNJ 1987*: 71). However, since Chinese statistics on co-operation agreements do not distinguish between barter trade and real ICAs, the figures are somewhat inflated. Many agreements included were known to be cases of simple inter-provincial barter trade in raw materials, fuel, equipment, and technology rather than genuine ICAs. The number of economic unions formed also increased sharply around the mid-1980s. By 1986, there were 32,000 unions, out of which some 1,000 were enterprise groups (*ZGJJNJ 1987*, IV: 12). Again a word of caution is necessary, as the figures on economic unions also include many non-industrial economic unions formed by rural households. The number of economic unions formed by industrial enterprises at the county level and above numbered only 6,833.

Despite the rapid increase in numbers the significance of domestic ICAs in breaking down ministerial, provincial, and enterprise autarky should not be overestimated. To begin with, though in some localities unions already accounted for 20 per cent of the local gross industrial output (*ZGJJNJ 1987*, V: 7) their share in industrial output nationwide was still fairly insignificant (*GYJJ*, 1987, 7: 73).

Second, since enterprise unions were keen to internalize their benefits co-operation very often involved only enterprises within a given administrative boundary. Third, a sample survey of Shanghai domestic ICAs reveals that co-operation was mainly confined to processing enterprises (*GYJJ*, 1987, 8: 101–2). There was little co-operation between processing and non-processing enterprises. The survey also reveals that most co-operation agreements involved only a simple form of co-operation, namely the relocation of land- and labour-intensive manufacturing processes and the transfer of commodities in the late product cycle from urban to rural enterprises by way of technical assistance, licensing, and joint venture. Finally, the sample survey of Shanghai domestic ICAs also indicates that the participating enterprises were mainly small- and medium-scale enterprises. Co-operation among large-scale enterprises accounted for only 7 per cent of the sample agreements.

According to the findings of the Shanghai sample survey, the main barriers to more meaningful co-operation were (a) the lack of proper markets for key inputs, (b) the lack of legislation to protect intellectual property rights, and (c) the imbalance in the distribution of co-operative benefits.

Co-operation usually led to the expansion of the production capacity of the partner firm which needed financing. However, the lack of a proper financial market in China made it difficult for partner firms to obtain the necessary funds. Co-operation normally involved the transfer of technology and skills from urban to rural enterprises. However, the lack of proper markets for technology and skilled labour meant that it was difficult to determine their real market prices. Hence, it gave rise to many price disputes between the two partners. Co-operation also generally involved the transfer of trade marks, patents, designs, and other forms of intellectual property from urban to rural enterprises. But the lack of legislation to protect these property rights increased the risks of co-operation for urban enterprises.

Finally, the distribution of net co-operation benefits appeared to be highly uneven. Owing to the preferential tax treatment rural enterprises as well as their local authorities normally captured the lion's share of co-operation benefits (*GYJJ*, 1987, 5: 92–4). Co-operation profits were usually distributed to each partner before tax. The distribution formula was based on each partner's equity contribution. However, since the profit tax rate for urban enterprises was much higher than that for rural enterprises, the net profits after tax received by the urban partner were lower than those received by the rural partner. To make up for this loss, urban enterprises tended to demand a higher share of profits before tax. To counter this demand, rural enterprises tended to inflate the costs of production. In response to this the urban enterprise, in turn, tended to assign accountants to monitor the cost accounting of the rural enterprise. This practice inevitably gave rise to many conflicts between the two partners.

Urban authorities also stood to lose from the co-operation since the output produced by joint ventures was not counted as theirs but as that produced by the host authorities. They also stood to lose in terms of tax revenues since the output of joint ventures was subject to product taxes in the host territories, and the bulk of these tax revenues accrued to the host authorities. As a result, urban authorities had little incentive to encourage their enterprises to enter into any joint venture agreement with enterprises in other territories.

The delegation of enterprises to key cities

Since existing administrative boundaries constituted a severe obstacle to real mergers and co-operation among industrial enterprises, the key city concept was promoted to remove this obstacle. According to this concept, the economy would be divided into several economic areas, each headed by a key city. It was envisaged that apart from a limited number of strategic enterprises of national importance, which would continue to be administered by the central ministries, most enterprises would henceforth be transferred from the central and local authorities to the city administration.

The main advantages of the key city approach to industrial co-operation are twofold: first, the delegation of enterprises to city administration enables a city to organize within its area of influence inter-enterprise co-operation across existing administrative boundaries. Second, it provides a strong incentive for firms located in the city centre and on its periphery to co-operate as the former need the co-operation of the latter to widen their market and to ensure the source of supply of much needed raw materials. The periphery for its part needs the co-operation of the city to obtain much-needed capital and technology.

The implementation of the key city concept proceeded on two fronts. First, there was a drive to transfer the centrally directed or ministerial enterprises and the locally directed, or provincial enterprises, to the key cities. Second, around 1983 a movement to abolish prefectures (*diqu*) and to put counties (*xian*) under the direct administration of a city was initiated. It was envisaged that this step would enable the cities to consolidate the development of county, village, and township enterprises and integrate them into a sub-contracting network with the city's large and modern enterprises (*JJGL*, 1983, 3: 17). Furthermore, it was hoped that this move would also facilitate agro-industrial linkage.

Though by the mid-1980s there was an increase in the number of industrial enterprises that came under the formal jurisdiction of key cities the actual gain in control power by cities over these enterprises was much less than expected. Several reasons account for this. First, in many cases ministerial and provincial authorities delegated only unimportant enterprises with poor performance to the cities but retained the important ones, especially those performing well finan-cially. As a result, in most cities the ministerial and provincial enter-prises still accounted for the lion's share of the city's industrial output or assets even though their number had been reduced. For example, in Nanjing in 1986 the number of ministerial and provincial enterprises was cut from around 2,000 to 76, yet these 76 enterprises accounted for 70 per cent of the city's industrial fixed capital assets (*CSJJ*, 1987, 6: 52).

Second, though ministerial and provincial authorities relinquished direct control over the input and output decisions of the delegated enterprises they still controlled the allocation of funds and scarce materials and issued 'informal' but irresistable 'guidance' to them (*GYJJ*, 1987, 8: 87; *CSJJ*, 1987, 2: 77). Third, owing to the cities' limited power many city industrial enterprises were reluctant to sub-ject themselves to administration by the cities. To overcome this, some key cities were elevated to the status of provincial authorities. They became independent planning units directly responsible to the State Councils and were formally granted wide-ranging decision-making power in planning, investment, the allocation of funds, fuel, materials, etc. However, up to 1986 most of this intended delegation of power from ministerial and provincial authorities to the cities was not en-forced (*CSJJ*, 1987, 2: 45). Interviews with 72 mayors of key cities, conducted by a Sichuan study group in 1987, reveal that 70 per cent of the mayors conceded that there had been no significant increase in the real control power of the cities over the delegated enterprises whereas some 23 per cent maintained that cities had gained some power but that this in most cases remained to be enforced (*CSJJ*, 1987, 6: 59). Finally, as more and more ministerial, provincial, county, village, and township enterprises came under the jurisdiction of cities the municipal authorities found themselves inundated with paperwork and unable to oversee enterprises effectively (*JJGL*, 1983, 9: 29).

The slow progress in the delegation of industrial enterprises to key cities was mainly due to the reluctance of the established interest groups, such as ministerial, provincial, and county authorities to give up their control power. It was also due to the growing doubts about the rationality of the key city concept. For this concept apparently did not deal with the root of the problem of ministerial and provincial autarky. The delegation of enterprises to key cities and the formation of key economic areas headed by key cities did abolish old administrative boundaries as had been expected but only to replace them with new ones. As a result a new type of administrative or regional autarky, namely city autarky, emerged. For example, some key cities designated as centres of certain economic areas began to build up their own local empire by maximizing the number of local enterprises producing all kinds of goods with the aim of creating self-sufficiency. At the same time they were avoiding co-operating with other areas (*CSJJ*, 1987, 6: 39).

THE IMPACT OF THE CHANGES

Did the administrative reforms and the industrial reorganization of Chinese industry in the first half of the 1980s achieve some of their original objectives, such as the reduction of administrative costs, the breaking down of ministerial, regional, and enterprise autarky, and the increase in the average size of Chinese industrial enterprises? Many claims have been made in the Chinese press about dramatic savings in administrative personnel through the simplification of the administrative hierarchy during this period.

To test this claim, Table 3.2 contrasts the growth of administrative expenditures at both the government and the enterprise level in the pre- and the post-reform periods. During the pre-reform period (1957–78) the growth of administrative expenditures lagged behind that of total expenditures but in the aftermath of the reforms the growth of administrative expenditures was 1.7 times that of total expenditures. A similar trend can also be found at the enterprise level. Administrative expenditure data are not available for enterprises. However, the number of administrative staff employed can be used as a proxy to gauge the trend. As Table 3.2 shows, the growth of administrative staff at the enterprise level after the reforms was almost three times that of the total staff. Thus, at both the government and the enterprise level, the share of administrative expenditures in total expenditures rose rather than fell. Hence the claim of administrative cost savings through administrative reforms cannot be substantiated.

TABLE 3.2. *Growth of Administrative Expenditures and Staff at Government and Enterprise Level, 1957–1978 and 1978–1986 (annual average %)*

	1957–1978	1978–1986
At government level		
Total expenditures of which:	6.4	9.7
Basic construction expenditures	6.4	5.1
Education, science and health		
expenditures	6.9	16.4
Administrative expenditures	3.3	16.0
At enterprise[a] level		
Total employees	6.9	1.9
Administrative staff	5.1	5.4

[a] State-owned enterprises only.

Sources: *ZGTJNJ 1981*: 118 and 1987: 627–8; *GHDSSWN*, 1984: 153 and Sun, 1984: 263.

The effects of the administrative reforms and of the promotion of inter-enterprise lateral linkages on the breaking down of regional autarky can be tested by a transport-production comparison (Rawski, 1976 and Lyons, 1985). It is reasonable to assume that a reduction in regional autarky would increase transport needs and, hence, the growth of transport would exceed that of output or the transport elasticity with respect to output would increase. Table 3.3 contrasts the growth of rail transport and output for a number of industrial commodities for the pre- and post-reform periods. It shows that for most industrial commodities, contrary to the prediction, rail transport elasticity with respect to output did not increase but fell. Hence, the claim that regional autarky has been reduced as a result of the administrative reforms is also not substantiated. However, it should be noted that the above test is not conclusive. The declining rail transport elasticity may have been due to a shift from rail to other modes of transport. Unfortunately, comparable data of non-rail transport for industrial commodities are not available. Hence this particular position cannot be tested.

TABLE 3.3. *Elasticity of Rail Transport with Respect to Output in Pre- and Post-Reform Chinese Industry*

Commodity group	1970–1978	1978–1986
Coal	0.82	0.50
Coke	0.88	0.31
Petroleum	0.40	0.05
Iron and steel products	1.02	0.77
Cement	0.44	0.58
Timber	0.88	1.07
Chemical fertilizer and insecticides	0.44	0.70
Average, unweighted	0.70	0.57

Sources: World Bank, 1983, II: 114, 345; *ZGJJNJ* 1987: 170–1, 284–7, 418; *ZGBKNJ 1980*: 364.

In order to test the ministerial autarky hypothesis it is reasonable to apply the extra-branch production (EBP) ratio (Pryor, 1973: 243). This ratio compares the output value of various goods produced by enterprises outside the designated branch ministry with that within the designated branch ministry.

Ministerial autarky implies a high EBP ratio as every branch ministry for the sake of self-sufficiency tends to produce goods which are supposed to be produced by another branch ministry designated for this purpose. Table 3.4 presents the EBP ratios for certain industrial commodity groups for which relevant data are available. It shows that in most cases the EBP ratio did not decline but increased. This suggests that a greater share of industrial output was produced by enterprises

TABLE 3.4. *Extra-Branch Production Ratios in China's Industry, 1978 and 1987*

Industrial group	1978	1987
Light industry	1.09 (1978)	2.38 (1987)
Machinery	1.74 (1978)	2.08 (1985)
Electronics	0.07 (1982)	0.46 (1987)
Iron and steel		
Steel	6.3 (1982)	7.0 (1985)
Iron	1.1 (1980)	2.0 (1985)
Rolled steel	2.1 (1980)	2.8 (1985)
Coke (machine made)	23.6 (1980)	25.4 (1985)

Sources: *ZGJJNJ 1986*: VI 69; Ma and Sun, 1981: 325; *ZGJXDJNJ 1984*: I: 14, VI: 3; 1986 : VII: 3, VIII: 21–3; *JJYJZL*, 1988, 115: 1; *ZGGTNJ 1986*: 514.

outside the designated branch ministry. Hence, the claim that the administrative reforms were effective in reducing China's ministerial autarky during this period is also not statistically confirmed.

Finally, enterprise consolidation is aimed at increasing the average size of enterprises in order to reap the benefits of economies of scale. To test whether China has achieved this objective we need a direct measure of the average size of Chinese industrial enterprises. Unfortunately, the size classification of industrial enterprises in Chinese statistics is based on a set of multiple criteria which includes volume of output, labour force, capital stock, etc. Hence, it does not lend itself to the calculation of a single size indicator. However, a recent study of concentration in Chinese industry reveals that the eight-firm concentration ratios for Chinese industry did not increase but actually declined in the 1980s (Chen *et al.*, 1991: 196–7).

However, significant progress appears to have been achieved in the reduction of enterprise autarky in the four major technological processes in the machinery branch, namely in casting, forging, electroplating, and heat treatment. As has been mentioned, most enterprises had their own workshops engaged in these processes in the past. For example, in 1980, there were some 20,000 workshops each of which turned out a minute volume of output. Between 1981 and 1985, under the direction of the SEC, 7,528 workshops in 41 cities were closed down. The concentration and specialization of these processes in the remaining workshops resulted in the saving of 240 million kilowatts of electricity, 263 thousand tons of coal, 61 thousand tons of coke, 34 million tons of water, and 1.3 million square metres of factory space (*ZGJXDJNJ 1986*: 132).

In summary, the administrative reforms and the reorganization of China's industry in the first half of the 1980s were designed to rationalize the existing industrial hierarchy in order to reduce bureaucratic waste and improve allocative efficiency. The resistance to change by established interest groups and the lack of complementary reforms in other areas of the economic system meant that the achievement of these reforms was limited. Thus, starting in the mid-1980s the government had to introduce more radical reforms to revitalize Chinese industry.

4 Changes in the Industrial System II: Increased Enterprise Autonomy

The comprehensive reform of China's industrial system began with the expansion of state enterprise autonomy. On the eve of the reforms in 1978, China's state industrial sector was under a system of centralized planning copied from the Soviet Union (Howe and Walker, 1989). Decisions on current input and output choices as well as investment were made at either the central or the local government level and were conveyed to individual enterprises in the form of detailed obligatory targets and rules. Individual enterprises had very little discretionary power within the constraints imposed from above (Ma, 1982: 198–210).

The system of centralized planning enabled China to carry out large-scale mobilization of the resources necessary for rapid industrial growth. Gross industrial output grew at an annual average of 12.5 per cent during the period 1951–80 (*ZGTJNJ 1981*: 497). This growth rate was well ahead of that achieved by India and other industrialized countries including Japan. In terms of net output the real growth rate was estimated at 10 per cent a year by the World Bank for the period from 1957 to 1979 which was again above the average of other low- and middle-income countries (World Bank, 1983, I: 118).

However, the system of centralized planning has also taken a heavy toll on China's industrial efficiency. World Bank studies reveal that total factor productivity in China's industry stagnated from 1957. This means that output growth was achieved, as in most of the Central and Eastern European countries, through the massive influx of productive resources, particularly the influx of capital and labour, rather than through an increase of their productivities (World Bank, 1983, I: 118). The increasing costs of industrial growth prompted the government to decentralize decision making in China's state industrial system in the late 1970s.

The decision to decentralize was initiated at the Third Plenary Session of the 11th Central Committee of the Chinese Communist Party (CCP) held in late 1978. It started with an experiment in expanded enterprise autonomy carried out in six enterprises in Sichuan in late 1978. In the following year the experiment was extended to the whole country. By the end of the first half of 1980, over 6,000 enterprises, comprising 15 per cent of China's 42,000 key industrial enterprises, were drawn into the experiment. These 6,000 enterprises accounted for 60 per cent of the gross output value, and 70 per cent of the profits of China's key industrial enterprises (*ZGGYJJGL*, 1983: 134).

Initially it was planned to enforce enterprise autonomy in all state industrial enterprises by the end of 1981 (*GWYGB*, 1980, 14: 423). However, at a Central Committee Working Conference held at the end of 1980 it was decided to halt the reforms temporarily due to the growing disequilibrium in the economy. In the following years the enterprise autonomy reform was overshadowed by the incentive reform under the industrial responsibility system. It was not until 1984 that the enterprise autonomy reform received a new impetus. In that year the Party decided to dismantle gradually the centralized planning system and the State Council decreed that 10 expanded rights be granted to state-owned industrial enterprises (*JJTZGGSC*, 1987: 3–14, 54–60, and 174–5). Since 1985 reforms have centred on granting greater autonomy to large- and medium-sized enterprises. Enterprise autonomy reform received a big boost in 1992 with the passing of regulations on 'Transforming the Management Mechanism of State-Owned Industrial Enterprises'. These regulations aim at the strict enforcement of enterprises' 14 expanded rights (*ZGJJTZGGNJ 1993*: 54–62).

This chapter assesses (1) in what areas enterprises have gained freedom of decision making under the reforms and how much they have gained; and (2) how effectively enterprises have been able to exercise their increased authority. However, to keep the analysis manageable we confine the discussion to enterprise input, output, and investment decisions.

RELAXATION OF PLAN CONSTRAINTS

The gaining of discretionary decision-making power by an enterprise in a planned economy can be measured in terms of the details of command communicated to the enterprise by the higher authority. The less detailed the commands the greater the discretion enjoyed by the enterprise (Pryor, 1973: 281). Two indices can be used to measure the detail of command. One is the number of product groups covered in the mandatory plan. An enterprise's discretion is increased if the number of product groups covered in the plan is reduced (Pryor, 1973: 307). Another indicator is the number and detail of obligatory targets or directives received by the enterprise. Theoretically, the smaller the number and the less detailed the directives the more discretion an enterprise enjoys.

Measured in terms of the first index Chinese state industrial enterprises gained increased discretion in output decisions as both the number of products and the share of industrial output subject to mandatory planning were substantially reduced. The former fell from 120 in 1979 to 60 in 1987 and the latter declined from 40 per cent in 1984 to 17 per cent in 1987 (Xie and Luo, 1990: 45). By 1993 only 36 products or 7 per cent of industrial output were reportedly still subject to mandatory planning (*ZGJJTZGGNJ 1993*: 254).

With respect to the second index of command planning, the number and detail of obligatory targets, it is understood that on the eve of the reforms in 1978 enterprises received eight formal obligatory plan targets. Output, quality, variety, and profit, together with delivery contract, were enterprise fund forming indicators, i.e. fulfilment of them was a precondition for the forming of an enterprise fund (see *ZGGYJJFQHB 1949–81*: 132). Cost and the other three input targets (material and fuel consumption and the use of working capital) were the additional enterprise fund conditions. The fulfilment of these would affect the rate at which an enterprise was able to deduct monies for the enterprise fund. Monies accumulated in the enterprise fund could be used by an enterprise for capital investment, collective consumption, and bonus payment (Riskin, 1987: 344).

In 1979, with the introduction of the expanded enterprise autonomy experiment the enterprise fund system was replaced by the profit-retention scheme. This reduced the number of formal plan targets tied to enterprise-retained profit to four items. A World Bank survey reveals that most enterprises in 1982 still received four specified targets, namely output, variety, quality, and profits (Tidrick and Chen, 1987). However, it was found that these targets exerted little constraint on enterprise behaviour because of their softness and the fact that enterprise profit-retention rates were negotiable.

With the introduction of the tax-for-profit system in 1983 and the subsequent adoption of the contract responsibility system (CRS) since 1987 the importance of plan targets for state enterprises declined further. Under the CRS, though an enterprise continued to receive plan targets from its supervisory agencies, its retained profit now largely depended on its actual profit rather than on the fulfilment of its plan targets. Hence, the number of obligatory targets for most enterprises was practically reduced to just one, namely, profit.

PROCUREMENT OF MATERIALS

Under the pre-reform system state-owned enterprises had only a limited choice in respect to their sources of material supply. The supply of most materials was planned and administered at three levels. Materials of strategic importance or first-category materials, such as steel, petroleum, coal, etc., were planned and allocated at the central government level, i.e. by the State Planning Commission and the State Material Bureau. Specialized materials, such as zinc, copper, textile machinery, etc., known as second-category materials, were planned and allocated by the individual branch ministries. All other materials were known as third-category goods and were either planned by the local government or left to the enterprises.

Under the reforms the number of materials under mandatory planning was drastically reduced. The number of first-category materials under mandatory planning at the SPC and State Material Bureau level was cut from 210 in 1979 to 12 in 1992 (*DDZGDJJGL*, 1985: 291 and *ZGJJTZGGNJ 1993*: 254). The number of both second- and third-category materials under mandatory planning at the ministerial and the local government level also experienced a decline under the reforms.

With the reduction in the number of materials under plan allocation the number of materials available at the market channels rose. The market channels include (1) marketing by enterprises (self-marketing) and (2) materials trading centres. The number of materials available under the self-marketing arrangement of an enterprise depended on the proportion of output it was allowed to market itself. This proportion increased significantly with the start of the reforms. Materials trading centres were set up by the State Material Bureau at various government levels to handle the trading of materials not subject to plan allocation, the number of which increased from 110 in 1984 to 400 in 1992 (*CD*, 29 Aug. 1992).

The share of market channels in enterprise material procurement increased steadily in the 1980s. Available estimates show that this share rose from 24 to 45 per cent in the first half of the 1980s (*JJCK*,

15 Sept. 1987). A survey of state-owned industrial enterprises reveals that by the end of the 1980s this share had risen to somewhere between 59 and 66 per cent (Jefferson and Rawski, 1994: 51).

HIRING OF LABOUR

Until the reforms state-owned industrial enterprises in China had limited power to determine their work-force. A labour quota was assigned from above in the form of a mandatory target (*DDZGDJJGL*, 1985: 363). A survey by the World Bank in 1982 reveals that enterprises did have a certain degree of flexibility in hiring labour as they managed to exceed the given quota by hiring non-planned labour, such as temporary workers, seasonal workers, children and other dependants of their workers' families, as well as peasants from the countryside (Tidrick and Chen, 1987). However, enterprises had very little flexibility in firing workers. An enterprise's power to determine the composition of its work-force was in the past also limited since the total wage fund, the total number of workers employed, and average wage payment were all set by the authorities from above (*JJGL*, 1984, 2: 17). These, together with the centrally set wage rate, more or less predetermined the composition of the work-force of an enterprise.

An enterprise's power to recruit the right kind of worker was also limited before the reforms. Very often labourers were administratively assigned to an enterprise by the Labour Bureau regardless of its specific requirements (Ma, 1982: 182) or additional workers were simply recruited from among the children and other dependents of the workers' families. Once recruited, workers became tenured labour which the enterprise could not dismiss even if they were found to be unsuitable or redundant (Liu Guoguang, 1980: 23).

The reforms gave enterprises increased flexibility in the hiring of labour. Since 1985 the labour quota for most large- and medium-sized enterprises has no longer been fixed but has been allowed to fluctuate according to output volume but subject to a fixed unit labour cost (*DDZGDJJGL*, 1985: 363–4). For small enterprises under either the contract or leasing system the labour quota was completely abolished (ibid).

The reforms also increased the enterprise's freedom to recruit and dismiss labourers within certain constraints. For enterprises experimenting with expanded autonomy these rights were formally restored by Decree No. 175 in July 1979 (*ZGGYJJFQHB 1949–81*: 137). Four years later these rights were extended to all state industrial enterprises by Decree No. 54 of 1983 (*GWYGB*, 1983, 8: 272). The extent to which an enterprise's right to dismiss workers was enforced is difficult to ascertain. Available evidence suggests that this right remained largely theoretical in the 1980s. This is also confirmed by the findings of enterprise surveys in Shanghai and Tianjin in 1987 (*JJYJ*, 1988, 4: 69 and *GYJJGLCK*, 1988, 10: 3 and 11–12). In the early 1990s, however, there was increased pressure by enterprises to enforce their right to fire redundant workers. In the first half of 1993, for instance, China's coal industry reportedly laid off 187,000 workers (*SCMPIW*, 9–10 Oct. 1993).

An enterprise's flexibility in selecting new workers and dismissing unsuitable ones, however, was definitely enhanced by the introduction of the contract labour system. The experiment to replace tenured labour by contract labour began in 1980. Labour Decree No. 11 of 1983 extended the new system to the employment of all new workers (*GWYGB*, 1983, 6: 214). As a result, the number of contract workers increased rapidly from 1983. By 1993 some 33 per cent of workers in all state-owned industrial enterprises were contract workers (*ZGTJNJ 1994*: 100).

The contract labour system enhanced the enterprise's freedom to hire, discipline, and fire workers. This is because under this system an enterprise hired workers no longer for life but for a specific period of time. A probationary period was usually provided for, during which the enterprise was allowed to fire a worker without any fuss. Furthermore, the new system allowed an enterprise to specify the duties to be performed by the workers and, hence, to safeguard its right to discipline them when they were caught not performing their duties.

To increase enterprises' authority to discipline and even lay off tenured workers an optimal labour combination programme was first introduced in 1985 in Qingdao. This allowed the director of an enterprise to select his/her own management team and the latter were allowed to select their own work-force from among the tenured workers. Once selected, they were offered a one- or two-year contract. Tenured workers who were not selected were placed in an internal 'waiting-for-employment' arrangement. They continued to receive the basic pay but not the occupational and other supplementary payments. Moreover, pressure was put on them either to retire early or to be replaced by their dependants. During the waiting-for-employment period they were usually given various kinds of temporary odd jobs until they were reappointed (*ZGQYGL*, 1988, 3: 128). Under the internal waiting-for-employment arrangement the enterprise wage fund would not be cut despite the reduction in the number of effective workers. The enterprise was allowed to use the available surplus wage fund to increase the wages of the selected workers. By 1987 the programme had been adopted by 76 municipal-owned enterprises and covered about 10 per cent of their work-force and, as a result, they reported an 8 per cent reduction in employment (*ZGQYGL*, 1988: 122–3). As a result of its success in shedding surplus workers the system was soon emulated by other municipalities and provinces (*ZGJJTZGG*, 1987, 10: 28) to such an extent that in many places over 50 per cent of enterprises had adopted the programme by the late 1980s (Xie and Luo, 1990: 266).

The reforms also gave enterprises greater power in determining the pay of workers. Since 1983 the enterprise wage fund was no longer fixed but was allowed to fluctuate either wholly or partially in line with an enterprise's performance. The full floating of the wage fund was, however, confined to certain industrial areas. For example, enterprises in coal, metallic and non-metallic ore mining, as well as the construction industry were allowed to have their entire wage fund (W) linked to their output (Q) subject to a fixed unit labour cost (lc) (*GYQYGL*, 1987, 11: 107–8):

$$W = Qlc.$$

The wage fund of large- and medium-sized industrial enterprises under the CRS was allowed to be fully linked to the amount of taxes and profits delivered to the state according to the following formula:

$$Wt = Wo(1 + rdP_t/Po)$$

where Wt is the current wage fund, Wo is the base-year wage fund, Po are the base-year taxes and profits delivered, dPt are the incremental taxes and profits delivered in the current year, and r is a coefficient in the range of 0 to 1. In most enterprises, r averaged 0.7 (*GYQYGL*, 1988, 2: 139).

In the early 1990s, 55 per cent of state-owned industrial enterprises linked their wage fund with employment while 40 per cent still engaged in wage planning for an absolute increment as allocated by the state (Li Yuan, 1993: 94). Since the wage fund was no longer completely fixed from above the government had to rely increasingly on progressive income tax in order to control the level of wage increments. In 1984 a progressive bonus and wage adjustment tax system was introduced.

Apart from the total wage payment enterprises also gained greater autonomy in designing their own wage system and in the promotion of workers. This is discussed in more detail in the next chapter.

Since labour was no longer subject to mandatory planning and allocation and since an enterprise was allowed to recruit and dismiss workers to a certain degree a labour market emerged in the major cities of China. By 1992 some 15,000 labour services markets which are known as 'Job Introduction Bureaux' had been set up (*ZGJJTZGGNJ 1993*: 328). These markets were formal labour markets set up by local Labour Bureaux. Most of them were in coastal areas and catered mainly for rural, collective, and private enterprise labour. Wages formed in these markets were subject to government control. The formal labour market for urban and state enterprises remained relatively underdeveloped in the early 1990s due to the limited labour mobility between these enterprises. This limitation was, in turn, due to the fact that most workers still relied on their enterprise for the supply of free housing, medical care, education, and other social services.

INVESTMENT DECISIONS

In the Chinese context fixed asset investment is divided into two categories: (1) the replacement and renovation of existing plant and equipment, which is known as investment in technical updating and transformation, and (2) the expansion of an existing enterprise through new investment in plant and equipment, which is known as capital construction investment. However, as technical updating and transformation investment inevitably lead to the expansion of an enterprise, the distinction between these two investment categories is blurred. In order to distinguish them clearly, official guidelines very often have to rely on specific criteria, such as the scale of investment expenditures etc.

Before the reforms capital construction investment in China was planned by the government, and enterprises had little discretion in respect of this category of investment. Capital construction investment was in turn subdivided into large, medium, and small project categories. The criteria used to classify projects into these three categories were in general based on either the scale of investment expenditure or the designed output capacity of a project (*ZGTJNJ 1983*: 589). Large- and medium-sized projects were subject to the control of the central authorities (the SPC and the SEC) whereas small-scale projects came within the purview of the decentralized authorities, namely the branch ministries and the local government (Ma, 1982: 406–7).

Before the reforms an enterprise was allowed to decide only on technical updating and transformation investment, provided that these could be financed through its own internal fund. However, an enterprise's internal fund available for this kind of investment tended to be rather limited in the past for several reasons. First, the size of the depreciation allowance which provided the principal source of finance for this kind of investment was very small due to the very low depreciation rate allowed. This rate, which averaged 3.6 per cent, was set in 1952 and was never adjusted until the late 1970s (Liu Guoguang, 1980: 166–7). Second, only part of the limited depreciation allowance was earmarked for technical updating and transformation investment. The other part was earmarked for major repair expenditures (Ma, 1982: 350).

Third, the fund deducted for depreciation allowances had to be remitted to the central government budget and was, therefore, outside the control of an enterprise. Hence, its limited financial resources in the past gave an enterprise little opportunity to exercise its autonomy in respect of this investment category.

In view of the practical difficulties in distinguishing between the two investment categories and the fact that very often an enterprise would carry out what constituted essentially capital construction under the guise of technical updating and transformation investment, the second category of fixed asset investment was drawn into central-ized planning as well in 1982; and plans for both categories of invest-ment were merged into one, which became known as the fixed asset investment plan (Ma, 1982: 350).

Despite the centralization of technical updating and transforma-tion investment planning, enterprise autonomy in both categories of investment was significantly enhanced under the reforms in the 1980s. To begin with, enterprises gained greater investment autonomy as a result of the decentralization of the vetting power for investment pro-jects. Specifically, local government was granted the vetting power for all non-productive fixed investment projects and productive fixed investment projects[1] with a value of less than 30 million *yuan* (Gao, 1987: 35).

The decentralization of the power to vet investment projects in itself does not necessarily imply greater enterprise investment autonomy. However, under the reforms the interest of the decentralized authorities became increasingly congruent with that of the enterprise as both were interested in output expansion, increased employment, and higher revenues. Where the relationship between the two was good, approval of investment projects became automatic. In these circumstances the decentralization of power to vet investment projects naturally led to greater enterprise autonomy in investment decision making (Tidrick and Chen, 1987).

Enterprises also gained increased investment autonomy through the increased availability of both internal and external funds. Enterprises' internal funds for investment were enlarged by a higher depreciation rate. The basic rate of depreciation for fixed assets, for instance, was raised from 4.1 per cent in 1978 to 5.7 per cent in 1992 (*ZGTJNJ 1994*: 29). The enterprise's share of depreciation allowances was also raised from the previous 30 to 100 per cent in 1987. In addition, the enterprises' internal funds were augmented by three new sources: (a) the production development fund formed under the profit-retention scheme; (b) the capital repair fund which was, under the reforms, allowed to be used for technical updating and transformation investment as well; (c) income from the sale or rental of idle or surplus assets.

An enterprise's external fund for investment was enlarged by a multiplication of its sources. Under the reforms an enterprise was allowed not only to borrow from the banking system but also to attract investment from other domestic and foreign enterprises. Of late, enterprises have also been allowed to issue bonds and shares to raise capital from the public.

The increase in the availability of financial resources at the level of enterprises and decentralized authorities is most evident from the growth of extra-budgetary revenues and decentralized investment financed by extra-budgetary funds. During the period 1978–92 extra-budgetary revenues grew at an annual average of 19 per cent while the average rate of growth of state budgetary revenues was only 9 per cent

---

[1] Productive investment projects refer to those in material production sectors; non-productive investment projects are those in non-material production sectors. The latter include investment in public utilities, housing, construction, education, culture, hospitals, etc.

(*ZGTJNJ 1994*: 221). As a result, the share of the latter in total revenues declined from 76 to 49 per cent whereas the share of extra-budgetary revenues rose from 24 to 50 per cent in the same period. Among the three categories of extra-budgetary revenues those of state-owned enterprises and their supervising agencies experienced the fastest growth. In 1992 their share accounted for 75 per cent of total extra-budgetary revenues. Most of these revenues were in fact owned by the enterprises themselves (*ZGFZYGG*, 1988, 11: 240). About half of the extra-budgetary revenues owned by state-owned enterprises came from their depreciation allowance and capital repair fund and the other half from their retained profits (*ZGFZYGG*, 1988, 11: 240).

Similarly there was a rapid growth of decentralized investment by enterprises financed by their extra-budgetary fund in the same period. Its share in total fixed asset investment increased from 51 to 90 per cent whereas the share of centralized investment (in the state budget) fell from 49 to 6 per cent in the period from 1978 to 1993 (*ZGFZYGG*, 1988, 11: 24 and *ZGTJNJ 1994*: 145). Most of the decentralized investments were financed by bank loans and self-raised funds.

Investment requires not only finance but also construction materials and equipment. As long as the allocation of these materials and equipment was under strict government control enterprises had little autonomy in investment decision making. Under the reforms, however, as has been discussed in the previous section, enterprises were able to obtain materials and equipment through various formal and informal market channels as a result of the derationing of supplies of materials. Hence, an increase in the marketization of the allocation of materials also contributed significantly to the greater autonomy of enterprises with respect to investment decisions.

Despite the gains of enterprises in investment autonomy under the reforms the extent of their autonomy should not be overstated. Surveys of enterprise investment activities reveal that most of the decentralized investment projects were in fact either decided directly by, or undertaken under, the influence of the decentralized authorities above the enterprise level, namely local government (*CZJR*, 1987, 10: 146–7; *ZGFZYGG*, 1988, 1: 43).

The pivotal role of local government in enterprise investment decisions can be attributed to several factors. One is the power of local authorities to vet investment projects which gave them the opportunity to influence enterprise investment decisions. Another factor is the general shortage of internal funds for decentralized investment.

Superficially enterprise internal funds experienced a sharp increase under the reforms because of the greater nominal profit retention by the enterprise. Thus, for instance, the rate of nominal profit retention, e.g. the share in after-tax profits, by state-owned industrial enterprises under independent accounting jumped from 4 to 44 per cent in the period from 1978 to 1992 (*ZGTJNJ 1993*: 419).

However, from the early 1980s enterprises' retained profits were increasingly siphoned off by both the central and the local authorities through various exactions and mandatory 'contributions' imposed upon enterprises. The central government exactions included (a) the compulsory purchase of government and key enterprise bonds, (b) a compulsory contribution to the state energy and transport development fund, and (c) a construction tax.

The increased autonomy of enterprises and local authorities in investment decisions, in the absence of any hardening of their budget constraints and of scarcity prices for inputs as well as for outputs, soon resulted in over-investment and the widespread misallocation of investment resources in the early stage of the reforms. To regain centralized control over investment resources the compulsory pur- chase of government bonds was first introduced in 1981. As from 1983, both local governments and enterprises were required to pay 15 per cent of the accruals to their own funds to the central authority as a contribution to the state energy and transport development fund (*GWYGB*, 1983, 21: 997–8). In addition, they were required to pay 10 per cent of their internally financed investment as a construction tax. Since 1987 they have also been required to purchase key enterprise bonds equivalent to 15 per cent of their internally financed investment (*GWYGB*, 1988, 4: 102–3).

The local government apportionments imposed on state-owned industrial enterprises consisted mainly of compulsory contributions to various local infrastructural development funds as well as to social welfare project funds. According to a sample survey of 100 enterprises in 23 cities in 1984 these 'contributions' accounted on average for 8 per cent of enterprise retained profits (CESRRI, 1987: 133). The various exactions imposed on enterprises by both the central and local governments significantly reduced the amount of enterprises' disposable retained profits. Consequently the effective profit-retention rate of enterprises was much lower than the nominal rate.

Enterprises' retained profits were also subject to a squeeze from below. By government regulation most of the enterprises' retained profits (at least 60 per cent) had to be put into a production development fund. But several surveys in the mid-1980s show that most enterprises tended to yield to the pressure of their workers and staff and diverted most of the retained profits either to bonus payments or into the collective welfare fund, the latter being used to finance the construction of housing (*GYQYGL*, 1987, 4: 128; *GYJJGLCK*, 1988, 10: 15). Consequently, out of the disposable retained profits only a minute amount could be made available for productive investment projects. For example, in Tianjin in 1986 only 15 per cent of the retained profits of the sample enterprises surveyed were made available for productive investment (*GYJJGLCK*, 1988, 10: 13).

Yet another factor which enhanced the role of local government in enterprises' investment decisions was the underdevelopment of the capital market. This was, in the early 1990s, still in its infancy, as will be discussed in detail in Chapter 7. The general shortage of internal funds, together with the underdevelopment of the capital market, forced enterprises to rely mainly on central and local government grants and loans as well as on bank credits to finance the bulk of their investment. This strategy, however, made enterprises even more susceptible to local government influence since access to such funds inevitably required consultation with, and approval of, the local government. For example, one survey found that between 50 and 73 per cent of bank loans, granted by the branch offices of the Bank for Industry and Commerce to finance enterprises' technical updating and transformation investments, were destined for projects arranged by the local authorities (*ZGFZYGG*, 1988, 11: 28).

SUMMARY

Chinese state-owned industrial enterprises gained considerable autonomy to organize their production and investment activities under the reforms. However, the extent of the autonomy they enjoyed differed considerably with respect to various areas of decision making. This is confirmed by the findings of two enterprise surveys in Shanghai and Tianjin in 1987 (*JJYJ*, 1988, 4: 69; *GYJJGLCK*, 1988, 10: 3; 11–12). These surveys reveal that enterprises had considerable decision-making freedom in relation to output, material acquisition, marketing, and joint ventures with other enterprises; whereas their decisions in the areas of pricing and the appointment of management personnel and workers and their remuneration were still subject to stringent government regulation.

In the early 1990s, despite the acceleration of enterprise autonomy reforms, an enterprise survey in 11 provinces and municipalities carried out in 1992 reveals that most of the expanded rights of the enterprises were not yet fully enforced (*ZGJJTZGGNJ 1993*: 179). According to this survey, enterprises have been able to exercise their increased autonomy effectively in only five areas, namely output, material acquisition, marketing, wage and bonus determination, and joint ventures or mergers with other enterprises. Their autonomy with regard to pricing, the disposal of retained profits and the firm's assets, personnel management, and internal administrative arrangement was still highly attenuated. Their autonomy in investment, foreign trade, and the employment of labour, as well as their right of refusal to various levies and mandatory contributions imposed by the government, was practically nil.

5 Changes in the Industrial System III: Incentive Reforms

Changes in the decision-making structure necessitate corresponding changes in the incentive system. Since both theory and practice suggest that in a decentralized decision-making environment proper incentives to allocate resources efficiently over time exist only under private ownership (Blommestein and Marrese, 1991: 50) decentralization of decision making needs to be accompanied by privatization. However, privatization of state industrial enterprises is ideologically unacceptable in China. Hence, an alternative incentive system needs to be found. Since the late 1970s China has experimented with numerous new incentive systems in an attempt to enhance the financial discipline of its state industrial enterprises. This chapter analyses these incentive changes and evaluates how effective they have been in motivating enterprise management and workers to strive for greater industrial efficiency.

ENTERPRISE INCENTIVES

As in other socialist countries two types of incentive exist for Chinese industrial enterprises: one for the enterprise as a whole and the other for its staff and workers. The incentive provided for the enterprise as a whole is its net income or profit share. Following Stiglitz, the profit[1] of state-owned industrial enterprises may be shared between the state and the enterprise in the following ways. If P is the profit and a and b are distribution parameters, P_e, the enterprise share, and P_s, the state share, then

$$P_e = aP + b. \qquad (1)$$
$$P_s = (1 - a)P - b, \qquad 0 < a < 1, \qquad (2)$$

where different patterns of profit distribution can thus be derived by assigning different values to the two distribution parameters. For instance, if

---

[1] The profits of state-owned enterprise in the Chinese context include capital and rental charges.

(1) $a = 0$, the enterprise receives a lump sum equal to b and the rest of the profit accrues to its owner, the state;
(2) $b = 0$, this is the pure profit-sharing scheme;
(3) $a = 1$, and $b < 0$, this resembles the rental system, under which the enterprise pays a fixed sum to the state for the use of capital and is entitled to keep the rest of the profit.

Alternatively, profit distribution may be a mixture of the above three extreme forms: for example, if $b < 0$, the enterprise pays the state a fixed fee and the state is entitled, in addition, to a given percentage, $1 - a$, of the profit. If $b > 0$, the enterprise receives a fixed sum plus a share in the profit. Given the assumptions of (a) freedom of choice, and (b) a competitive economy, the equilibrium levels of a and b, or the optimal pattern of profit distribution between the state and the enterprise, depend not only on the incentive effects but also on the risk sharing and supervision cost as well as fiscal revenue aspects of altern-ative distributive systems (Stiglitz, 1974; and Cheung, 1969).

THE ENTERPRISE FUND (*QIYE JIJIN*) SYSTEM, 1978–1979

Since 1978 China has experimented with five main types of profit-sharing scheme. Initially the enterprise fund system similar to that adopted during the First Five-Year Plan period was reintroduced in 1978. This system was first introduced to a very limited number of enterprises (largely in Sichuan) in 1978. In 1979 it was extended to about 50 per cent of the state enterprises. Under this system an enter-prise was given a lump sum equivalent to a certain percentage of its wage bill. The size of this percentage hinged upon the degree to which the enterprise had fulfilled the eight obligatory input and output targets and the delivery contract (*ZGGYJJFQHB 1949–81*: 132–3). Of these targets, five were basic targets which had to be fulfilled to enable an enterprise to qualify for the enterprise fund. These were out-put, product mix, quality, profit, and the delivery contract. The fulfilment of these five targets would entitle an enterprise to assign 3 per cent of its wage bill to the enterprise fund. An enterprise which fulfilled each of the other targets (cost, material consumption norms, labour productivity norms, and working capital norms) could earn an additional 0.5 per cent of its wage bill to be assigned to the enterprise fund. Thus, an enterprise could earn altogether up to 5 per cent of its wage bill as enterprise fund if all nine targets were fulfilled. The enterprise fund was to be fed from enterprise profits. For enterprises with a planned loss the fund was to be fed from state subsidies.

The major defect of the enterprise fund system is that it induced an enterprise to fulfil and even overfulfil the obligatory targets assigned from above. This, however, is not compatible with the goal of the reform, which is to increase enterprise autonomy. Furthermore, by tying the enterprise fund to (a) the wage bill and (b) plan fulfilment and overfulfilment enterprises were encouraged not only to strive for a larger wage bill and number of employees but also to conceal their real production capacity and to bargain for a soft plan (*JJGL*, 1979, 4: 18). Hence, less than one year after its re-establishment, this system was replaced by another one known as the profit-retention system.

THE PROFIT-RETENTION (*LIRUN LIUCHENG*) SYSTEM, 1979–1980

The profit-retention system is essentially a pure profit-sharing scheme where the enterprise share, P_e, is planned as a fixed percentage, a, of its actual profit, P_t:

$$P_e = aP_t. \tag{3}$$

The norm, a, is determined in such a way as to enable an enterprise to retain sufficient funds from its profit to meet its decentralized investment expenditures and incentive pay which hitherto had mainly been fed from the state grant or the wage bill and were included in production costs. Thus this system represents an attempt to make profit the sole success indicator of an enterprise.

The profit-retention scheme is superior to the previous enterprise fund system for the following reasons. First, it is more compatible with the aim of the reforms of increasing enterprise autonomy since an enterprise's share in profit was now directly tied to actual profit; the attainment of some plan targets as a condition for an enterprise's share in profits was abandoned. Second, it had a greater incentive effect as the profit which the enterprise could retain was no longer fixed but allowed to rise with increased profits. Thus it provided enterprises with a stronger incentive to strive for maximum profits. Third, it forced enterprises to share part of the risk with the state in meeting enterprise investment, welfare, and incentive pay expenditures. Last, but not least, it reduced the burden and, hence, the cost to the state of the direct supervision of enterprises.

However, the profit-retention system also has some limitations. To begin with, to encourage an enterprise to maximize profit in an environment devoid of scarcity prices could lead to considerable waste. Enterprises might be misled by irrational prices to adopt incorrect production techniques and to produce the wrong goods. Furthermore, in the absence of a competitive buyers' market enterprises had little incentive to cut costs, introduce new products, or adapt their product mix to buyer demand as they had no difficulty in achieving their sales objectives. Secondly, irrational prices also gave rise to large and unjustified inter-enterprise profitability differentials which undermined the objectivity of the incentive system.

Finally, the 'individualized' norms or rates of profit retention set for each enterprise also caused problems. The profit-retention rate was calculated as a ratio of the enterprise's base-year expenditures on product development, staff welfare, and bonuses to its base-year profit. Since the size of the welfare and bonus expenditures was linked to the size of its wage bill in the past, the profit-retention rate for individual enterprises in practice hinged on the size of their past wage bill and profit. This means that an enterprise which had performed well in the past with a higher profit and higher labour productivity and, hence, a lower wage bill ended up getting a lower retention rate, whereas an enterprise which had performed poorly, with lower labour productivity and a higher wage bill, was given a higher retention rate. Moreover, an enterprise which had performed well in the past had already exhausted its profit potential and, hence, its actual profit was unlikely to experience any significant further increase. Thus an enterprise which had performed well in the past was penalized on both counts and ended up receiving a relatively lower profit share than its poorly performing counterpart because of its lower retention rate and relatively constant profit base.

Due to the above-mentioned shortcomings the profit-retention scheme was amended several times after its introduction. First, in view of the existence of non-scarcity prices an enterprise was no longer rewarded solely on the basis of its profit performance. The decrees of January 1980 and April 1981 again added the fulfilment of several plan targets as conditions for enterprise profit retention (*ZGGYJJFQHB 1949–81*: 142–4; *GWYGB*, 1981: 761).

Second, to motivate an enterprise to improve on its past profit performance so as to exploit fully its profit potential, enterprises were no longer rewarded on the basis of their current performance alone. Past performance was also taken into account. Specifically, if an enterprise's current profit, P_t, was equal to, or smaller than, its base year profit, $P_t - 1$, the enterprise's share in profit, P_e, was calculated as under the original formula:

$$P_e = a P_t. \tag{4}$$

If, however, an enterprise's current profit was greater than its base year profit, then enterprise profit retention was broken down into two parts: a basic retention and an additional retention. The basic retention was awarded for the achievement of profit equivalent to that achieved in the preceding year and the additional retention was awarded for an improvement of the profit over the base year. Thus enterprise total retention, P_e, may be expressed as follows:

$$P_e = a P_{t-1} + b (P_t - P_{t-1}). \tag{5}$$

To encourage enterprises to improve on their past profit the enterprise additional profit retention rate, b, was set higher than the basic retention rate, a. However, due to the well-known 'ratchet effect', the expected incentive effect did not materialize. Specifically, enterprises tended to conceal reserves and to be very cautious about improvements on their previous profit as they were afraid that an improvement in current profit would increase the base year profit in future. To alleviate this fear, the base year profit was later made constant for a given period of several years (*GWYGB*, 1980: 424).

Third, it was increasingly realized that it was not correct to put all enterprises under the same profit-sharing formula. Different profit-sharing formulas[2] were deemed necessary to induce optimal

---

[2] Non-uniform profit-sharing formulas should not be confused with non-uniform or an individualized system for an enterprise's rate of profit sharing or rate of payment to the state. From the optimal incentive point of view different profit-sharing formulas for different groups of enterprises may be deemed necessary in order to take account of their different profit potential and environmental constraints. Hence, the rate of profit sharing or payments to the state may vary among groups of enterprises or branches of industry. Yet for individual enterprises within a particular group or branch adopting a common profit-sharing formula, objectivity in the incentive system requires that the rate should be uniform. Consequently, a uniform enterprise profit-sharing system is not inconsistent with different groups of enterprises or industrial branches adopting different profit-sharing formulas. In an individualized enterprise profit-sharing system the rates are determined for each enterprise. This practice enables an enterprise to increase

performance from different groups of enterprises with different profit potential and different environmental constraints. Thus, from April 1981, the system of placing all enterprises under a uniform profit-sharing scheme was formally abandoned. The decrees of October and November 1981 allowed different varieties of profit-sharing scheme to coexist, each designed for particular conditions of enterprises. Which variety of the scheme was to be chosen was decided by an enterprise's supervisory agencies in consultation with the Ministry of Finance (*GWYGB*, 1981: 756–69).

Once chosen the scheme was supposed to remain in effect for three to four years. The varieties included (1) the pure profit-sharing scheme ($P_e = a P_t$), designed for enterprises with more or less stable profit performance; (2) the basic-cum-additional profit-retention scheme ($P_e = a P_{t-1} + b (P_t - P_{t-1})$), designed for enterprises with large and unexploited profit potential; (3) the overplan profit-retention scheme for overfulfilment of planned profit target $P_e = a (P_t - P')$, where P' is the planned profit and a the retention rate for overplan profit, designed for enterprises suffering from declining profit due to conditions beyond their control; (4) the profit-contract system for enterprises with little profit or suffering from loss; and (5) the tax-for-profit system for enterprises with stable output as well as profit performance.

THE PROFIT-CONTRACT (*LIRUN BAOGAN*) SYSTEM, 1981–1983

The profit-contract system is essentially a rental system. In its pure form an enterprise undertakes to pay the state a fixed sum equivalent to the actual amount of profit delivered to the state in the base year, P_b, and the state allows the enterprise to retain all excess profits. Thus, an enterprise's share is

$$P_e = P_t - P_b; \qquad (6)$$

whereas the state's share is

$$P_s = P_b. \qquad (7)$$

In China, this pure form of the profit contract system was seldom adopted. The most prevalent form is a mixed one where an enterprise

its profit share not by improving its profit performance but by bargaining with the authorities to change its sharing rates (see Pryor, 1973: 260–1).

undertakes to pay the state a fixed amount of profit, P_b, scheduled to grow at an annual constant rate, r, and the state, in addition, is entitled to a given percentage, d, of the excess profit. Thus an enterprise's share, P_e, is

$$P_e = P_t - P_b(1 + r) - d[P_t - P_b(1 + r)]. \tag{8}$$

Hence

$$P_e = (1 - d)[P_t - P_b(1 + r)]. \tag{9}$$

The state's share, P_s, is

$$P_s = P_b(1 + r) + d[P_t - P_b(1 + r)]. \tag{10}$$

The profit-contract system was adopted because of its greater risk-sharing and incentive effects. Under the profit-sharing scheme an enterprise's risk was minimal. If the worst came to the worst its profit share was nil but it could never be negative. The incentive effect of such a scheme was also limited for an enterprise's maximum profit share was limited to the approved profit-retention rate. Under the profit-contract system enterprise risk increased as its profit share became negative if its profit performance was unsatisfactory. However, if it performed well, it could keep the entire increase of profit for itself under the pure profit-contract system. In a mixed profit-contract system an enterprise's profit share would still be larger than that under the profit-retention system[3] even though an enterprise could not keep the entire excess profit for itself.

Because of its stronger incentive effect the profit-contract system proved popular among Chinese industrial enterprises. Originally, the profit-contract system was intended for enterprises with small profits. In 1981, the state expected a huge deficit as a result of its readjustment programme. To ensure stable state revenues from delivered profits of enterprises the profit-contract system was extended to all other enterprises as well (*GYJJ*, 1982, 5: 32). Within a few months of its initiation in 1981 65 per cent of all state-owned enterprises at the county level and above had adopted the system (*GYJJ*, 1982, 5: 18). By early 1982,

---

[3] Under the mixed profit-contract system the percentage share of an enterprise, T_e, is $(1 - d)[P_t - P_b(1 + r)]/P_t$ or $(1 - d)[1 - P_b(1 + r)/P_t]$. Hence if $P_t = 0$, $T_e < 0$ and if $P_t \rightarrow \alpha$ $T_e = 1 - d$. $(1 - d)$ was set higher than a and b of the pure profit-retention system as an enterprise's share of risk was larger under the mixed profit-contract system. According to one source $(1 - d)$ was at least 40 per cent whereas the maximal profit-retention rate under the profit-retention system was only 30 per cent (*GYJJ*, 1982, 5: 18).

the rate of adoption had risen to more than 80 per cent (*CBR*, Nov.–Dec. 1983: 15).

However, the spread of the profit-contract system proved to be short-lived. Its shortcomings became increasingly evident in the course of its implementation and, hence, by 1982 it attracted a lot of criticism. To begin with, the profit-contract system provided enterprises with a stronger incentive because the enterprise share of profit could be increased. But it also decentralized the country's financial resources and thereby exacerbated the problem of the state's loss of control over their utilization. Over the years enterprises were successively provided with an increased share in profit under the reforms. Enterprise profit share soared from 3 to 20 per cent during the period 1978–82 (*GWYGB*, 1980: 420; 1983: 472).

Since enterprise profit was the main source of state revenues the latter dwindled as the enterprise share increased.[4] Hence, the state was forced to cut back on its own investment in such strategic sectors as transportation and energy. On the other hand, investments financed by enterprises and local authorities' own funds soared. Most of these were poured into the processing industries and were thus aggravating the problem of shortage of raw materials, energy, and transport (Byrd, 1983: 332).

Furthermore, the anticipated strong stimulus to increase productivity provided for by the profit-contract system did not materialize. Most efficiency indicators lagged behind their target rates in Chinese industry in 1981. For example, over half of the 78 major industrial products recorded a fall in quality and over half of the 152 industrial material and energy consumption indices experienced an increase in 1981 (Chai, 1983).

One of the main reasons for the failure of the profit-contract system to stimulate productivity growth is that an enterprise's fixed payment to the state (that is, P_b and r in equation (9)) was not uniform for all enterprises but was individually set. This gave an enterprise the opportunity to bargain with the state for a lower P_b and r so as to increase its profit share without improving its performance (*GYJJ*, 1982, 5: 18).

Another major reason for the failure of the profit-contract system to stimulate productivity growth was the indiscriminate use of the

---

[4] Theoretically it may be possible for the state to fix r at a relatively high level so as to ensure a certain state profit share. In reality, r was usually fixed at a low level as a result of the state underestimating the inflation rate in the years covered by the contract.

escape clause or subsidies. As mentioned earlier, theoretically, an enterprise was forced to shoulder a greater risk under the profit-contract system since its profit share would be negative if its performance was not satisfactory. In fact, however, this never happened as authorities were always willing to bail out faltering enterprises by either exempting them from payment of fixed fees or granting reductions therefrom. Thus, enterprises were actually responsible only for profits and not for the loss they incurred (*GYJJ*, 1982, 5: 19).

THE TAX-FOR-PROFIT (*LI GAI SHUI*) SYSTEM SINCE 1983

For the reasons described above the search for a better enterprise-incentive system continued. In 1983, the Chinese authorities decided to place all state-owned enterprises under the tax-for-profit system. This system is somewhat similar to the previous profit-retention system as it is essentially a profit-sharing system. It differs, however, from the latter in that enterprises' payments to the state are in the form of income tax.

Prior to the reform Chinese state-owned enterprises were subject to one single tax, i.e. the industrial and commercial tax which is in essence a turnover tax. With the introduction of the tax-for-profit system the industrial and commercial tax was split into four parts: (a) product tax, (b) value added tax, (c) business tax, and (d) salt tax. In addition, seven new taxes were introduced, namely (a) resource tax, (b) real estate tax, (c) land-use tax, (d) vehicle tax, (e) municipal maintenance and construction tax, (f) income tax, and (g) adjustment tax (*JJTZGGSC*, 1987: 684–5). Thus, if P_t is enterprise profit and t the income tax rate then the enterprise share is given by

$$P_e = (1 - t) P_t \qquad (11)$$

and the state share is given by

$$P_s = {}_t P_{t'} \qquad (12)$$

The tax-for-profit system in its ideal form as described above is superior to the previous profit-retention and contract system for the following reasons. First, under the previous profit-retention and contract systems the rates of enterprise payments to the state were not uniform across enterprises. Hence, it introduced an element of arbitrariness and opened a means for enterprises to increase their profit share by bargaining with the authorities for a lower rate instead of improving their own performance. Under the tax-for-profit system enterprises' payments to the state were in the form of taxes, the rates of which were uniform across enterprises. Hence, it minimized the element of arbitrariness and strengthened the objectivity of the incentive system.

Second, under the previous profit-retention and contract system the rates of enterprises' payments to the state were rather unstable. This introduced an element of uncertainty into the expectations of enterprises. Hence, an enterprise was reluctant to reveal its true production capacity for fear of a future increase in the rate of payment to the state. Under the new system enterprise payments to the state assumed the form of tax the rates of which were not only uniform but also stable, at least for a number of years. Hence, the element of uncertainty was reduced and enterprises could be expected to be motivated to reveal their real production capacity without fear.

Third, under the previous profit-retention and contract system profit had become the main success indicator and objective of an enterprise. However, as prices had not yet been reformed, encouraging enterprises to maximize profit might give rise to considerable negative side effects. Under the new tax-for-profit system several specific taxes were introduced to eliminate the negative effects of the arbitrary price system. These included resource and land-use tax to substitute for the rental charges for the usage of land and other natural resources. They also included a product tax which was designed to wipe out excess profit accrued to commodities due to their higher fixed prices. Last but not least, they also included a real estate tax, vehicle and vessel tax, as well as municipal maintenance and construction tax to remove the unfair advantage enjoyed by some lucky enterprises in an especially favourable location and environment.

Fourth, under the profit-contract system the enterprises' share of profit could grow unchecked, a process which exacerbated the problem of over-decentralization of the country's financial resources. Under the tax-for-profit system the income tax rate on enterprise profit could be made progressive so that when enterprise-retained profit reached the maximum level most, if not all, of the increased profit could be made to accrue to the state.

Finally, under the tax-for-profit system an enterprise no longer delivered its profit to the supervisory agency but paid taxes directly to the state instead. Thus, the financial relationship between an enterprise and its supervisory agency had changed substantially. Specifically, the supervisory agency no longer had any claim on the residual income of the enterprise. Thus it had less incentive to supervise the enterprise's activity closely. Enterprise autonomy was thereby increased.

Unfortunately, up to the early 1990s the pure income tax system as described above was not fully implemented. For large- and medium-sized enterprises a mixed system of income tax and profit retention was used whereby an enterprise would first pay a uniform 55 per cent income tax on its profit. The after-tax profit might be retained by an enterprise entirely if it was equal to that retained by the enterprise in the base year of 1983. If it exceeded that base level the excess would be shared between the state and the enterprise in the form of an adjustment tax. The adjustment tax rate, t_a, was calculated as follows:

$$t_a = [P_b(1 - t) - P_{eb}]/P_b, \tag{13}$$

where P_b stands for the base year profit, t for the 55 per cent income tax rate, and P_{eb} for the base year enterprise profit retention (SSYCWSC, 1987: 237).

For small enterprises a mixed system of income tax and the profit-contract system was used under which an enterprise would pay a progressive income tax and, if an enterprise's after-tax profit was found to be higher than its base year (1983) profit retention, a part was siphoned off by the state in the form of contract fee. Both the adjustment tax rate and the contract fee were to be determined individually for each enterprise by the respective authorities in consultation with the enterprise supervisory agencies (SSYCWSC, 1987: 15, 235).

The successful implementation of the pure income tax system depends ultimately on the construction of a correct system of direct and indirect taxes. The 1994 tax reform package, which focused on enterprise income and turnover tax (SCMPIW, 15–16 Jan. 1994; Xu and Ma, 1993: 74–6), aimed to achieve this objective. The main thrust of enterprise income tax reform is to equalize the tax burden between domestic and foreign enterprises and to eliminate the gap between the nominal and the actual tax burden for domestic enterprises. Hitherto, Chinese domestic state-owned enterprises were subject to 55 per cent income tax rate whereas foreign-invested enterprises were taxed at only 33 per cent. The reform in 1994 reduced the income tax rate for domestic enterprises to a uniform rate of 33 per cent. In the past, the actual income tax rate for domestic enterprises was lower than the nominal rate as they were allowed to treat the repayment of loans as tax deductible. The reform in 1994 abolished this practice and required enterprises to pay their loans from their after-tax income.

The 1994 indirect tax reform was designed to bring the Chinese tax structure more in line with international practice. Specifically, it aimed to establish an indirect tax system consisting of value added tax (VAT), business tax, and consumption tax (*SCMPIW*, 8–9 Jan. 1994; Xu and Ma, 1993: 70–6). VAT applies to commodity transactions and covers all stages from production to retail sales. VAT is levied at 13 per cent for necessities and 17 per cent for all other products. Business tax applies to service transactions and carries a tax rate between 3 and 20 per cent. Consumption tax was introduced as a replacement for the product tax. As mentioned earlier, the latter was designed to wipe out the differences in the profit margins of enterprises due to the controlled price system. As the price structure became increasingly marketized and rationalized the original function of this tax diminished. Under the 1994 tax reform, the product tax was renamed consumption tax and applied to only 11 special commodities and luxury items; the purpose was to achieve certain policy objectives, such as the discouragement of cigarette smoking and alcohol consumption as well as the conservation of energy.

THE CONTRACT RESPONSIBILITY SYSTEM (*CHENGBAO JINGYING ZERENZIH*) SINCE 1987

A large variety of contract responsibility systems (CRS) have been practised in China since 1987. However, the most popular form was the two-guarantee-and-one-link-up system (*liangbao yi gua*). Under this system the state and an enterprise entered into a contract, the duration of which averaged three to four years. During the contract period the enterprise would guarantee the state three things: (1) obligatory delivery of a certain amount of profit; (2) completion of the planned tasks of technical renovation of the enterprise; and (3) the link-up of the growth of its wage bill with that of its efficiency indicators. The state, on the other hand, held out the promise that the enterprise could retain any profit in excess of the obligatory delivery. The actual amount of profit delivered was individually determined for each enterprise (*QYCBZN*, 1988: 341). Several schemes were used to determine this amount. Which scheme was adopted for each enterprise depended on its profit potential. For enterprises with an average profit potential a method known as '*shang jiao lirun dinge baogan*' was used, according to which the enterprise undertook to pay the state a fixed sum equivalent to the base year profit delivery. This was normally the actual amount of the income and adjustment taxes payable in the base year. For enterprises with a high profit potential the enterprise would undertake to pay the state a fixed sum equivalent to its base year profit delivery plus either an annual increment or a certain percentage share of its excess profit. The former scheme is known as '*shang jia lirun dizeng baogan*' and the latter as '*shang jia lirun jishu baogan, chao shou fencheng*'. Finally, for a loss-making enterprise a scheme known as '*jian kui baogan*' was adopted, according to which an enterprise would undertake to guarantee the planned reduction of its loss and in return was allowed to retain any savings from any reduced loss compared with the plan.

From the above description it is clear that the CRS is essentially similar to the old profit-contract system. Basically it is a rental system under which an enterprise was made to bear a higher risk by guaranteeing the state a given amount of obligatory delivery regardless of its profitability. But at the same time an enterprise was also provided with stronger incentives as it was allowed to retain all or most of its excess profit. However, an enterprise was subject to more constraints under the CRS than under the old profit contract system. An enterprise undertook not only to guarantee the obligatory delivery of profit but also to achieve certain plan tasks, such as the technical renovation of the enterprise etc. In some cases other mandatory planned input and output indicators were also included in the contract. Furthermore, an enterprise was supposed to limit the growth of its wage expenditures to that of its efficiency indicators.

Thus, the CRS represents a retreat in the development of the Chinese industrial incentive system on the following counts. First, the CRS was a retreat from a uniform incentive system to an individualized one. This is because under the CRS enterprises' payments to the state were no longer in the nature of a tax and, hence, the rates of payment were no longer uniform between enterprises. The individually set rates left room for bargaining between the parties to the contract and thereby softened the budget constraint of the enterprise. Second, the CRS was also a retreat from a decentralized decision-making system to a centralized one as the CRS tended to incorporate numerous planned indicators into the contract and thereby limited enterprises' autonomy.

None the less CRS should be viewed as a tactical retreat dictated by reality. Under the existing property rights arrangements, the market structure, and the price system of the late 1980s it was neither correct to place all enterprises under the same incentive system nor possible to give an enterprise full autonomy in decision making. A differentiated incentive system coupled with limited enterprise autonomy was necessary to induce optimal performance from enterprises conditioned by differentiated internal and external environmental factors. In this sense, the CRS represents an interim incentive system prior to a complete reform of China's economic system.

ENTERPRISE INCENTIVE REFORM IN THE 1990S

Enterprise incentive reform in the first half of the 1990s was centred on perfecting the CRS, the renewed attempt to implement the bankruptcy law, and corporatization of state-owned enterprises.

As mentioned earlier, one of the weaknesses of the CRS is that income tax and adjustment tax were mixed together and contracted out to the enterprises and the contract rates became individualized. Consequently, enterprises' payments to the state were no longer in the nature of a uniform tax. As a remedy, an attempt was made in the early 1990s to separate the tax from the profit contracted. The new target of the contract was after-tax profits, with loans to be repaid after tax. The objectives of this measure were to restore the uniform income tax rate system and to subject all enterprises to an equal tax burden.

Another weakness of the CRS is that because the term of the contract was fixed for such a short period (three to five years), it encouraged enterprises to maximize short-run profit at the cost of long-run profit. To correct this behaviour the target of the contract was changed in the first half of the 1990s from profit delivery to the conservation and growth of enterprise assets (*ZGJJTZGGNJ 1993*: 71).

At the same time, to further enhance the financial accountability of enterprises the pressure on loss-making enterprises was increased by the renewed attempt on the part of the government to implement the bankruptcy law. This law was enacted in the latter half of the 1980s but had not been enforced. In the early 1990s loss-making enterprises, instead of being declared bankrupt, were forced to merge with other enterprises. By the end of 1992 over 10,000 enterprises had been merged. The number of enterprises declared bankrupt, however, soared in the first half of the 1990s. By the end of 1994 it had reached 1,000. However, fewer than half of these were state-owned enterprises (*SCMPIW*, 5–6 Nov. 1994).

To further strengthen enterprise financial accountability corporatization was also put on trial in the early 1990s. The idea originated from Professor Li Yining and was geared to simulating private enterprise behaviour within state-owned enterprises, but without privatization (Zhou, 1993: 125–44). This is to be achieved by converting state-owned enterprises into joint stock companies with the state still controlling a dominant share of the company and the rest of the shares owned by individuals, other institutions, or even foreigners. The state is expected to exercise its ownership function through state holding companies or state investment banks. The management of the company is separated from its ownership. The board of directors assumes full independent decision-making power and serves as an agent of the shareholders. Performance is monitored by the annual shareholders' meeting and by the prices of company shares in the stock markets as well as by the threat of take-over by other companies if the management team fails to peform. In late 1994 there were some 20,000 joint stock companies (*SCMPIW*, 10–11 Dec. 1994). But most of these were collective enterprises and only some 300 have listed their shares in the stock markets and just six companies have listed their shares overseas.

WORKERS' INCENTIVES

The discussion of the post-reform Chinese industrial incentive system has so far focused primarily on incentives provided for an enterprise as a whole. This and the following section will deal with incentives provided for the personnel working in an enterprise.

As in other socialist countries the main incentive provided for Chinese workers is the incentive pay which workers receive in addition to their basic wage. While the basic wage is relatively stable the incentive pay is variable in accordance with a worker's performance.

Initially a worker's incentive pay consisted mainly of a regular bonus or an above-norm piece-rate wage. Prior to the introduction of the profit-sharing scheme regular bonuses and above-norm piece-rate wages were financed from the wage bill and included in production costs (*ZGGYJJFQHB 1949–81*: 102). Since the introduction of the profit-sharing scheme regular bonuses and above-norm piece-rate wages were financed from enterprise-retained profit and, hence, were no longer included in the cost of production (*ZGGYJJFQHB 1949–81*: 138; *GWYGB*, 1981: 577).

With the introduction of the CRS workers received incentive pay in the form of an efficiency wage instead of a bonus or an above-norm piece-rate wage. An efficiency wage is essentially a wage increment in addition to the basic wage which is linked to, and therefore varies with, enterprise and worker performance. Efficiency wages were, once again, financed from the wage bill and included in production costs (Liu Jieshan *et al.*, 1988: 59).

Incentive pay was initially distributed on an egalitarian basis (*GWYGB*, 1981: 339). Monthly assessment meetings were held to determine the individual contributions and each worker's entitlement to the incentive payment (Shirk, 1981: 585). Such meetings were not only time consuming but also unproductive as they could hardly arrive at an objective assessment of individual contributions. As a result the total available incentive fund was simply divided equally by the number of workers. An informal rotation system was also in use whereby everyone was given a turn to receive a bonus during the year so as to save the enterprise from being sanctioned by the higher authorities for egalitarian distribution of the bonus.

The egalitarian way of distributing incentive pay defeated the very purpose of its introduction. Hence, to counteract egalitarianism the intra-enterprise responsibility system (IRS) was introduced. The IRS was designed to tie the incentive pay for workers more closely to their performance. Under the IRS a variety of incentive pay schemes were adopted which can be classified according to the following characteristics: (1) whether the award was given on a group or individual basis; (2) the kind of award given; and (3) the method of measuring a worker's performance.

The industrial process, however, requires extensive division of labour and work needs to be performed by groups. Hence, it is not possible to separate exactly the contribution of one individual from that of another. Thus, unlike the responsibility system in agriculture an award in industry cannot be given on a purely individual basis. Hence a mixed system was generally used in Chinese state-owned industrial enterprises where awards were given both on a group and an individual basis (*QYNBFPZDGGDZCYSJ*, 1988: 197–359; Xu, 1988: 324–6).

The mixed system used is akin to the work-point method of distribution of collective income in a production team in pre-reform Chinese agriculture. Under this system the performance of groups within the enterprise and their entitlement to the enterprise incentive fund were determined first. Then individual performances within the group were assessed and used as a basis to distribute the incentive fund awarded to the group. Specifically, group or individual performance was measured in terms of certain specific criteria, such as merit points earned, extra output produced, extra work done, etc., which in turn served as a claim against the group incentive fund. Thus, the entitlement of an individual worker to enterprise incentive fund, Yi, was determined by the number of merit points earned or extra output produced by the worker, Wi, and the bonus value of the merit points or extra output produced, w. Thus,

$$Yi = Wi \cdot w. \tag{14}$$

The bonus value of a merit point or the additional output produced was, in turn, arrived at by dividing all merit points earned or all extra output produced by all workers within the group into the designated group incentive fund, P. Thus,

$$w = P/\Sigma Wi. \tag{15}$$

Substitute (15) into (14),

$$Yi = Wi(P/\Sigma Wi). \tag{16}$$

Thus, the incentive pay for individual workers depended not only on their own effort in terms of Wi but also on the group effort which determined the group incentive fund available, P. Hence, to maximize individual incentive pay one needed to maximize not only individual merit points but also the group bonus. Thus, the mixed system is designed to combine the advantages of an individual incentive plan with that of a group plan. It aims to relate individual performance more closely to individual pay while encouraging employees to work together in a co-operative spirit to increase the amount of group bonus money (Lawler, 1973: 120).

The kind of reward provided under the IRS assumed various forms. In addition to the regular bonus and above-norm piece-rate wages, an efficiency wage and floating promotion were also used. In an above-norm piece-rate wage system workers received incentive pay only for the excess output produced over the norm. In the efficiency-wage system a part or the entire wage of workers was made variable in accordance with the performance of the whole enterprise as well as that of workers. In the floating-promotion system workers were given a temporary wage increase through promotion which could be withdrawn if the promoted worker's performance failed to live up to expectation. The most prevalent forms of award in the late 1980s were the bonus and above-norm piece-rate wages and they remained popular in the early 1990s (*ZGJJTZGGNJ 1993*: 325).

With regard to the measurement of performance basically four different methods were used (Yue, 1988: 154–64). The first method is the point system under which individual and group performance were assessed in terms of merit points. The performance indicators used were usually a set of targets which were disaggregated into numerous detailed targets and assigned to groups within the enterprise. The targets received by each group were further disaggregated into even more detailed targets which were then assigned to individual workers within the group. At the end of the period both individual performance and group performance were then assessed in terms of the degree to which the assigned targets had been fulfilled. Basic points could be earned for target fulfilment. Additional points could be earned if the targets were overfulfilled. If, however, some of the major targets were not fulfilled the basic wage of the group and the workers would be cut.

The second method is the contract system. Under this system a group or an individual contracted with the enterprise for a fixed amount of inputs and was held responsible for meeting a set of specific indicators, such as output and profit. They were entitled to the basic wage alone if the contracted targets were fulfilled. A bonus, however, would be provided if the assigned targets were overfulfilled. If the assigned targets were underfulfilled the basic wage of the group or the individual would again be cut.

The third method is the above-norm piece-rate wage system. Under this system norms specifying the amount and quality of output or work during a period were established. For overfulfilment of the norms the group and individuals received extra pay according to a predetermined scale, in addition to the basic wage. If the norms were underfulfilled, the basic wage of the group and the workers would be cut.

The fourth method is the linkage system (*guagou*) under which the growth of the group's or the individual's incentive pay was tied to the growth of the performance indicators of both the enterprise and individual workers. The third and fourth methods were found to be the more popular ones in Chinese state-owned industrial enterprises in the late 1980s (*QYNBFPZDGGDZCYSJ*, 1988: 197–359; Xu, 1988: 324–6).

By tying incentive pay to performance IRS represents a distinct improvement over the previous worker incentive system. None the less several limitations of the new incentive pay system deserve to be mentioned. To begin with, since the award was mainly given in the form of a bonus and above-norm piece-rate wages, leaving the basic pay unchanged, it is important to know whether the weight of these elements in the total pay package was significant enough to encourage the desired behaviour. The growth of their share, however, was initially slow, as a result of several constraints imposed by the government. Under the profit-sharing scheme the bonus was financed from retained profit. However, not all retained profit could be distributed as bonus. Theoretically, the bulk of it, or about 75 per cent, had to be fed into a production development fund (Liu Jieshan *et al.*, 1988: 180). Furthermore, a ceiling was imposed on the actual amount of bonus distributed: it was not allowed to exceed an amount equal to two-and-a-half times the monthly basic wages of the workers. Though this ceiling was lifted in 1984 growth of the bonus was still constrained by a heavy progressive bonus tax. In 1988 the bonus tax rate for bonus pay in excess of two-and-a-half times the monthly basic pay ranged from 20 up to 200 per cent (Liu Jieshan *et al.*, 1988: 408). Under the CRS workers received an efficiency wage which varied with enterprise and individual performance. Hence, theoretically, workers' entire pay became incentive pay. In practice, however, both upward and downward flexibility of efficiency wages were limited.

Upward flexibility was constrained by a wage adjustment tax the rate of which in 1988 started at 20 per cent for a wage increase in excess of 7 per cent and rose to 200 per cent for a wage increase in excess of 27 per cent (Liu Jieshan *et al.*, 1988: 99). The downward flexibility of efficiency wages was also limited by the provision that wage cuts exceeding 20 per cent of the approved wage bill were not allowed (ibid.). However, by 1993, the reintroduction of incentive pay boosted the share of the bonus and above-norm piece-rate wages in the total money wage bill of workers in state-owned industrial enterprises from 3.6 per cent in 1978 to 25 per cent (*ZGLDGZTJZL 1978–85*: 132; *1978–87*: 180; *ZGTJNJ 1994*: 115).

Second, the existence of a sufficiently large incentive pay is no guarantee of its adequacy, for the degree of the award differential is equally important. Unfortunately, there are relatively few data on intra-enterprise wage differentials. However, inter-enterprise award differential data are available and these can be used to shed light on the adequacy of intra-enterprise award differentials. As is evident from Table 5.1, the inter-enterprise per capita bonus differential was significantly wider in the post-reform period than in the pre-reform period. The coefficient of variation of the enterprise per capita bonus increased from 0.67 to 0.82 per cent from 1987 to the first half of 1989.

TABLE 5.1. *Distribution of Per Capita Bonus among Industrial Enterprises, 1987 and 1989*

Monthly per capita bonus (*yuan*)	Percentage share of enterprises	
	1987[a]	1989 (first half)[b]
0–9.9	7.1	8.7
10–19.9	19.4	16.8
20–29.9	26.2	16.3
30–39.9	19.4	16.6
40–49.9	13.1	13.6
50–59.9	8.0	8.8
60–69.9	3.6	5.9
70–79.9		4.9
80–89.9		2.2
90–99.9	3.3	1.3
100–109.9		1.3
110 and over		3.7
Average per capita bonus (*yuan*)	32.6	42.0
Coefficient of variation	0.67	0.82

[a] A sample of 749 enterprises out of which 91.2 per cent are state-owned, 7.7 per cent are collectively owned, and 0.6 per cent are under 'miscellaneous forms of ownership'.

[b] Out of the 763 enterprises 90 per cent are state-owned, 8.9 per cent are collectively owned, and 1.1 per cent are under 'miscellaneous forms of ownership'.

Source: *KDJDS*, 1989, 2: 34–263.

In spite of this increase the inter-enterprise money wage differential remained rather narrow. As Table 5.2 indicates the coefficient of variation of the inter-enterprise per capita money wage was much less than that of the inter-enterprise per capita bonus. There was an increase in the inter-enterprise wage differential from 1987 to the first

TABLE 5.2. *Distribution of Per Capita Monthly Wage among Industrial Enterprises, 1987 and 1989*

Monthly per capita wage (*yuan*)	Percentage share of enterprises	
	1987[a]	1989 (first half)[b]
0–99.9	9.0	1.6
100–119.9	22.9	8.7
120–139.9	27.8	16.1
140–159.9	22.7	22.7
160–179.9	10.8	16.2
180–199.9	4.0	13.0
200–219.9		11.0
220–239.9	2.8	3.6
240–259.9		2.2
260 and over		5.0
Average per capita monthly wage (*yuan*)	135.5	171.1
Coefficient of variation	0.24	0.30

[a] Same as Table 5.1.
[b] Same as Table 5.1.

half of 1989, yet the range of per capita money wage among enterprises remained rather limited. This relatively narrow range can be explained by several factors. One of them is the apparent limited weight of the bonus in workers' total pay. As a result, the increased inter-enterprise per capita bonus differential did not widen the gap of the inter-enterprise per capita wage significantly.

Another factor is the above-mentioned wage adjustment tax which appeared to be quite effective in controlling excessive wage increases in some enterprises. And yet another factor is the linkage system which tied the growth of wages to the growth of enterprise profits. Under the prevalent distorted prices, the linkage system introduced an element of arbitrariness and inequity into the award of wage increases among enterprises. This is because the growth of enterprise profits was not necessarily due to the growth of enterprise labour productivity. Hence, workers in some enterprises might receive a wage increase without having to increase their labour productivity, simply because of the distorted prices. Furthermore, since wage increases were financed from the wage bill and included in production costs under the CRS system, a wage increase would push up production costs and curb profit growth.

The elasticity of cost increase and profit reduction with respect to wage increases depends on the weight of labour costs in the total costs of an enterprise. Hence, enterprises using capital-intensive techniques of production would be favoured as they were able to pay larger wage increments since these had hardly any effect on their costs or their profits. Enterprises with labour-intensive production techniques, on the other hand, were disadvantaged as they were constrained in their wage increases by their higher elasticities of cost increase and profit reduction with respect to wage increases. This inequity in the distribution of wage increases between enterprises fuelled the demand by workers in disadvantaged enterprises to catch up with the wage increases in advantaged enterprises. This led to a general equalization of wage increases across enterprises.

Third, the method of performance measurement is also important for an effective incentive system. An award closely tied to performance needs specific and objective performance measures if it is to be accepted by individual workers (Lawler, 1973: 133). As mentioned earlier, the prevalent methods of performance measurement were the piece-rate and the linkage systems which measure performance in terms of output and a set of performance indicators.

Though the piece-rate method of performance measurement is more specific and objective it measures only a narrow aspect of performance, namely output. The upshot of this was that other equally important aspects of performance, such as quality, cost, etc., were ignored or performed poorly (*GYJJGLCK*, 1982, 4: 20–2). The linkage system, which uses a set of indicators as a measurement of performance, is more comprehensive yet it is less specific and objective. Individual workers had to take into account a host of indicators to qualify for a reward; hence, the relationship between their effort and reward was made less visible than when a single specific and objective indicator was used (*JJGL*, 1983, 10: 41–2). Moreover, the set of indicators normally also included measures, such as profit, quality, etc., which were beyond the individual worker's control.

Fourth, to maximize the incentive effect, the norm used as a basis for evaluating an individual worker's performance should be set neither too low nor too high. In China, however, most industries had no uniform national established norms. Norms were usually set by individual enterprises based on dubious methods and statistical records. Since managerial incentive pay tended to be linked with that of the workers, as will be discussed in more detail in the next section, both the factory manager and the workers had an incentive to press for a lower norm by presenting invalid data.

Lastly, the costs of the incentive plan also need to be considered. These costs are mainly those of measuring and monitoring group and worker performance. These can be very high due to the fact that the industrial process usually involves many individuals working together, with the result that it is not easy to separate individual contributions from each other. Hence, the administrative costs of linking incentive pay more closely to individual performance might in fact outweigh its benefits. Unfortunately, relatively little information is available about these matters.

MANAGERIAL INCENTIVES

To complete the analysis of Chinese industrial incentive systems the bonus scheme for managerial personnel deserves special consideration since it differs from that of production workers. Traditionally China, unlike its Eastern European counterparts, did not rely on bonuses and other incentive pay to motivate its managers. The pay of managerial staff had no variable element and their main material reward for successful performance was promotion (Eckstein, 1977: 104). The lack of a well-developed incentive pay scheme for managerial personnel in the past can be attributed to several factors (*GYQYGL*, 1982, 2: 46): First, there is the general belief that managers should be motivated by moral rather than material incentives. Second, the role of managerial staff in production was considered less important than that of production workers. Production workers were given the status of front-line workers. Staff working in supportive units, such as repair and tool departments, were considered less important and were classified as second-line workers. Managerial staff were considered least important and were classified as third-line workers (*GYJJGLCK*, 1982, 5: 50). Third, there was the general fear that giving managers a bonus might increase the income differential between the rank-and-file and the managerial staff.

With the reintroduction of bonuses and other incentive pay for workers in 1978, managerial staff also received bonus payments which were linked to those of production workers. The bonus level for managerial staff was based on the average bonus for production workers. Typically, it was set lower than that of second- and first-line workers (Shirk, 1981: 586). As with production workers, the initial method of determining the bonus entitlement of managerial staff through monthly evaluation meetings was soon replaced by an egalitarian distribution method (*GYQYGL*, 1982, 2: 39).

To counter egalitarianism, IRS for managerial staff was introduced in the early 1980s and under it various schemes were developed to measure managerial performance. But unlike the performance of production workers, the results of managerial work cannot be measured directly by specific criteria, such as output and profit, or in terms of a set of specific plan targets. Hence, a more comprehensive evaluation procedure had to be developed (*GYQYGL*, 1982, 5: 86).

Among the various procedures developed in the early 1980s, the most popular was the points system (*GYQYGL*, 1982, 7: 37). Under this system the job performance of leading cadres was assessed in terms of three groups of indicators designed to measure both the quantity and quality of their work. The first set of indicators measured the results of their work indirectly, namely in terms of the fulfilment of plan targets under their responsibility. Thus for instance, for a cadre heading the finance section of an enterprise the fulfilment of certain financial targets, such as profitability, working capital per unit of output etc., was deemed essential.

The second set of indicators measured the quality of their work in terms of such specific criteria as punctuality in submitting various reports, accuracy of their reports, etc. The third set of indicators measured their work attitude in terms of such attributes as friendliness and co-operation in dealing with other departments in the enterprise.

Basic points were attached to each indicator which added up to 100 points in total. Additional points could be earned for overfulfilment and there were penalties for underfulfilment as well. The total number of points earned individually was then used as the basis to calculate the individual manager's claims against that portion of the bonus assigned for distribution to eligible managerial staff.

The strength of the points system lay in its comprehensiveness or in its attempt to measure all aspects of the job performance of managers. However, the goal of comprehensive assessment was achieved at the cost of simplicity and objectivity. As the number of performance indicators, some of which were non-specific in nature, soared it became very difficult for the individual to visualize the relationship between his/her job performance and the paid-out reward. Furthermore, due to the large number of indicators covered and the dubious ways in which norms were set for individual indicators (*GYQYGL*, 1982, 7: 40), differences in the number of points and, hence, in bonus entitlement tended to be very limited. Thus, the introduction of IRS for managerial staff failed to eradicate completely the egalitarianism in the distribution of bonuses among eligible managers. For instance, a survey of IRS for managerial staff in Shanghai in the early 1980s revealed that the maximum differential between the highest and the lowest monthly bonus pay for managers was only three to five *yuan* and the minimum differential was reduced to a mere couple of cents (*GYQYGL*, 1982, 7: 41).

Under the CRS theoretically both the positive and negative incentives for managers were significantly enhanced. As stipulated in the regulation governing the contract system (*QYCBZN*, 1988: 48) top managers, upon fulfilment of the contract, were allowed to earn an amount more than triple that of the average worker. In cases of non-fulfilment their salary could be halved. However, up to the early 1990s the implementation of this new managerial incentive system made little progress. For various reasons managers were reluctant to cash in their bonus entitlements. One of the major reasons was that they were afraid of widening the manager–worker income differential because of the possible political repercussions. Another reason was that the bonus for both managers and workers came from the same source, namely retained profits. Managers feared that the cashing in of their bonus entitlements would reduce the amount of the bonus fund available for distribution to the workers and would thereby undermine worker morale (Liu Jieshan *et al.*, 1988: 291).

Consequently, managerial incentives under the CRS saw few practical improvements. This is evident from the narrow income gap between managers and workers found in enterprise surveys. Thus, for instance, a sample survey of 322 state enterprises carried out in Shanghai in 1987 shows that the manager–worker income differential seldom exceeds 50 per cent (*JJYJ*, 1988, 4: 69). This finding is confirmed by a more comprehensive national sample survey of 1,296 enterprises (*GYJJGLCK*, 1988, 4: 11) which shows that the earnings of most managers were not significantly higher under the CRS than under the previous bonus system. Most received only a modest increment to their salary after the change to the CRS system. A survey of 769 state-owned enterprises in Sichuan, Jiangsu, Jilin, and Shanxi conducted by the Institute of Economics of the Chinese Academy of Social Sciences in 1989 also reveals that managerial personnel did not take advantage of the enterprise incentive reform to increase their income, and that while production workers' wages rose in real terms by 3.2 per cent annually, wages of managerial personnel rose by only 1.8 per cent from 1980 to 1989 (Groves *et al.*, 1994: 206).

Proposed managerial incentive reforms in the first half of the 1990s include the severance of the link between managerial income and that of production workers. Instead it has been proposed that the growth of managerial income should be linked with the growth of enterprise assets (Li Yuan, 1993: 95).

IMPACT OF THE INCENTIVE REFORMS

The key test of whether China's incentive reforms in its state industrial system were successful or not lies in the answers to the following questions: (1) whether it had basically changed the attitude of enterprise managers from an output to a profit orientation; (2) whether it had hardened enterprise budget constraints; (3) whether it had tightened the link between workers' pay and their productivity; and (4) whether it had increased enterprise total factor productivity (TFP).

With regard to the first question, available evidence suggests that China's state industrial enterprises have become increasingly profit oriented. This is confirmed by the findings of a number of national sample surveys of factory managers. Thus, for instance, the earliest nation-wide sample survey of 359 factory managers in 1984, carried out by CESRRI, found that of the 14 enterprise objectives listed in their questionnaire, profit-related objectives were regarded by managers as the most important, whereas 'fulfilment of output quotas' and 'doubling of output value' were regarded as the least important (*JJYJ*, 1985, 11: 3). A second survey by CESRRI of 1,296 factory managers in 1987 also confirms the previous findings. The respondents were asked what were the enterprise's main constraints. The majority of them (63.3 per cent) regarded profit-related factors, namely 'supply of raw materials and their prices' and 'marketing of output and their prices' as the most important constraints on their enterprise whereas only 4.7 per cent of managers regarded plan targets as the enterprise's main constraints (*GYJJGLCK*, 1988, 4: 6). A more recent nation-wide survey of 300 large and medium-sized state industrial enterprises by a Hong Kong team in collaboration with the Institute of Economics of the Chinese Academy of Social Science

(CASS) in 1989 again found that profit and profit-related objectives were considered by most managers as the most important enterprise objectives (Chai and Tisdell, 1992: 14–15).

With regard to the second question, the softness of a state enterprise budget constraint is, according to Kornai (1980: 306–9), conditioned by the following factors: (1) the enterprise's price-making power; (2) a soft tax system; (3) free state grants; (4) a soft credit system; and (5) extensive fiscal redistribution of profits 'from the strong to the weak'. One of the implications of a soft enterprise budget constraint is that the survival and growth of an enterprise is independent of its profitability. This suggests not only that enterprises care little about profit and loss but also that their investment activity and liquidation bear little relation to their profit performance. Another implication is that under the impact of extensive redistribution of profits among enterprises the individual enterprise's profit share is not related to its original profit, i.e. loss-making enterprises also pay out profit shares. Furthermore, it can be expected that the size of the workers' bonus has little to do with their enterprise's actual profit, for loss-making enterprises also pay bonuses. Thus the softness of the state enterprise budget constraint can be tested in terms of the increased interdependence between (a) the enterprise's profit share and its actual and reported profit; (b) enterprise investment activity and its actual profitability in the preceding years; (c) liquidation of an enterprise and its profitability; and (d) an enterprise's bonus payment and its profitability.

The test results based on the above criteria, using the nation-wide sample survey of 300 state enterprises conducted by a Hong Kong team in 1989 are mixed (Chai and Tisdell, 1992). On the one hand, enterprise budget constraints appear to have hardened, the profit share of large and medium-sized state industrial enterprises was highly correlated with their reported profits during the period 1984–8, with the estimated correlation coefficient ranging from 0.881 to 0.931. Moreover, enterprise investment activity was found to be closely related to past profit performance.[5] On the other hand, there were still

---

[5] The estimated regression equation between the two is as follows:

$$\text{(a) } 1984: G_K = 0.196 + 1.733\,\Pi_{t-1}, R^2 = 0.481,$$
$$(5.20)\ (16.59)$$

$$\text{(b) } 1988: G_K = 0.143 + 1.532\,\Pi_{t-1}, R^2 = 0.348,$$
$$(5.71)\ (12.57)$$

several soft spots in enterprise budget constraints. For example, it was still almost unheard of in the second half of the 1980s for enterprises to be declared bankrupt due to persistent losses. Furthermore, loss-making enterprises still paid bonuses, as indicated by the loose correlation between the growth of enterprises' expenditure on workers' bonuses and welfare payments and their retained profits per worker.[6] The continued softness of enterprise budget constraints is most evident from the inelastic demand for bank loans by state industrial enterprises with respect to the interest rate change, as shown in Table 5.3.

TABLE 5.3. *Perceived Enterprise Demand for Bank Loans in Response to a Rise in Interest Rates*[a]

Enterprise response	No. of responses	%
(1) Unchanged	240	84.8
(2) Decline by 10–20%	20	7.1
(3) Decline by 20–30%	15	5.3
(4) Decline by 40–50%	2	0.7
(5) Decline by 50% and more	6	2.1
TOTAL	283	100.0

[a] The question asked was: 'If the interest rate rises by 5 per centage points, by how much would you reduce your request for a bank loan?'

Source: Chai and Tisdell, 1992: 1.

With respect to the third question, an early study by Jefferson and Xu (1991) found that workers' compensation both in kind and in money was increasingly tied to their productivity. However, this study is based on a very small sample of only 20 enterprises in Wuhan in the late 1980s. Moreover, since their sample includes not only large and medium-sized state enterprises but also small state and collective

where G_K stands for an enterprise's rate of fixed capital investment and Π_{t-1} for its rate of profitability lagged by one year. The *t*-values are in parentheses.

[6] The estimated relation between the two variables is as follows:

(a) $1984: \ln B/L = 1.29 + 0.188 \ln P/L, R^2 = 0.212,$
   (44.9) (8.76)

(b) $1988: \ln B/L = 1.01 + 0.132 \ln P/L, R^2 = 0.118,$
   (40.7) (6.15)

where *ln B/L* stands for the logarithm of bonus and other welfare expenditures per worker and *ln P/L* is the logarithm of retained profits per worker. The *t*-values are in parentheses.

enterprises their results may not be representative of typical state enterprise behaviour. A more recent study by Groves *et al.* (1994) using the 1989 survey data of 769 state-owned enterprises carried out by CASS found that in four out of the five industries bonuses were significantly positively correlated with productivity and that the causality goes both ways—from productivity to bonuses and from bonuses to productivity.

Finally, concerning the last question, the continued softness of the budget constraints of the enterprises, coupled with the limited development of the factor market and its imperfection, suggests that China is far from attaining economic efficiency in its state industrial system (Tisdell, 1992, chapter 9). Recent studies by Groves *et al.* (1994) and Jefferson and Rawski (1994), however, indicate that TFP has increased in the state industrial sector under the reforms. But their findings should be regarded as tentative. Official statistical data of state-owned industrial enterprises are fraught with over- and underreporting factors (Zhou, 1993: 139) and it is very difficult to measure accurately the actual output and input of these enterprises. Another study by Hu, Hai, and Jin (1994) concluded that TFP had not increased but had declined in the state industrial sector during the years 1984–8. In any case, as of 1994, both the productivity and profitability of China's state industrial sector left much to be desired. In the first quarter of 1994, 50 per cent of state-owned industrial enterprises were reportedly suffering a loss. If the hidden subsidies in the form of low-priced inputs are included the percentage share of loss-making enterprises soared to 80 per cent. Furthermore, there is evidence that both capital and labour productivity remained very low in these enterprises. For instance, in recent years 70 per cent of the country's investment went to the renovation of these enterprises; and yet their output grew by only 20 per cent (*CD*, 24 Aug. 1994). In the period from 1989 to 1991 the output growth of these enterprises declined and their labour productivity growth stagnated, yet their expenditure on wages grew at double-digit rates (*CDBW*, 11–17 Sept. 1994).

6 Reforms of the Price System

There are basically four types of prices in China: industrial ex-factory, agricultural purchase, wholesale, and retail (Zuo, 1985: 31–2). Industrial ex-factory and agricultural purchase prices are basically the producer prices received by industrial and agricultural producers when they sell their output whereas wholesale and retail prices are basically the consumer prices paid by the end-users and final consumers of the industrial and agricultural products (Gu, 1987: 156–62).

Industrial ex-factory prices and agricultural purchase prices are the basic constituents of the Chinese price system in the sense that all other prices are derived from them. Thus, for example, industrial and agricultural wholesale and retail prices are formed by adding the circulating expenses and profit margins of the wholesaler and retailer plus taxes to the industrial ex-factory and agricultural purchase price (Hu, 1982: 404–5).

Although wholesale and retail prices are based on industrial ex-factory and agricultural purchase prices the link between the two sets of prices was very tenuous in the past since the government often changed one set of prices without changing the other by simply manipulating taxes and/or profits at the wholesale and retail level (Donnithorne, 1967: 440). The discussion in this chapter is limited to the formation of industrial ex-factory, agricultural purchase, and retail prices. It focuses primarily on changes in pricing principles and the major implications of these changes.

INDUSTRIAL EX-FACTORY PRICES

Though in the past both the setting and the adjustment of Chinese industrial prices were cost oriented there is strong evidence to suggest that relative industrial prices diverged widely from their actual costs. This is because, first of all, prices were adjusted infrequently, despite the changing cost conditions. Most of the Chinese industrial ex-factory prices were formed in the early 1950s. During the period 1953–78 there were only two major price adjustments, plus several minor corrections. Furthermore, the scale of the price adjustments was limited. In the interests of price stability and other government price policy objectives the rate of price adjustment usually fell behind that of cost changes. Finally, and most important of all, the official costs upon which Chinese industrial prices were set and adjusted underestimated actual costs. For Chinese cost calculations in the past were based on average rather than marginal costs. The opportunity cost of capital, land, and other natural resources in the form of capital and rental charges was not included. Until recently depreciation charges were set at about 3.7 per cent on average (Liang and Tian, 1979: 18) which was too minute to reflect the physical wear and tear of fixed assets. Furthermore, the obsolescence of capital equipment was not accounted for.

The divergence between relative prices and costs is evidenced from the wide variation in the rate of profitability calculated in relation to the total amount of fixed and working capital among industrial branches on the eve of the reforms. The ratio between the highest and lowest profitability amounted to 38 to 1 in 1979 (Hu, 1982: 45; Gao, 1982: 162). Generally speaking in the heavy industry sector, prices and profits were exceptionally high in the processing branches and exceptionally low in the extracting branches. In the light industrial sector, prices and profits were very high in branches using non-agricultural products as raw materials whereas prices and profits were known to be relatively low in branches using agricultural products as raw materials (Gao, 1982: 162).

Scarcity prices are indispensable if the market and prices are to play a greater role in China's economic system. Thus, as the new leadership in China attempted to blend Chinese socialism with the market in the late 1970s there was growing pressure for a price reform.

The reform of China's industrial prices can be divided into two stages. In stage one, from 1979 to 1984, reform measures centred on improvements in cost calculations and on the adjustment of controlled prices. The objective of the reform was to make controlled prices reflect more closely the actual costs of production. In stage two, from 1985 on, the focus shifted to price decontrol.

Cost calculation

As has been mentioned before, production costs were significantly underestimated in the past in China due to the fact that the opportunity cost of non-labour factors of production was not properly accounted for. Thus, as from the early 1980s, there were attempts to introduce full cost accounting for these factors in order to remove this inadequacy. First, the rate of depreciation was raised in an attempt to account for the costs of capital more accurately. Initially, the depreciation rate was raised only in selected enterprises and localities. In 1985 the State Council decreed a new depreciation scheme under which the average rate of depreciation was raised from 4.1 to 5.7 per cent. Second, both fixed and working capital charges were first introduced in 1980 for enterprises under the expanded autonomy experiment (*ZGGYJJFQHB 1949–81*: 139 and 146). They were suspended, however, upon the introduction of the tax-for-profit scheme in 1983 (*GWYGB*, 1983: 575). The working capital charge was reinstated in 1984 (*GWYGB*, 1984: 331). Third, in the past banks also charged enterprises interest on loans to finance working capital, although the rate was very low. The reforms raised the rate from 5 per cent in 1979 to 10.98 per cent in 1993 (*ZGTJNJ* 1994: 549). In the past enterprises' fixed-asset investments were mainly financed by interest-free and non-repayable state grants. From the early 1980s bank loans were increasingly used to finance both modernization and basic construction investments. Interest charges for this type of loan varied according to duration and across industrial branches. They were adjusted upwards several times under the reforms. Attempts were also made to account for the cost of land and other natural resources. Rental charges on land and other natural resources were introduced under the tax-for-profit system in 1984 in the form of land-use and natural-resource tax (Gong and Chen, 1984: 42–67).

On the whole, the new method of cost calculation represented an improvement. However, from the opportunity cost point of view several objections can still be raised. For instance, depreciation rates remained very low compared to those in other countries. Moreover, there was no revaluation of assets and the new depreciation charges were simply calculated on the basis of the arbitrary, historical or book value instead of replacement value (Dai, 1983: 6). Interest charges for bank loans also appear very low in relation to the rate of inflation. The real interest rate on bank loans for most industrial enterprises was, for most of the time, in fact negative. Furthermore, the practice of allowing enterprises to repay both interest and principal on bank loans before the calculation of taxable profits and income tax payments meant that a large part of the cost of bank loans was absorbed by the state in the form of lower tax receipts (World Bank, 1988*a*: 123).

Finally, charges for fixed capital provided by the state prior to the reforms remained unaccounted for.

Price adjustment

A number of price adjustments for major industrial products were undertaken after 1979. The relevant information is presented in Table 6.1. These price adjustments were undertaken with two objectives in mind: to realign relative prices with relative costs in order to reduce the disparity of relative prices and profitability among industrial branches; and to realign the domestic prices of traded goods with international prices.

A few key points emerge from the data in Table 6.1. First, price adjustments followed closely the pattern of the past. In the heavy industry sector prices were raised for products of the extracting (logging)

TABLE 6.1. *Adjustment of Industrial Ex-Factory Prices, 1979–1992*

Period	Upward	Downward
1979–1984	Coal, crude oil, coke, pig iron, steel ingot, billet, some steel products, non-ferrous metals, cement, plate glass, cotton cloth.	Cars, general machinery and parts, measuring instruments and apparatus, cutting tools, chemical fibres, polyester cloth.
1985–1988	Coal, crude oil, natural gas, electricity, ferrous and non-ferrous metals, soda ash, sulphuric acid, calcium carbide, cement, cotton cloth and textiles, silk, paper, cigarettes, sugar, washing powder, soap, colour TVs, bicycles, milk powder.	Electronic parts and cellular glass.
1989	Crude oil, electricity, generators, paper and silk.	
1990	Coal, crude oil, petroleum products, non-ferrous metals, stainless steel, glass, cotton textiles and garments, sugar.	
1991–1992	Coal and chemical fertilizer.	

Sources: Xie and Luo, 1990: 249; Hu, 1987: 271; *ZGWJNJ* 1985 : 145, 348–9; *JJTZGGSC*, 1989, II: 669; *CP*, various issues; *ZGJJTZGGNJ 1993*: 299–300; *SCMPIW*, 25–6 Dec. 1993.

and raw materials branches, such as fuel, ferrous and non-ferrous metal, construction and chemical materials, in response to increasing costs. But prices in the processing industry branches, such as machinery and electronics, were reduced in response to productivity increases and cost reductions (Hu, 1985: 28). In the light industry sector prices were raised in those branches which use agricultural raw materials, such as cotton textiles, clothing, and sugar. However, branches using non-agricultural raw materials, such as chemical fibres and polyester clothing, experienced price cuts. Second, since 1989 there has been only an upward adjustment of prices in response to cost increases due to inflationary pressures.

Price decontrol

Attempts to increase the flexibility of the pricing of industrial products was achieved through the introduction of a mixed price system consisting of both fixed and free prices. This system was meant to get the best of both worlds, namely to reap the benefits of both the fixed and the free price system while avoiding some of their costs. The decontrolling of some prices allows prices to fluctuate according to changing cost and demand conditions, whereas the retention of some control prices allows the government to maintain some degree of overall price stability as well as to set certain prices with government objectives in mind (Hare, 1976: 201).

Altogether three different categories of prices have been introduced since 1979: fixed, guidance, and market prices. Guidance prices are also known as floating prices. Under these, enterprises are allowed to determine prices within upper and lower limits (limit prices) or adjust prices below a ceiling (ceiling prices) or above a floor (floor prices)— each of these boundaries being set by the government. Market prices are determined by buyers and sellers in response to demand and supply conditions.

The decontrol of prices in the industrial producer goods sector featured the dual price system under which two sets of prices, fixed and uncontrolled market prices, coexisted for the same product. The dual price system began, under mandatory planning in the early 1980s, with the introduction of floating and market prices in addition to the existing state fixed prices for industrial goods. At first it applied only to a few industrial producer goods but later it was extended to cover most of them. In 1984 the State Council decreed that enterprises were allowed to market on their own behalf surplus output over and above the mandatory quotas at prices within the 20 per cent limit fixed by the state (Xie and Luo, 1990: 280). The dual price system was formally in place in 1985 when the 20 per cent limit was cancelled (ibid.). Thus, from 1985 most industrial producer goods were sold under two prices, i.e. fixed prices for planned delivery and market prices for surplus over and above the quota. The gap between market and fixed prices for selected producer goods could be quite large, with the market price being triple the fixed price (*CP*, 1990, 10: 18). The coexistence of two prices for a single product, with the market price significantly higher than the fixed price, created a potential non-exclusive rental income. In order to capture this rental income producers frequently attempted to divert to market sales outputs destined for planned delivery. This practice resulted in a steady decline of planned deliveries and most producer goods ended up being sold at the higher market prices (*CP* 1990, 9: 4).

To correct the dysfunctional mechanism of the dual price system two measures were introduced in the late 1980s and the early 1990s. First, attempts were made to narrow the gap between the two sets of prices by imposing a ceiling on market prices and by an upward adjustment of the state fixed prices. The former was achieved in 1988 and 1989 when the market prices of an increasing number of producer goods were subject to state-fixed maximal limits (*ZGWJNJ 1989*: 144 and *CP*, 1990, 5: 37). The latter was implemented in 1990 when the fixed prices of crude oil, coal, steel products, ferrous and non-ferrous metals, chemical industrial raw materials, plate glass, and cotton textiles were adjusted upwards by 10 to 40 per cent (*CP*, 1991, 5: 54).

Second, an attempt was made to eliminate the dual price system altogether by phasing out the fixed prices through decontrol of the prices of most industrial producer goods (*ZGJJTZGGNJ 1993*: 249 and 296). In 1992 the prices of a large number of heavy industrial producer goods including coal, steel products, glass, and chemical raw materials, as well as machinery and electronic parts and components, were decontrolled. Altogether more than 600 industrial producer goods and transport prices were freed. As a result, the number of industrial producer goods and transport prices still subject to fixed prices was reduced from 737 to 89 by the end of 1992. At the same time the government expanded sales under market prices for those products the prices of which remained controlled (*ZGJJTZGGNJ, 1993*: 296).

Price decontrol of industrial consumer goods was first introduced in 1982 when 160 so-called minor industrial consumer goods were placed in the market price category. In 1983 another 350 minor consumer goods were added. By 1984 virtually all the minor consumer goods were in the market price category (Xie and Luo, 1990: 255). During the second half of the 1980s market prices were extended to non-minor consumer goods as well. In 1985 sewing machines, wristwatches, radios, and electric fans were sold at market prices and in 1986 the market price category was further extended to include bicycles, black-and-white TV sets, refrigerators, washing machines, tape recorders, up-market cotton textiles, and synthetic textiles. Finally, in 1988 the best brands of wines and cigarettes were included as well. In the late 1980s, however, a temporary reversal of price control occurred because of inflation and price increases for certain durable consumer goods in the market price category had to be vetted by the authorities (*ZGWJNJ 1989*: 15). But in the early 1990s price decontrols continued. By the end of 1992 only a few basic consumer goods, such as salt, basic medicines, newspapers, and books were still subject to fixed prices (*ZGJJTZGGNJ 1993*: 293).

The results of the decontrol of industrial ex-factory prices are shown in Table 6.2 which indicates that while in 1978 virtually all industrial ex-factory prices were fixed by the government an overwhelming proportion of them were determined by market forces in

TABLE 6.2. *Distribution of the Three Categories of Industrial Prices (%)*

	Coverage of manufacturing sales				
	1978	1987	1988	1990	1992
Producer goods					
Fixed prices	97.0	64.0	65.0	44.6	20.0
Extracting branches			95.0		
Raw material branches			75.0		
Manufact. branches			41.0		
Floating prices	0.0	23.0		19.0	15.0
Market prices	3.0	13.0	35.0	36.4	65.0
Consumer goods					
Fixed prices	100.0	50.0 ⎱	40–50	29.8	10.0
Floating prices	0.0	18.0 ⎰		17.2 ⎱	90.0
Market prices	0.0	32.0	40–50	53.0 ⎰	

Sources: *CP*, 1990, 4: 2; 1990, 9: 10; 1990, 10: 13–14; 1992, 8: 25, 30; *ZGWJNJ 1989*: 60; Zhang Zhuoyuan *et al.*, 1988: 25; *ZGJJTZGGNJ 1993*: 298.

the early 1990s. Specifically, 80 per cent of industrial producer goods were sold at market and floating prices in 1992. For industrial consumer goods the share was even higher and reached 90 per cent in the early 1990s.

Despite the greater impact of market forces on the price of industrial goods the significance of administered prices should not be underrated. A glance at Table 6.2 shows that for upstream products, such as energy, fuel, and raw materials, administered prices were still very significant. Since upstream products make up more than 70 per cent of the value of downstream products (*CP*, 1989, 4: 12) administered prices still played an important role in the pricing of industrial goods in the early 1990s.

Impact of the reforms

The impact of the industrial price reforms is shown in Table 6.3. In general the industrial ex-factory price level as a whole almost tripled between 1978 and 1993. Prices of producer goods grew faster than those of consumer goods. In the producer goods sector the extracting

TABLE 6.3. *Industrial Ex-Factory Price Indices and Growth Rates, 1978–1993 (1978 = 100)*

Year	All industries	Producer goods				Consumer goods
		Total	Extracting branch	Raw material	Processing branch	
1984	119.1	133.2	149.9	126.8	111.0	104.7
1985	129.5	147.1	163.1	140.6	124.0	109.2
1986	134.3	154.1	164.1	151.2	128.5	111.6
1987	145.0	166.1	187.2	161.5	137.8	120.6
1988	166.7	188.9	204.6	183.4	158.0	140.8
1989	197.7	224.6	246.3	213.3	188.6	166.5
1990	205.8	234.4	252.1	226.0	197.1	172.4
1991	218.6	253.2	284.4	252.7	204.6	177.9
1992	233.5	276.8	320.0	278.4	219.7	183.6
1993	289.5	370.1	469.5	390.9	269.6	201.1
Average annual growth rate (%)						
1978–1984	3.0	4.9	7.0	4.0	1.8	0.8
1984–1993	10.4	12.0	13.5	13.4	10.4	7.6

Sources: *C P*, various issues; *ZGJJTZGGNJ 1993*: 268; *ZGTJZY 1994*: 47.

branches experienced the largest and the processing branches the lowest price increases. As a result, the major distortion in China's pre-reform industrial price structure, namely the relatively low prices of producer goods in general and of those in the extracting branches in particular, was significantly rectified during this period.

To measure the extent of the reduction of the industrial price distortion under the reforms we compute the rates of profitability, in relation to the total amount of fixed and working capital among the industrial branches, for state-owned enterprises employing independent accounting. Increased price flexibility should improve the relationship between relative prices and relative costs and, hence, reduce the variation in the rate of profitability of enterprises across industrial branches. As shown in Table 6.4, between 1981 and 1992 both the average profitability and its variation across industrial branches were significantly reduced. The coefficient of variation of profitability fell from 0.846 in 1981 to 0.260 in 1992. However, it should be noted that in addition to price reform, other factors, such as increased competition due to the reduction in barriers to entry, were also responsible for the convergence of profitability among state-owned industrial enterprises (Naughton, 1992: 14–41).

TABLE 6.4. *Profitability of State-Owned Independent Accounting Enterprises in Selected Industrial Branches,[a] 1981, 1984, and 1992 (%)*

	1981	1984	1992
Coal	3.5	2.0	−3.0
Petroleum extraction	45.4	35.7	−1.2
Chemical industry	26.1	29.9	9.8
Machine buildg. industry	10.8	17.5	5.7
Transport equipment	7.2	16.0	10.8
Electronic apparatus	10.7	23.0	10.9
Building materials	15.0	18.4	11.9
Logging and transport of wood	13.7	14.4	6.8
Food	63.9	56.7	3.6
Textiles	63.6	27.1	4.8
Unweighted average	26.0	24.1	6.0
Variation coefficient	0.846	0.582	0.260

[a] Only branches for which profitability data are available for all three years.

Sources: *ZGTJNJ 1981*: 261–2; *1985*: 379–80; *1993*: 438.

AGRICULTURAL PURCHASE PRICES

Under the old agricultural purchase system the government acted as a monopsony in the purchase of most farm and sideline products. These were classified into three categories. The first included products that were vital to people's livelihood, such as food grain, cotton, edible oils, etc. These goods were subject to unified purchase (*tong gou*) (Ma, 1982: 295). The second category included most of the important farm and sideline products, such as live pigs and economic crops which were subject to assigned purchase (*pai gou*) (Ma, 1982: 296). Small and diverse commodities, such as spices, local specialities, small animals, and aquatic products were known as third-category products. These commodities, together with those of the first and second categories in excess of state unified and assigned purchase quotas, were subject to negotiated purchase (*yi gou*).

Under the unified and assigned purchase scheme farmers were obliged to deliver to the state a given quota of commodities at an official quota price. Under unified purchase a price premium above the basic procurement price was paid for additional sales to the state. Under negotiated purchase both the sales quantity and the price were negotiated between the state commercial agencies according to the demand and supply conditions.

Price changes, 1979–1984

The pre-reform Chinese agricultural price system was dominated by quota and above-quota prices established by the government. Under the strategy of forced industrialization farm surpluses were extracted to help finance the expansion of the urban industrial sector. Hence farm purchase prices were deliberately set low in relation to costs, with the result that by 1977 the production of many agricultural items was unprofitable (Lardy, 1983*a*). To restore financial incentives to farm production the first step taken by the government was to raise quota prices for various products in three different ways, starting in 1979. First, prices for quota deliveries of 18 farm products were raised. In 1979 the quota prices of the following products were increased by the following percentages: grain by 20, soybean by 15, oil-bearing crops by 24, cotton by 15, and live pigs by 26, respectively. For such commodities as hemp, sugar-cane, sugar-beet, eggs, beef, lamb, animal skins, and aquatic products, price increases ranged from 20 to 50 per cent (*RMRB*, 25 Oct. 1979). In 1980 and 1981 quota purchase prices for certain products, such as soy beans, cotton, tobacco, etc., were raised once again (*GYJJGLCK*, 1984, 8: 37–8). Second, the government also raised the above-quota price for grain from 30 to 50 per cent. Third, the above-quota price for above-quota delivery was extended to other farm products including cotton, which hitherto had not been entitled to these prices (*GYJJGLCK*, 1984, 8: 23–32; Sicular, 1988: 684).

The second step taken by the government to restore price incentives for farm products was the reintroduction of negotiable and market prices which had been abolished during the Cultural Revolution. In 1979, the system of negotiated purchase prices was reintroduced. Farmers who had fulfilled their procurement quota were allowed to sell their excess output to the government voluntarily at negotiated prices. With the revival of the rural free market as early as 1978 and its expansion in subsequent years farmers were also allowed to sell an increased proportion of their output at market prices. At first, market trade was limited to the output of second- and third-category products in excess of the state procurement quota. By 1980 all first-category products except cotton were allowed on the markets after state delivery quotas had been fulfilled (Sicular, 1988: 689). Thus by 1984 farmers faced four categories of prices: quota, above quota, negotiable, and market prices. The relative importance of these four price categories in terms of agricultural marketing is given in Table 6.5.

The changes in agricultural procurement prices between 1978 and 1984 significantly enhanced price incentives for farm production. To begin with, the raising of the state quota price and the above-quota

TABLE 6.5. *Percentage Share of Various Categories of Agricultural Purchase Prices, 1978–1992*

	1978	1984	1985	1991	1992
Quota price	84	34			
Above quota price	8	34			
Negotiated price	2	14			
Market price	5	18			
Contract prices			37.0	22.2	15.0
State guidance prices			23.0	20.0	
					85.0
Market prices			40.0	57.8	

Sources: Field, 1988: 562; *CP*, 1991, 8: 27; 1992, 8: 28; *ZGJJTZGGNJ 1993*: 294.

price, together with the greater opportunities for farmers to sell a larger proportion of their produce at the higher above-quota, negotiable, and market prices contributed directly to the subsequent huge upsurge in the average agricultural purchase prices received by farmers. Table 6.6 shows that the weighted average of state agricultural procurement prices rose by 53.7 per cent in the period of only seven years from 1978 to 1984. This contrasts with a mere 48.7 per cent increase over the 22 years from 1957 to 1978.

Second, the extension of bonus prices for above-quota deliveries of farm produce other than grain, coupled with the commitment of the government to act as a buyer of last resort at this price, implies that farmers faced a stepwise average and marginal revenue curve (Wyzan, 1985). As indicated in Figure 6.1, farmers received quota prices, Pq, for quota delivery, Qq, and above-quota prices, Paq, for above-quota

TABLE 6.6. *Index of Agricultural Purchase and Industrial Retail Prices, 1979–1993 (1978 = 100)*

	Average farm procurement price[a] (1)	Retail price of industrial products in rural areas (2)	Relative price of agricultural products (3) = (1) / (2)
1979	122.2	100.0	122.2
1980	130.8	100.9	129.7
1981	138.6	101.9	136.0
1982	141.6	103.6	136.7
1983	147.8	104.6	141.3
1984	153.7	107.8	142.6
1985	166.9	111.3	150.0
1986	177.6	114.9	154.6
1987	198.9	120.4	165.2
1988	244.7	138.7	176.4
1989	281.4	164.7	170.9
1990	274.1	172.2	159.2
1991	268.6	177.4	151.4
1992	277.7	182.9	151.8
1993	314.8	204.4	154.0
Annual average growth (%)			
1978–1984	7.4	1.2	6.1
1984–1993	8.3	7.4	0.9

[a] All figures refer to state purchase prices only. Figures for 1978–84 include quota, above-quota, and negotiated prices, and 1985–90 figures include contract, proportion, and negotiated prices.

Source: ZGTJNJ 1991: 230; 1994: 231.

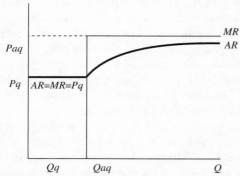

FIG. 6.1. Perverse State Demand Curve Facing Chinese Farmers, 1978–1984

delivery, *Qaq*, which was higher than the quota price. Consequently farmers faced a positively sloped rather than a negatively sloped demand curve, i.e. the more they produced the higher were the average and marginal revenues they received. Furthermore, the marginal revenue was higher than the average revenue for excess output produced beyond the quota purchase price.

Third, since the government acted as a buyer of last resort for output at above-quota prices farmers were in practice assured that the negotiated and market prices or the marginal price they received would not fall below the above-quota price. Such an assurance transferred the entire burden of the market risk from the farmers to the state and thereby reduced the farmers' uncertainty with regard to price expectations.

The changes in agricultural purchase prices in the period from 1979 to 1984 also significantly improved the structure of agricultural purchase prices. Before the reforms this was characterized by three 'lows', the relatively low prices of: (a) agricultural products in general as compared to industrial products; (b) crops as compared to non-crop products; and (c) food grain as compared to industrial crops. These three 'lows' were reflected in the relatively low profitability of agricultural production in general, and of crop and grain production in particular.

The effect of the 1979–84 price changes on relative prices and profitability in the different categories of farm products can be seen in Tables 6.6 to 6.8. Table 6.6 compares the increases in average farm purchase prices with those in retail prices of industrial products in rural areas. It shows that from 1978 to 1984 the annual average increase of agricultural purchase prices was significantly higher than that of retail prices of industrial products. As a result there was a significant improvement in the agricultural terms of trade during this period. Table 6.7 shows that during the same period grain prices grew faster than those of industrial crops. Hence, both the relative prices and the profitability of grain production, as compared to other farm products, were significantly improved in this period.

The improvement in the Chinese agricultural purchase price structure in the first phase of the reforms is also evidenced by Table 6.8. It shows that the average profit per *mu* of both grain and industrial crops increased during the period 1978–85. But the rate of increase was significantly higher for grain. The same table shows that the coefficient of variation of profitability between various crops was significantly reduced between 1978 and 1985. This indicates that the relative prices of crops were brought more in line with their relative costs during this period.

TABLE 6.7. *Indices of Agricultural Purchase Prices, Selected Products, 1979, 1984, and 1992 (1978 = 100)*

	1979	1984	1992	Average annual growth rate[a]	
				1978–84	1984–92
I. *Crops*					
1. Grain				3.9	14.4
Wheat	121.5	121.7	176.0		
Rice	120.7	120.7	200.3		
Corn	120.5	120.7	190.0		
Soy beans	114.9	160.9	323.3		
2. Industrial crops				3.3	9.0
Vegetable oils and oil seeds	123.9	124.7	220.0		
Cotton	117.0	125.1	270.6		
Tobacco	100.3	122.6	160.3		
Sugar crops	121.9	137.6	263.3		
II. *Non-crops*				6.0	15.6
Timber	115.0	185.4	532.4		
Livestock	122.6	133.6	304.7		
Fresh vegetables	111.5	126.8	438.6		
Aquatic products	117.5	127.5	563.5		

[a] Unweighted average

Sources: *ZGTJNJ 1991*: 257–9; *1993*: 265–7.

TABLE 6.8. *Profits per* Mu *of Major Crops, 1978, 1985, and 1991 (in* yuan*)*

	1978	1985	1991
Grain crops	4.2	48.2	63.4[a]
Rice	8.8	73.9	107.0
Wheat	−0.5	40.0	49.0
Corn	2.5	37.9	47.4
Soy beans	6.2	41.2	50.2
Industrial crops	12.6[a]	84.4[a]	186.4[a]
Peanuts	10.3	61.9	118.2
Rapeseed	−2.6	27.1	38.8
Cotton	16.5	81.9	191.1
Sugar-cane	33.9	156.9	424.6
Sugar-beet	5.0	94.2	159.4
Coefficient of variation	1.10	0.56	0.877

[a] Unweighted average

Source: *ZGWJNJ 1989*: 72, 75; *ZGNYNJ* 1992: 468–79.

Price changes since 1985

One of the serious side effects of the increase in the agricultural procurement price in the period from 1978 to 1984 was the huge subsidies
incurred by the government in marketing the agricultural products it
purchased (Walker, 1984: 801). Higher purchase prices mean a higher
bill for state procurement. Because of the fear of inflation and its ad-
verse effect on the living standard of the urban population, the retail
prices of agricultural products were not adjusted accordingly. With
the retail price, Pr, kept below the average procurement price, P, the
gap between the two $(P - Pr)$ had to be bridged by government subsidies. The government subsidy bill, S, can be written as

$$S = Q(P - Pr), \qquad (1)$$

where Q is the output purchased. It is clear from equation (1) that the
subsidy bill was directly related to the output purchased and the average purchase price. As farmers were faced with an upward sloping
average revenue function there was a positive relation between Q and
P. Thus as output soared average purchase prices and the government's subsidy bill also soared. The price subsidy bill for cereals,
cotton, and oil-bearing crops alone soared from 1.1 to 20.1 billion
yuan between 1978 and 1984! Its percentage share in total government
expenditures increased from about 10 per cent in 1978 to 13 per cent in
1984 (*ZGTJNJ 1990*: 244 and 229).

The growing financial burden of agricultural price subsidies was one of the major reasons that prompted the government to introduce further changes in the agricultural price system towards the end of the first phase of the reforms. Thus, from 1983, the system of above-quota sales at bonus prices was abolished, first for oil-bearing crops, and then for cotton, and in 1985 for grain (*GYJJGLCK*, 1984, 8: 37). For each product multiple prices were replaced by a single state purchase price, known as a proportionate price, which was fixed at a level equivalent to the weighted average of the old quota price and the above-quota price.

The reform of the agricultural purchase price system finally culminated in the abolition of the old compulsory procurement system in 1985. By the middle of that year, with few exceptions, all agricultural products were freed from the compulsory delivery quota (*WWP*, 18 Aug. 1985). For grain, cotton, and oil crops a two-track system, i.e. a combination of contract and market purchase, was introduced in its place. Under the contract-purchase system farmers signed an agreement with the state which obliged them to sell a proportion of their output to the state at the state-fixed contract price. They were allowed to sell the remainder to the market at market prices. The contract prices were to be set at the new proportionate price level. To meet the state's needs beyond the contracted amount state commercial departments would buy from the market at market prices (Sicular, 1988: 694). To reduce market price fluctuations the state promised to buy any amount at the old quota price if the market price were to fall below the old quota price. Thus the old quota price constituted a floor for the market price.

For all other farm products state procurement was to be done in the market at either guidance or market price. As a result the proportion of agricultural purchases bought at government fixed prices declined drastically from 1985. By 1992 the number of fixed-price farm products had dropped to six and they accounted for only 15 per cent of agricultural purchases (see Table 6.5). Purchases at guidance and market prices, on the other hand, rose to 85 per cent of all agricultural purchases in 1992. In that year more than 800 counties experimented with the complete decontrol of grain prices (*ZGJJTZGGNJ 1993*: 297).

The reform of agricultural purchase prices since 1985 was meant to reduce state price subsidies for the marketing of agricultural products as well as to increase the role of the market in agricultural price determination. However, it had serious repercussions for farm price incentives. To begin with, under the two-track system the contract price is a weighted average of the previous quota price and the above-quota price. This meant a significant drop in the average price received by farmers for their sales to the state. Second, the perversity in the state demand function facing the farmer was removed as the state no longer guaranteed to act as a buyer of last resort at the higher above-quota price but only at the lower quota price. In Figure 6.2 the state demand curve facing the farmer in the first stage of the reforms is the unbroken curve. Under the two-track system introduced in the second period of the reforms, if farmers had a 'bad' year so that they could only sell $\bar{Q}1$ (where $\bar{Q}1 < Q$ and Q is the trend value of sales of the crop under normal weather conditions), the average and marginal revenue of farmers was equal to the contract price, Pc. If farmers had a good year and produced $\bar{Q}2$, they would sell Q units at Pc and the remainder ($\bar{Q}2 - Q$) to the market at the market price. The market price might be higher or lower than the contract price depending on market conditions. However, it would never fall below the old quota price as the government promised to act as a buyer of last resort at this price. Thus the new state demand curve and its associated marginal curve (the broken curves) were no longer sloping upward but downward. Third, since the floor price was now set at the lower quota price rather than the higher above-quota price the marginal purchase price received by farmers for their sales beyond the contracted amount to the state was also much lower. As can be seen from Figure 6.2, MR under the new system is significantly lower than that under the old one for output beyond $\bar{Q}$.

Fourth, as the role of the market expanded farmers were also subject to the greater risk of price instability. The greater variability of purchase prices had its origin in two sources. First, there was more fluctuation of government fixed prices as the government switched from quantity to price planning (Lardy, 1983b). Fixed or contract prices were manipulated more frequently according to the demand and supply situation in order to guide farm production decisions (Sicular, 1988: 703). Second, there was also a greater fluctuation in market prices due to the lagged response of farmers to price incentives. The simple cobweb model shows that price and output fluctuate in a cyclical pattern because of this lagged response. The amplitude of the cycle will diminish over time as long as the elasticity of demand is larger than the elasticity of supply.

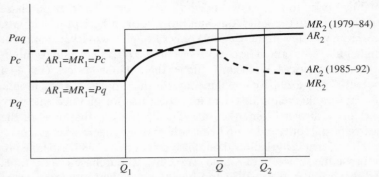

FIG. 6.2. Two Kinds of State Demand Curve Facing Chinese Farmers, 1984 and 1985–1992

In China the farmers' response to price changes was very elastic. Demand elasticity was low, however, as government agencies and industrial enterprises which demanded farm products were less price responsive. They were guided more by political and administrative considerations than by economic ones and very often they did not face hard budget constraints in their demand for farm products (Sicular, 1988: 704). This is confirmed by a Chinese study which shows that the price elasticity of supply averaged 0.57 whereas that of demand was only 0.29 in the period 1978–87 (*SLJJJSJJ YJ 1990*: 21). Since elasticity of supply was greater than that of demand the amplitude of the price and output cycles tended to increase rather than to decrease over time. The greater instability of agricultural purchase prices is evidenced by the large fluctuation in the annual growth rates of farm purchase prices during this period. The standard deviation of the annual increase of agricultural purchase prices rose from 8.5 during the years 1979–84 to 10.4 during the years 1985–92 (*ZGTJNJ 1993*: 262).

Finally, farm incentives were also hit by the rapid increase in input prices. Hitherto the compulsory procurement quotas, coupled with the planned supply of low-priced agricultural inputs, were the key instruments of state agricultural production planning. With the end of compulsory quotas there was no longer any necessity for central rationing of farm inputs. Hence the state-planned supply of low-priced farm inputs was abolished. In its place a two-track input supply system was introduced under which a part of the inputs was still allocated at planned price to those farmers who had signed a contract-purchase agreement with the state. A greater proportion of agricultural inputs, however, was now made available only through the market channel at higher market prices. The coexistence of two prices for a single input, with market prices significantly higher than planned prices, created a potential non-exclusive rental income for the supplier of farm inputs. To capture this rental income inputs destined for planned sale were very often diverted to market sale. The upshot was that most of the scarce farm inputs ended up being sold at the higher market prices.

The reform in agricultural purchase prices since 1985 also failed to improve the structure of China's agricultural purchase prices. Table 6.8 shows that between 1984 and 1993 the growth of industrial prices caught up with that of agricultural purchase prices, with the result that there was little improvement in the relative prices of agricultural products in this period.

Among agricultural product prices those for grain continued to surge ahead of those for industrial crops, as Table 6.7 shows, leading to the further improvement in their relative price. However, the rise in crop prices lagged behind that of non-crop prices. Consequently, the relative prices of crops continued to worsen. The limited improvement in the Chinese farm purchase price structure is corroborated by the larger coefficient of variation of profitability among various crops shown in Table 6.8. This indicates an increased divergence between relative prices and their relative costs during this period.

RETAIL PRICES

On the eve of reforms there were basically three types of retail prices at which consumer goods were sold to households in China: list, negotiated, and market prices. List prices were charged by the state or co-operative commercial organizations for important industrial and agricultural products, i.e. the first- and second-category goods subject to state unified purchase and arranged purchase. These prices were set by the government. Negotiated retail prices were those charged for commodities subject to negotiated purchase. These included the small and diverse third category of industrial and agricultural commodities. They also included the first- and second-category agricultural commodities that farmers were allowed to sell to the state or co-operative commercial organizations under the negotiated purchase scheme once their unified and arranged purchase quotas were met.

The negotiated price was set according to demand and supply conditions within limits controlled by the government whereas market prices were determined by supply and demand in the free market. Among the three types of retail prices the list price was by far the most important one in the early 1980s, since about 80 per cent of retail sales were transacted at this price. Only some 20 per cent of retail sales were transacted at negotiated or free market prices (see Table 6.9).

One of the major features of China's pre-reform retail price system was price stability. According to the official retail price index price rises during the period from 1952 to 1978 averaged less than 1 per cent per annum (*ZGTJNJ 1989*: 250). The key to Chinese retail price stability in the past was the freezing of the prices of basic necessities. This implies that most of the increases in producer prices of these commodities were not passed on to consumers. Consequently most of the goods were sold at a loss, which necessitated government subsidies. The number of items requiring price subsidies soared from 1 to 38 and their share in state revenues increased from less than 1 to almost 22 per cent between 1953 and 1980 (*CP*, 1990, 6: 13–14).

Another major feature of China's pre-reform retail price system was the detachment of the structure of retail prices from that of producer prices. The principal components of the retail price were (1) the

TABLE 6.9. *Retail Sales by Type of Retail Price, 1978–1992*

	List price	Guidance price	Market price	Total
1978	80.0	20.0[a]		100.0
1985	47.0	19.0	34.0	100.0
1986	35.0	25.0	40.0	100.0
1987	33.7	28.0	38.3	100.0
1988	28.9	21.8	49.3	100.0
1989	31.3	23.2	45.5	100.0
1990	30.0	25.0	45.0	100.0
1991	20.9	10.3	68.8	100.0
1992	5.6	0.8	93.5	100.0

[a] Percentage share of retail sales under negotiated and market prices.

Sources: 1985–92: *CP*, 1991, 8: 27; 1992, 8: 29; 1993, 7: 50. 1978–84: *ZGWJNJ 1989*: 351; *CN*, 1 March 1980: 1.

industrial ex-factory price or the agricultural purchase price, (2) the turnover tax, and (3) the profit mark-up. If the turnover tax rate and the profit mark-up are uniform then relative retail prices are organically tied to producer prices. In China, however, the rates of turnover tax and profit mark-up differed significantly between commodities in the past. The rate of turnover tax ranged from 0.4 per cent for radios to 61 per cent for cigarettes. And in 1983 the profit mark-up ranged from −9.9 per cent for coal to 46 per cent for electricity (Zhang Zhuoyuan *et al.*, 1988: 43–9).

These differentiated rates of turnover tax and profit mark-up had been introduced to achieve certain policy objectives, one of which was to make the distribution of real income less unequal than that of money income. This was achieved by charging low rates for necessities and high rates for luxuries. Another objective was to guide the population's demand for consumer goods. Thus, for instance, low rates were set on books for educational reasons while the high rate for cigarettes was intended to curb tobacco consumption.

The system of differential turnover taxes and profit mark-ups separated the producer price structure from the consumer price structure and thereby detached production from consumption, resulting in the simultaneous coexistence of shortages and surpluses in the consumer goods market. This meant that goods in demand remained underproduced because of the low relative producer prices whereas goods that had little appeal to the public were produced in large quantities and gave rise to excess inventory due to their relatively high producer prices.

The reform process in the retail price sector resembles that of the producer price sector. In phase one the reform measures centred mainly on price adjustment. In line with increases in agricultural purchase prices retail prices for food and light industrial products using agricultural raw materials were adjusted upward in order to reduce state subsidies during the years 1979–84. To minimize the inflationary impact, the retail prices of light industrial products using industrial raw materials were adjusted downward during that period (Xie and Luo, 1990: 250–1; Wang and Qiao, 1988: 145–7).

During the first phase of the reforms attempts were also made to decontrol the retail prices of the so-called third-category agricultural and industrial products. As shown in Table 6.10, basically all third-category commodities were decontrolled by 1984. However, it was not until the second phase of the reforms that the decontrolling of retail

TABLE 6.10. *Decontrol of Consumer Prices, 1979–1994*

Year	Commodity coverage
1979	Third-category agricultural products
1982	160 third-category industrial products
1983	350 third-category industrial products
1984	Basically all third-category industrial products
1985	First- and second-category agricultural and industrial products,[a] pork, vegetables, fowl and eggs
1986	Bicycles, black and white TVs, refrigerators, washing machines, tape recorders, certain types of cotton textiles and chemical fibres
1988	Best brands of cigarettes and wines
1991	All brands of cigarettes
1992	Grain and edible oil in major cities, coal, colour TVs, detergents, wire, nails, yarn, cloth, cotton piece goods
1994	Coal

[a] After state purchase quota for these products has been met.

Source: See Table 6.1.

prices was extended to the first- and second-category commodities as well. By early 1994 the government had even lifted the price control of coal—which accounted for 76 per cent of China's energy consumption (*SCMPIW*, 4–5 Dec. 1994).

The retail price reforms in recent years have significantly liberalized China's retail price system. As shown in Table 6.9, the proportion of retail sales at list prices declined from 80 to 6 per cent whereas that at market and guidance prices increased from 20 to about 94 per cent between 1978 and 1992.

The retail price reforms also checked the soaring trend of price subsidies. In the first phase of the reforms (1978–84) the upward adjustment of retail prices lagged behind that of purchase prices and, hence, price subsidies continued to soar. Since 1984, however, the growth of retail prices has caught up with that of purchase prices, leading to a levelling off in the growth of price subsidies (*ZGTJNJ 1993*: 238). This was not achieved without costs, however, for the rate of inflation during the years 1984–93 was more than triple that in the first phase of the reforms.

Finally, the retail price reforms also reduced the extent of consumption disequilibrium. Prior to the reforms, because of the existence of administered prices and quantity rationing, Chinese consumers had not been able to spend money on more desirable goods, the supply of which was limited—leading to an under-consumption of these goods. The unspent money balance spilled over to other goods, the supply of which was less restricted and, hence, led to over-consumption of these goods (Chai, 1992: 733). Under the reforms retail prices were decontrolled and the rationing of consumer goods was in fact eliminated with the introduction of the two-track system under which both controlled and unregulated market prices coexist for the same good (Chai and Tisdell, 1992: 5). Under this system, though consumers remained rationed in their purchases from the controlled market at controlled prices, they were no longer rationed in their purchases in the uncontrolled market. Hence, excess demand or under-consumption of some goods, in the form of involuntarily held money balances and their spillover to other goods—leading to their over-consumption, was significantly reduced.

SUMMARY

The preliminary results of the price reforms are mixed. On the one hand, the reforms significantly increased the flexibility of the Chinese price system. Prior to the reforms, most producer and consumer prices were set by the government. By 1992, 80 per cent of industrial producer goods and 90 per cent of industrial consumer goods were sold at market and floating prices. In the case of agricultural purchase and retail prices, market and floating prices accounted for 85 and 94 per cent of the total sales in 1992 respectively.

The increased flexibility of the price system as a result of the reforms has significantly reduced the price distortion of producer and consumer goods. Relative producer prices are now more aligned with their relative costs and the divergence of producer prices from consumer prices has also been reduced. Moreover, with the introduction of the two-track system (the coexistence of two sets of prices for the same good), most producer and consumer marginal decisions are now made at uncontrolled market prices. The extent of production and consumption disequilibrium was also significantly reduced by the early 1990s.

On the other hand, the inertia of the price system remained. About one-fifth of industrial producer goods and 15 per cent of agricultural raw materials remain heavily regulated. They are key upstream products and their continued price regulation reduces the responsiveness of their prices to market forces and, hence, distorts relative prices between them and their downstream products. Moreover, a significant proportion of flexible prices are floating prices which are not entirely free from administrative intervention by the government.

7 Reforms of the Financial System

Prior to the reforms financial resources in China were highly central-ized. The mobilization and allocation of financial resources was done mainly through the state budget in conjunction with the state plan. This is evident from Table 7.1 which shows that household savings accounted for only 3 per cent whereas the state budget accounted for 46 per cent of total national savings on the eve of the reforms in 1978. Since the government was the main saver and investor financial inter-mediaries were neither necessary nor allowed. Hence, financial markets were closed, financial instruments were prohibited, and all financial institutions had been either confiscated or nationalized and were merged with the Peoples' Bank of China (PBC) (Jao, 1989: 2).

The PBC in the past was a monobank owned and controlled by the government. It combined the roles of central and commercial bank (Chai, 1981: 37). As a central bank it was the bank of issue and respons-ible for the regulation of banknotes and coin circulation in the coun-try. It was the sole source of credit as indebtedness between enterprises and other units within the state sector was forbidden. The Bank was

TABLE 7.1. *Composition of Savings, 1978–1991 (% of GDP)*

	Total savings	Household	Enterprise	Budgetary
1978	33.2	1.1	17.0	15.1
1979	34.6	3.1	21.4	10.0
1980	32.3	4.4	20.7	7.3
1981	30.3	3.4	20.0	6.6
1982	31.6	7.5	18.7	5.4
1983	31.5	9.9	15.9	5.7
1984	32.8	14.4	11.8	6.6
1985	34.5	13.4	14.0	7.0
1986	36.1	14.4	15.9	5.8
1987	39.1	16.2	18.4	4.5
1988	38.0	17.0	17.8	3.2
1991	40.4	18.7	19.9	1.8

Sources: World Bank, 1990; Yusuf, 1994: 80.

also the centre of settlement as it kept the accounts of all institutions in the state and collective sectors. All payments for transactions between and among them, with minor exceptions, were required to be transferred on their bank accounts. Finally, the Bank acted as a banker for the government. It kept the accounts of government departments, accepted their deposits, cleared their payments, and provided the government with loans. As a commercial bank, like its western counterparts, it accepted deposits from its clients (state enterprises and collective units), cleared their payments, and granted bank loans to satisfy their capital needs. In addition to the above-mentioned two banking functions the Bank, like its Soviet counterpart, also performed a crucial function in monitoring the implementation of the state plan.

The supply and allocation of credit was regulated by the Bank through an annual credit plan which specified the sources and use of funds by economic sectors and types of enterprises (Chai, 1981: 41). The function of interest in the past was not to ration credit but to encourage households to save and enterprises to economize in their use of loans. In practice, however, the incentive role of interest was rather limited as interest rates for both deposits and borrowing were fixed by the government at a very low level and were kept unchanged for a relatively long period (see Table 7.2). Enterprise deposits attracted an interest rate which was significantly lower than that for individual deposits. This not only discouraged enterprises from saving but encouraged them to use all available financial resources for internal investments.

The pre-reform monetary system featured two types of money: enterprise money (bank deposits) and household money (cash) (Chai, 1981: 39–42). These two kinds of money circulated in two distinct but connected circuits. Enterprise money circulated within the state and collective units which were not allowed to hold cash. They held money in the form of bank deposits and payments for transactions among them above a minimum amount were settled exclusively through transfer between deposit accounts. Household money circulated mainly in the private sector. Households and private enterprises held their money either in cash or as saving deposits and transactions in the private sector as well as between the private sector and the state or the collective sector took place in cash. Cash and bank deposits were not interchangeable. However, a part of the bank deposits was converted into cash through wages, bonuses, and other payments to individuals

TABLE 7.2. *Selected Interest Rates, 1971–1993 (% per annum)*

	1971	1979	1980	1985	1988	1990	1993
Deposit rates							
1. Individual							
Demand deposit	2.16	2.16	2.16	2.88	2.88	2.88	3.15
1-year time deposit	3.24	3.96	5.40	6.84	8.64	11.34	10.42
		(1.96)	(−1.60)	(−1.96)	(−9.86)	(9.24)	(−2.78)
5-year time deposit		5.04	6.84	8.28	10.80	14.94	
Treasury bond				9.00	10.0		
2. Enterprises							
Demand deposit	1.80	1.80	1.80	1.80	2.88	2.88	
1-year time deposit					4.32	8.64	11.34
Treasury bond					5.00	6.00	
Lending rates							
1. Industry and commerce							
Working capital	5.04	5.04	5.04	7.92	9.00	11.34	9.36
		(3.04)	(−0.96)	(−0.88)	(−9.50)	(9.24)	
3–5-year equipment loan		5.04	9.36	10.80	14.40		
2. Agriculture							
Working capital	4.32	4.32	4.32	7.20	9.00		
Individuals		4.32	4.32	7.92	9.00		

Note: Figures in parentheses are real rates.

Sources: *ACBF 1989*: 149–60; World Bank, 1988*a*: 263; Wu Xiaotang, 1992: 123; *ZGTJNJ 1992*: 662–3; *1993*: 670–1; *1994*: 548–9.

by the state and collective units and through payments for the purchase of agricultural products by the state. A part of the cash was then converted back into deposits through retail sales receipts, taxes, and other fiscal payments made by the private sector.

The supply of enterprise money came from the state budget and the PBC. The budget provided state and collective enterprises with fixed capital and quota working capital, both of which types of capital were interest free and non-repayable whereas the PBC provided them with credit to finance above-quota working capital. The control of enterprises' money supply was mainly implemented through the state budget and credit plan. The state budget specified the amount of fixed capital and quota capital whereas the credit plan specified the amount of credit to be allocated to enterprises.

The supply of household money was controlled by the PBC and implemented through a cash plan which regulated the flow of cash between the banking system and the non-banking sectors. The major channel for cash inflow or the withdrawal of currency from circulation was through retail sales receipts, which accounted for 70 per cent of total cash inflow (Liu Hongru, 1980: 168). The major channel for cash outflow or the injection of currency into circulation was through wages and other payments to individuals plus government purchases of agricultural products. These accounted for 70 per cent of total cash outflows (ibid.).

The size of the net increase or decrease of currency in circulation each year was planned by the government on the basis of the following quantity theory formula (Zhao, 1979: 103):

$$M = PQ/V$$

where PQ is the value of total retail sales, V the average velocity of money, and M the amount of money in circulation.

The planned amount of currency in circulation was derived by dividing the planned value of retail sales by the average velocity of money. The latter was estimated as the ratio between the value of total retail sales and the average amount of currency in circulation in the benchmark year. The estimated planned amount of currency in circulation was then compared with the amount already in circulation in the previous year. The balance between the two then determined the planned net increase or decrease of currency in circulation for the current year.

The basic notion behind the cash plan was to regulate the total amount of currency in circulation in such a way that it was just sufficient to allow households to purchase the planned volume of consumer goods at planned prices and to add to their savings at the desired rate. If the cash plan was accurate and strictly adhered to then the macro-equilibrium between supply and demand on the consumer goods market could be maintained and inflation pressures avoided. In practice, however, the PBC had little control over most of the factors affecting the amount of money in circulation (Blejer *et al.*, 1991: 13; Jao, 1989: 15). Consequently, more money than consumer goods was continuously fed into the economy. The resulting discrepancy between effective demand for and supply of consumer goods was not always bridged by a price increase, but rather by an increased proportion of money income the population were forced to hold in the form of liquid assets, particularly in the form of growing saving deposits.

FINANCIAL LIBERALIZATION

The impetus for change in China's financial system in the early 1980s came primarily from the decentralization of financial resources. Accompanying the decentralization of decision-making power through the reforms an increased proportion of the national financial resources was now held by the decentralized units, i.e. by households, enterprises, local governments, etc. As indicated in Table 7.1 government savings mobilized through its budget declined during the reforms and their share in total savings dropped from almost 46 per cent in 1978 to less than 5 per cent in 1991 whereas the share of savings by decentralized units soared dramatically. By 1991 the share of households, for instance, in total national savings reached 46 per cent. The decentralization of financial resources led to a greater separation of the saver from the investor. As a result there arose a need for financial intermediaries (World Bank, 1989: 28–9).

The main thrust of the financial reforms in China was financial liberalization, the objectives of which were (1) to correct excesses of financial repression in the past, and (2) to build a financial system which would mainly rely on market forces and on decentralized decision making. These two objectives are related to the larger aim of achieving a more effective mobilization of savings and a more efficient allocation of investable resources. The measures introduced to liberalize the financial sector include financial system reforms, the development of financial markets, liberalization of interest rates, and the relaxation of credit controls.

FINANCIAL SYSTEM REFORMS

The reforms of the financial system were aimed at enhancing the efficiency of banks by increasing competition between them and improving their management. Measures introduced to stimulate competition included the breaking up of the monobank, separating the central banking function from commercial banking, establishing new banks and non-bank financial institutions (NBFIs), as well as admitting foreign banks into China.

In 1984 a two-tiered banking system was created and the PBC was transformed into a central bank only. Its commercial banking activities were taken over by four specialized banks, each of them operating in a specific sector of the economy (*DDZGDJRSY*, 1989: 191–6). The Agricultural Bank of China (ABC) was re-established in 1979 and operated mainly in the rural sector. The Industrial and Commercial Bank of China (ICBC) was established in 1984 and handled mainly the domestic currency business of state enterprises in the industrial and commercial sectors. The Bank of China (BOC) acquired its independent status in 1979 and was mainly responsible for foreign exchange business. The Peoples' Construction Bank of China (PCBC) also became part of the specialized banking system in 1985 and was mainly responsible for the disbursing and control of the use of funds budgeted for basic construction and modernization investment. The PCBC was also allowed to take deposits from enterprises and use them to extend long-term credits to finance both basic construction and modernization investment.

In addition to the above-mentioned four specialized banks, nine national and regional commercial banks were established. These include the Bank of Communication (BOCs), the China International Trust and Investment Bank (CITIB), the Merchant Bank, the Everbright Bank of China, the Fujian Industrial Bank, the Guangdong Development Bank, and the Shenzhen Development Bank (*CDBW*, 13–15 Sept. 1992 and 11–17 Sept. 1994).

Changes in the banking sector were paralleled by the rapid development of NBFIs since 1979. As of early 1994, China had established over 60,000 rural credit co-operatives (RCCs), 1,500 urban credit co-operatives (UCCs), and over 590 trust and investment companies, as well as finance and leasing companies (*JJYJ*, 1994, 7: 28). Despite their rapid development, the share of NBFIs in total financial assets was still rather small in comparison with that of the banking institutions.

On the eve of the reforms only four foreign banks had branches in China, namely the Hong Kong and Shanghai Banking Corporation (Hong Kong), Standard Chartered Bank (UK), the Bank of East Asia (Hong Kong), and the Overseas Chinese Banking Corporation (Singapore). Since the beginning of the reforms entry restrictions for foreign banks in China have been gradually relaxed. By 1992 about 47 foreign-funded banking and financial institutions and 218 foreign bank representative offices had been set up in China (*CD*, 13–15 Sept. 1992). But the scope of their business was still subject to many restrictions. For instance, they were not allowed to engage in domestic currency transactions.

Measures introduced to improve the general management of banking enterprises included the decentralization of bank management and turning banks into independent enterprises. In the past the management structure of China's state banks was highly centralized and hierarchical. All policies originated at the head offices and were uniformly applied by the branch offices throughout the entire country. Regional and local offices merely applied regulations and directives issued at the centre and gave loans within overall and specific quotas assigned to them. Any surplus in deposit balances at local offices would be transferred to the head office and any deficit was made up by grants from the head office. Thus local banking officials did not have any incentives to mobilize more deposits or to ensure that credits were effectively used.

Under the new system the broad categories of credit continued to be centrally planned by the head office but greater latitude was given to local branches in respect of loan approval. Moreover, within the limits of the deposit and credit targets assigned to them they were allowed to grant more loans if they were able to attract more deposits.

Attempts were also made to turn Chinese state banks into independent enterprises responsible for their own financial gains and losses. The measures introduced to achieve this included profit retention and the profit and loss contract system. Until the reforms bank profits were largely remitted to, and losses were subsidized by, the budget. Hence, banks were not motivated to achieve efficiency and profitability in their operations. In 1985 profit retention was introduced by the ICBC and the ABC for their branch offices (*DDZGDJRSY*, 1989: 201). In 1988 the ABC introduced the CRS which up to then had only been used in industrial and commercial enterprises (*ACBF 1989*: 326). By 1989, even the branch offices of the PBC were reportedly operating under the profit-retention system (*FS*, 1990, 2: 2).

The reform measures described above helped China to achieve substantial diversification in its financial system. As Table 7.3 shows, on the eve of the reforms the PBC held over 90 per cent of the total assets of all financial institutions. At the end of 1989 its share had dropped to only 16 per cent whereas that of the five state banks had risen to almost 72 per cent. By 1991, the share of the five state banks was 82 per cent (*JJYJ*, 1992, 11: 27).

In spite of the diversification outlined above, the achievements of the financial system reforms up to the early 1990s were limited. The role of the PBC was not significantly different from what it had been

TABLE 7.3. *Assets of Banks and Non-Bank Financial Institutions, 1978, 1984, and 1989 (in billion yuan)*

	1978	1984	1989
Banks	207.3	816.8	2,785.2
Central Bank (PBC)	188.4	280.7	501.7
State banks	18.9	536.1	2,283.5
ICBC		326.7	772.5
ABC		128.7	373.1
BOC		80.7	677.4
BOCs			53.0
PCBC			407.5
NBFIs	18.9	90.2	371.9
RCCs	18.9	81.3	231.8
UCCs			19.6
CIB[a]			10.0
CITIB			15.7
Insurance companies	neg.[c]	neg.[c]	17.4
Investment trusts[b]		8.9	77.4
TOTAL	207.3	907.0	3,157.1

[a] China Investment Bank.
[b] Investment trusts within the banking system only.
[c] Negligible.

Sources: Bei, 1989: 256–67; Tam, 1991*a*: 27; Blejer *et al.*, 1991: 16.

in the past. It was still subordinated to the government and had to bear the responsibility of financing budget deficits and helping to fund ailing state-owned enterprises through 'a disguised process of monetized budget financing' via expanded credit extended by specialized banks but funded by new loans from the PBC (Tam, 1991*a*: 9–10). Hence, it was not in a position to carry out independent monetary policy.

Although the financial institutions were multiplying, competition between them remained relatively limited because each type was restricted to conducting business within its explicitly prescribed sphere. They were in fact assigned monopoly positions with respect to particular groups of clients or types of services (World Bank, 1988*a*: 271). Entry of new institutions into a particular market segment was still tightly regulated.

Similarly, while the banks had a greater profit orientation their budget constraints generally remained soft, for several reasons. First, a significant proportion of their lendings were direct loans which the banks had to extend to enterprises regardless of their profitability. Second, the budget constraints of the clients of the bank, the state enterprises, remained soft. This, together with the lack of a legal framework for dealing with non-performing loans, made it difficult to hold banks responsible for their own profits and losses. Finally, most local bank branch offices were subject to dual controls from both their head office and the local government. This enabled the latter, in pursuance of local government objectives, to order banks to lend money to local enterprises regardless of their ability to pay.

FINANCIAL MARKET DEVELOPMENT

There are four types of financial market in China: the informal credit markets, the commercial paper markets, the interbank money markets, and the long-term capital markets (K. W. Li, 1994: 85). Informal credit markets developed rapidly during the first stage of reforms and played a dominant role as a source of loans to rural households (Tam, 1991*b*). Methods like discounting, acceptance, and re-discounting of bills by banks were formally introduced in 1986 (*DDZGDJRSY*, 1989: 213).

The interbank money market was first started in 1986 (*DDZGDJ RSY*, 1989: 214). By 1992, 30 cities had established their own interbank market (*CD*, 13 Aug. 1992). The volume of transactions in these markets, however, remained thin. In March 1989, for example, interbank transactions in 11 cities totalled only 352.9 million RMB or less than 0.1 per cent of the Chinese GDP (Jao, 1989: 5). Most interbank transactions were between banks or branches in the same province. Local government pressure limited the interregional transfer of funds and, hence, the development of the money market on a national scale (Blejer *et. al.*, 1991: 10). The capital market was reopened in China with the introduction of various new financial instruments (see Table 7.4). During the first stage of the reforms the range of these instruments was limited to treasury bonds, which were first issued in 1981. In the second phase of the reforms broader measures were introduced, which included new government bonds, bank bonds, enterprise bonds, and shares.

Bank and enterprise bonds and shares were all introduced around 1985. All carried coupon rates higher than that of the one-year time deposits and these made them attractive alternatives to saving

TABLE 7.4. *Total Value of Securities Outstanding and their Composition, 1981–1990 (in billion* yuan *)*

	Government bonds		Bank bonds	Enterprise		Total
	Treasury bonds	Others		Bonds	Shares	
1981	4.9					4.9
1982	9.3					9.3
1983	13.4					13.4
1984	17.7					17.7
1985	23.7		0.5			24.2
1986	29.3		3.0	8.4		40.7
1987	34.2	8.5	6.0	8.6	1.0	58.3
1988	41.2	27.2	8.5	17.3	3.5	97.7
1989	45.5	42.6	7.5	26.9	4.2	126.8
1990	48.5	54.4	9.0	59.5	4.6	176.0

Sources: Jing *et al.*, 1991: 63.

deposits. Enterprise shares in China did not have true equity security, i.e. a long-term share in the residual earnings and assets of the issuing enterprise. They were a hybrid of bond and equity the maturity of which was short, ranging from one to three years. The return typically consisted of two parts: a fixed interest and a dividend linked to net profit (Ho, 1986). The owner of a share did not have the right to participate in the management of the enterprise.

There are two types of enterprise share in China. A-shares consist of those that are state-held and those held by legal persons; these shares are individually traded in *yuan*. B-shares are quoted in convertible foreign currencies and are reserved for foreigners. Trading in state-held shares is banned, in order to maintain the state's majority position in the company.

The total volume of securities issued and their composition are presented in Table 7.4, from which it can be seen that the size of the capital market in China was still rather small. At the end of 1990 the total outstanding securities were estimated at a value of 176 billion *yuan*, which was equivalent to only 10 per cent of China's GDP. In contrast, the corresponding shares for India and Malaysia in 1984 were 27 and 96 per cent respectively (World Bank, 1988*a*: 239). China's capital market was also narrowly based and was mainly limited to government bonds, which accounted for almost 60 per cent of total outstanding securities at the end of 1990. By 1992 the value of the total securities issued was 129.2 billion *yuan*, of which 42 per cent were state bonds and only 9.3 per cent were enterprise shares (*ZGJJTZGGNJ 1993*: 266). Finally, the capital market in the early 1990s accounted for only 8 per cent of the external financing of enterprises (Wu and Xie, 1993: 37).

The limited development of the capital market in China up to the early 1990s was primarily due to the fact that the issue, transfer, and pricing of securities in China was still very much regulated by the government. This reduced the liquidity of securities and hampered the development of secondary markets. A secondary securities market was formally opened in 1988 (World Bank, 1988*a*: 323). By the early 1990s two stock markets had been established, one in Shanghai and one in Shenzhen. In Shanghai 101 A-shares and 22 B-shares were traded while in Shenzhen 73 A-shares and 19 B-shares were traded (*SCMPIW*, 19–20 March, 1994). In addition, 700 securities-transaction facilities were set up in more than 100 cities (*CD*, 29 Aug. 1992). But the volume of securities transactions was limited. In 1991 it amounted to only 13.3 billion *yuan* or 5 per cent of the total securities (ibid.). The fact that the securities market in China was highly regulated was due to the incomplete nature of the enterprise and price reforms (World Bank, 1988*a*: 324). In an environment where enterprises were not yet fully responsible for their profit and loss and where prices were still distorted the government had good reason to be apprehensive that the free issue of bonds and shares would encourage enterprises to borrow beyond the limits of their debt-servicing capacities and that the financial resources mobilized might be used for wasteful purposes and would, therefore, fuel inflationary pressures.

LIBERALIZATION OF INTEREST RATES

The control of interest rates was relaxed by more frequent adjustments, by wider bands for regulated rates, and by a greater rate differentiation in the course of the reforms. Between 1979 and 1993 the deposit rate for individual one-year fixed deposits was raised from 3.96 per cent to 10.42 per cent and the lending rate for one-year working capital loans to industrial and commercial enterprises was raised from 5.04 to 9.36 per cent (Table 7.2).

Banks and NBFIs were also given a certain flexibility to raise interest rates under the reforms. From 1988 they were allowed to float the interest rate upward or downward by up to 30 per cent relative to the rate specified by the PBC (*ACBF 1989*: 325). There was also a greater differentiation in interest rates according to the length of the maturity period and the type of borrower. Thus, for example, there were nine categories of and about 30 individual rates for both deposits and loans in 1993 (*ZGTJNJ 1994*: 548–9). From late 1988 the rate of long-term savings deposits was linked to the retail price index in order to protect depositors from inflation.

Despite the above-mentioned reform measures the role of interest rates for financial intermediaries was still very limited. To begin with, interest rates were still administratively set by the PBC in consultation with the State Council. Second, increases in nominal rates were not sufficiently large to offset the open rate of inflation or to establish a positive real interest rate. This was true especially in the latter half of the 1980s and in 1993 (see Table 7.2). Third, until September 1988, the rate for enterprise deposits was set lower than that for individual ones. This rate differential encouraged intermediation between enterprises outside the banking system.

Finally, due to the incomplete nature of the enterprise reforms enterprises' demands for bank loans were not very responsive to changes in interest rates. As mentioned earlier, the results of a survey of 300 large and medium-sized state industrial enterprises in five of China's major cities in 1989 reveal that the interest rate elasticity of demand for bank loans by state enterprises was practically zero (see Table 5.3). The inelastic demand was partly due to the fact that enterprises were not yet fully responsible for their profits and losses. It was also due to the practice whereby until very recently enterprises were allowed to deduct from their pre-tax profits both the cost of interest and the repayment of the principal of their loans. This practice lowered the cost to enterprises of borrowing and reduced the interest rate elasticities of demand for bank loans.

RELAXATIONS OF CREDIT CONTROL

During the first phase of the reforms certain credit criteria were relaxed. The traditional distinction between budget funds for financing enterprise quota working capital and fixed capital, and bank credits for financing enterprise above-quota working capital was abandoned. Credits were increasingly used to finance not only enterprise above-quota working capital but also quota working capital as well as fixed capital requirements. Banks were also given more discretionary power in their lending decisions. Further, the traditional principle that credit be granted on the basis of the plan was relaxed. Projects approved by the plan no longer obtained automatic credits and banks had authority to reject the financing of a project which failed to pass its own feasibility and profitability tests. Finally, borrowers were no longer restricted to state and collective enterprises but individual enterprises and households were given loans as well.

From the mid-1980s efforts were made to eliminate overall direct credit controls on bank lending. Though credit ceilings continued to be assigned to specialized banks in accordance with the annual credit plan they were no longer mandatory but indicative (World Bank, 1988*a*: 298). However, direct credit control was reintroduced in the late 1980s as inflationary pressures mounted.

Sectoral credit allocation was largely discontinued after the introduction of the second phase of the reforms. Details of the credit plan were becoming largely indicative in nature (ibid.). However, the selective allocation of credit to priority sectors at subsidized interest rates continued. It is estimated that in the early 1990s two-thirds of all bank loans granted were policy-directed loans (Yusuf, 1994: 87). Moreover, particularly at the local level, bank lending was heavily influenced by government pressures to direct funding to particular enterprises (Blejer *et al.*, 1991: 10).

CHANGES IN THE MONETARY SYSTEM AND POLICY

With the relaxation of cash controls over state and collective enterprises and the surge of individual enterprises, household money or cash became an increasingly important means of settlement of transactions. Prior to the reforms cash accounted for only about 5 per cent of business transactions and the other 95 per cent were settled exclusively through transfer between deposit accounts. By the end of 1988 the proportion of business transactions settled by cash had soared to between 30 and 40 per cent, whereas the share of transactions settled through bank accounts had decreased proportionately (*FS*, 1989, 7: 37).

The liberalization of the financial system also prompted a reassessment of the instruments of monetary policy, for direct controls were no longer viable in a liberalized financial environment. Hence, new and effective indirect control mechanisms had to be developed and strengthened. The shift towards indirect monetary controls occurred mainly in the second phase of the reforms. Greater reliance was placed on reserve requirements and PBC lending to banks. Open market operations for the financial sector, however, were not adopted since China still lacked a broad, active and resilient market in government securities. The reserve requirement was first introduced in 1984, with the reserve ratio ranging from 20 to 40 per cent for different types of deposits (Jao, 1989: 16; World Bank, 1988a: 298). In 1985, however, this range was replaced by a uniform ratio of 10 per cent which was again raised to 12 per cent in 1987 in order to curb inflation. Since 1988 it has been fixed at 13 per cent (Wu Xioatang, 1992: 175). The required reserve was interest bearing and the rate of interest was adjusted upward from 4.32 per cent in 1984 to 7.2 per cent in 1989.

However, the reserve requirement has proved ineffective in containing the growth of bank liquidity and lending. This is evident from the fact that throughout the second half of the 1980s specialized banks consistently held excess reserves at the PBC. The ratio of these excess reserves to their deposits averaged 10 per cent (Blejer et al., 1991: 16). The excess reserve overhang was induced by several factors (World Bank, 1988a: 302). First, bank budget constraints were still relatively soft as banks were not yet fully responsible for their profits and losses, and, hence, their liquidity management was lax. Second, the differential between the lending and the deposit rate for their transactions with the PBC was so small that it encouraged banks to borrow money from the PBC and to hoard it for rainy days. Third, the fragmentation of the interbank market also impeded the flow of resources from banks with high reserves to other banks that would be able to lend them.

The PBC also tried to influence the banks' lending decisions by adjusting the terms of its own lendings to banks. In 1984 the deposit rate was identical to the lending rate for banks. From 1985, however, both of them were adjusted upward, with the lending rate about two percentage points higher than the deposit rate (World Bank, 1988a: 298–9; ACBF 1989: 154, 325). However, in view of the soft budget constraints of banking enterprises the effectiveness of these variations in interest rates in discouraging banks from borrowing from the

PBC was very limited. Moreover, the ability of the PBC to control bank lending was hampered by the ability of local governments to put pressure on their own PBC branches to extend credit to specialized banks to enable them to meet regional needs (Blejer *et al.*, 1991: 12).

In short, China's experience with indirect monetary controls in the second half of the 1980s suggests that in the absence of (1) real autonomy of the PBC, (2) any significant hardening of budget constraints for banks as well as for production enterprises, and (3) a genuine market for government securities, the effectiveness of indirect monetary policy instruments is likely to be very limited indeed.

The ineffectiveness of indirect policy instruments to contain China's monetary expansion in the second half of the 1980s can be seen in Table 7.5. In general, the growth of money supply can be decomposed into the growth of reserve money and the money multiplier (Tseng and Corker, 1991: 27). Table 7.5 indicates that while the money multiplier was rather unstable the growth of reserve money was the primary determinant of monetary expansion in the period from 1986 to 1989. The main factors affecting the reserve money supply can be grouped into 'autonomous' and 'policy' factors (Tseng and Corker, 1991: 28). Autonomous factors include changes in the central bank's net holdings of foreign assets and net claims on government. The 'policy' factor in China was limited to the central bank's lending to financial institutions as open market operations did not at that time exist in China. As may be seen from Table 7.5, net budgetary borrowing

TABLE 7.5. *Growth Rates of Monetary Variables in China and their Sources, 1986–1989*

	1986	1987	1988	1989
1. *Growth of broad money and its sources*				
Broad money	29.3	24.2	20.9	18.4
Reserve money	23.7	14.0	25.8	23.7
Broad money multiplier	4.9	8.8	−3.9	−5.2
2. *Factors affecting reserve money[a]*				
Autonomous factors	4.2	11.2	6.8	3.5
Net foreign assets	−3.8	4.0	1.8	3.0
Net budgetary borrowing	6.6	5.3	3.0	−1.4
Claim on financial institution	19.5	2.8	19.1	20.2

a Change as % of reserve money at the beginning of the period.

Source: Estimated from balance sheets of PBC (Blejer *et al.*, 1991: 16).

and change in foreign assets were the major sources of monetary disturbances in the period under discussion. The PBC not only was unable to contain the growth of reserve money generated by the growth of government borrowing and an increase in net foreign assets but fuelled its expansion by raising its lending to financial institutions. Thus, in the wake of the rapid monetary expansion and the rising inflation rate in 1988 the PBC was forced to restore direct credit controls to achieve monetary stability (Blejer *et al.*, 1991: 14).

In the early 1990s, however, even direct credit control 'had increasingly lost its effectiveness in containing the growth of money supply' (Wu and Xie, 1993: 36). This is because under heavy pressure from specialized banks and PBC local branches the credit ceiling had often been adjusted upward. Moreover, due to the rapid financial market development the difference between the increase in credit and that of the money supply grew and by 1992 only 43 per cent of the increased money supply was accounted for by an increase of credit. Hence credit control had only limited effect on the adjustment of money supply.

PRELIMINARY RESULTS

A successful financial reform should achieve the following goals. It should (1) deepen a country's financial system, (2) increase its capacity to save, (3) enhance its investment efficiency, and (4) achieve and maintain macro-stability without the deployment of direct macroeconomic control instruments (World Bank, 1989: 25–40).

Measured in terms of financial deepening, the performance of China's financial reforms is impressive. The greater availability of financial institutions increased the population's access to depository institutions, as evidenced by the growing density of depository institutions revealed in Table 7.6. The greater volume and variety of financial instruments also induced savings to be held increasingly in financial rather than in non-financial assets. The index of financial deepening, measured in terms of the ratio of broad money to GNP, increased by 400 per cent in the period from 1978 to 1992. Measured in terms of financial assets to GNP, it increased by 150 per cent.

By international comparison, China's financial depth in the early 1990s not only surpassed that of other Asian countries at a comparative stage of development but was comparable with that of some of the middle-income Asian countries. For instance, China's ratio of

TABLE 7.6. *Indicators of Financial Depth in China, 1978–1992*

	1978	1981	1984	1992
Density of depository institutions per 10,000 population[a]		1.02	1.08	3.50
Ratio of broad money[b] to GNP	0.12	0.19	0.29	0.60
Ratio of financial assets[c] to GNP	0.95	1.21	1.51	2.34[d]

[a] State banks and RCCs.

[b] Broad money in China is equal to M_2 (see Wu and Xie, 1993: 36) and M_2 is the sum of currency in circulation plus urban and rural household deposits.

[c] Includes M_2, deposits of enterprise and government agencies, assets of banks and NBFIs, bonds and shares.

[d] 1991.

Sources: *ZGTJNJ 1990*: 89, 665; *1993*: 81, 663; *ACBF 1989*: 169; K. W. Li, 1994: 40; *JJYJ*, 1992, 11: 31; *ZGTJNJ 1993*: 31 and 664.

financial assets to GNP was 2.34 in 1991. The corresponding ratios for India, Brazil, Malaysia, and South Korea in 1988 were 1.14, 1.75, 2.89, and 2.34 respectively (*JJYJ*, 1992, 11: 32).

However, measured in terms of other criteria the achievements of China's financial reforms are largely negative. To begin with, as mentioned earlier, the monetary authority was not able to maintain price stability without the use of direct monetary policy instruments. Broad money supply grew at an average annual rate of 29.9 per cent, i.e. more than double the 9 per cent rate of growth of GDP during the years 1978–90 (K. W. Li, 1994: 40; *ZGTJNJ 1991*: 31). The excess supply of money has led to the worst inflation in the history of the People's Republic, with the rate of retail price increases reaching double digit figures in the late 1980s and again in 1993 and 1994.

Second, financial reforms amidst rising inflationary pressure have contributed little to increasing the rate of saving. As Table 7.7 shows, the rates of saving of both rural and urban households were responsive to changes in per capita real disposable income and the real deposit rate of interest. During the first phase of the reforms the rates of saving of both rural and urban households soared in response to higher real interest rates and real disposable income per capita. However, in the second half of the 1980s, both rural and urban households' rates of saving declined because of the slowdown in the growth of their real

TABLE 7.7. *Savings Behaviour of Households, 1978–1992*

	Rate of savings		Real disposable income per capita		Real deposit rates
	Rural (1)	Urban (2)	Rural (3)	Urban (4)	(5)
1978	15.9		145		
1979	20.9		170		1.96
1980	21.9		191		−1.60
1981	23.0	0.4	219	447	3.00
1982	26.5	5.3	261	473	3.86
1983	28.8	4.3	298	493	4.26
1984	32.0	8.5	338	555	2.96
1985	30.1	2.4	352	558	−1.96
1986	27.9	6.0	353	631	1.20
1987	26.5	5.9	363	642	−0.10
1988	25.6	3.5	365	650	−9.86
1989	23.4	5.8	340	629	−6.46
1990	25.6	9.2	370	683	9.24
1991	22.3	7.4	375	724	4.66
1992	24.6	10.4	399	788	2.16

Notes: Savings include housing expenditures. Real disposable income is income in 1980 prices.

Sources: Column 1: Chai, 1991: 12; *ZGTJNJ*, various issues; Column 2: *ZGTJNJ*, various issues; Columns 3 and 4: Chai, 1992: 723; Column 5: see Table 7.2.

income and the negative rate of interest. In the early 1990s the rate of rural households' saving stabilized because of the positive real interest rate whereas that of urban households rose in response to both increased real income and a positive real interest rate.

Finally, there is little evidence that financial liberalization has increased investment efficiency. The incremental output–capital ratio (IOCR) rose during the first phase of the reforms but declined during the second (Chai, 1994: 505).

The greater autonomy of local authorities and enterprises in investment decisions, coupled with the greater role of financial institutions in the allocation of investment resources, appears sound in theory since central authorities do not have sufficient information to make detailed investment decisions. However, financial deregulation in an environment where prices are still distorted and enterprise budget constraints remain soft does not necessarily improve investment efficiency. In fact, it may worsen it. This is evident from the lopsided investment structure which emerged in China during the reforms.

Accompanying the dispersion of financial resources under the reforms were a greater decentralization of investment decisions and a rapid growth of investment by the non-state sector. Its share in total fixed asset investment soared from 18 to 30 per cent in the period from 1980 to 1993 (*ZGTJZY 1994*: 27). Within the state sector there was a rapid growth of investments by decentralized authorities financed by their own extra-budgetary funds. Their share in total investments in the state sector soared from 51 to 94 per cent in the period from 1978 to 1993 (*ZGTJNJ 1994*: 145).

The decentralization of investment brought about radical change in China's investment pattern. Prior to 1978, since basic construction investment accounted for the lion's share of China's total fixed asset investment, the structure of its basic construction investments can be viewed as a proxy for its investment structure. Most basic construction investments at that time were in general 'productive' investments. Specifically these investments were in energy, raw materials and transport. However, since the reforms investments have tended to be concentrated in 'non-productive' projects and projects in the processing industries where products command relatively high prices and, hence, high profits and tax revenues for local authorities. Investments in sectors with critical shortages, such as energy, raw materials, transport, and communications, became relatively neglected because of the relatively low prices of their products. As a result, the share of 'productive' investments fell from 79 per cent during the years 1953–80 to about 61 per cent in 1986. That of energy, raw materials, transport, and communications declined from about 50 per cent to 21 per cent during the same period (*ZGGDZCTZTJZL 1950–85*: 5).

To correct this lopsided investment structure the government was forced to step up its own investments in the neglected sectors. Consequently the declining trend of investments in these sectors has been arrested since 1987 and by 1992 the share of 'productive' investments had risen to 66 per cent (*ZGTJNJ 1993*: 146). However, since these investments were partly financed by the government borrowing from banks they fuelled inflationary pressures by their contribution to excess money supply during this period. Hence, the correction of the lopsided investment structure was mainly achieved at the cost of price stability.

THE REFORMS IN 1994

In the wake of high inflation in the late 1980s banking reforms were practically shelved and considerable recentralization took place. In 1994, however, banking reforms resumed. The main thrust of the reforms in 1994 was the strengthening of the central bank role of the PBC, the commercialization and internationalization of China's banking system, and a renewal of the attempt by the PBC to use indirect monetary control to achieve monetary stability.

The PBC is expected to transfer its previous non-central bank functions to other institutions. In the past one-third of the budgetary deficit was financed by the central bank. As from 1994 the Ministry of Finance was prohibited from borrowing from its PBC account or borrowing money from the PBC to finance debts; deficits are to be met only through the issuing of treasury bonds to the public (*CD*, 1 March 1994).

The number of local branches of the PBC was reduced and local branches were stripped of their authority to adjust loans. The main function of the PBC is to offer clearing services to, and financial supervision of, the banks, as well as to implement independent monetary policies through the use of such indirect control measures as reserve ratios, central bank lending rates, and open market operations (*SCMPIW*, 20–1 Nov. 1993).

In the past specialized banks handled both commercial and policy-related loans. To transform them into commercial institutions working for profit their policy-loans issuing function is to be taken over by three newly established policy banks: the State Development Bank (SDB), the Exports and Imports Bank (EXIM) and the Agriculture Development Bank (ADB). The SDB is to provide loans for financing fixed-asset investment in China's infrastructure and key industrial projects. EXIM is to supply loans for financing equipment and machinery imports as well as to engage in export promotion. Finally, the ADB is to finance agricultural projects and agricultural purchases (*SCMPIW*, 23–4 April 1994).

To internationalize China's banking system more Chinese cities are to be opened to foreign banks and they are to be allowed to conduct *yuan* business on a limited basis (*SCMPIW*, 5–6 March 1994). And to bring more competition to the banking market more commercial banks are to be established. The People's Livelihood Bank, China's first private commerical bank, was due to open in 1995; and there are proposals to turn urban credit co-operatives into banks.

In addition to the banking reforms there are other reform measures in the pipeline, including the liberalization of interest rates. The PBC is to allow the deposit and loan interest rates of commercial banks to float within a greater range. In the area of financial markets the stock quota system is to be abandoned in favour of a more flexible system of control. Under the quota system the government has set a limit on the number of shares to be issued each year.

The effectiveness of these reforms remains to be seen. The creation of a truly commercial banking system in China depends on transforming China's largest banks, the four specialized banks, into commercial banks. The prospects of this transformation do not appear to be good. To begin with, the specialized banks lack financial expertise and experience to make sound commercial lending decisions. Furthermore, even though they would be freed from having to lend to loss-making state enterprises they still carry massive debt owed by them which effectively gives them a negative asset value. With such large debts on their books it is very unlikely that they will be able to establish viable deposit–loan ratios. Similarly, the real internationalization of the Chinese banking sector will probably not take place until the the major state banks are capable of competing with foreign banks in the open market.

8 The Open Door Policy I: Trade Liberalization

The open door policy was an integral part of China's new development strategies adopted by the country's leadership since 1978 to modernize its economy. A comprehensive evaluation of China's open door strategy requires a detailed analysis of its six main features, which are trade liberalization, foreign direct investment (FDI) liberalization, utilization of foreign loans, exports of labour for construction work abroad, the development of special economic zones, and the development of the tourist industry. Within the space limitations of this book it is impossible to discuss all of these policy elements or to analyse them exhaustively. Instead this and the following chapter focus on the first and second elements, namely trade and FDI liberalization only.

In the past China regarded trade as a necessary evil. Imports were used to achieve greater self-sufficiency and exports only served to pay for imports. Trade was limited as much as possible and was not seen as having merit in itself or as a viable strategy for China's economic development. However, under the new policy which started in 1978 trade was considered as beneficial: it was now seen as augmenting domestic resources and as providing an additional source for rapid economic growth through the realization of static and dynamic gains of trade. Hence, trade was to be maximized whenever possible.

With the change in the official attitude towards the role of trade, from trade aversion to trade proclivity, the country's previous under-trading was viewed as deplorable, for China's share in world trade averaged only 0.6 per cent in the past (*GJMYWT*, 1980, 1: 1). Former Premier Zhao Ziyang declared at the Fourth Meeting of the Fifth National People's Congress at the end of 1981 (*TKP*, 14 Dec. 1981) that one of China's long-term strategies was to strive for a greater share in world trade.

To open the country to more and efficient trade the Chinese leadership realized that it would have to dismantle the various layers of 'insulation' which in the past had shielded the domestic economy from the world economy. These layers included the physical separation of domestic producers and consumers from their foreign counterparts through a foreign trade and exchange monopoly and the divorce of foreign and domestic prices through an artificial exchange rate system and an automatic system of variable taxes and subsidies. The discussion below first analyses the measures introduced since the late 1970s to remove these insulation layers and to make trading enterprises more interested in foreign trade. It then examines their efficiency, growth, and stability implications.

BREAKDOWN OF FOREIGN TRADE MONOPOLY

The steps taken to remove the physical separation of domestic economic units from foreign markets included the breaking of the foreign trade monopoly by way of decentralizing trading rights down to local authorities, industrial ministries, and production enterprises. This also meant a reduction in the scope of foreign trade planning.

In the past trading rights had been monopolized in the hands of a few national foreign trade corporations (FTCs). The decentralization of trading rights was initiated between July and September 1979 with the issuing of several important documents by the Central Committee of the CCP and by the State Council. These documents set out the principles according to which local authorities, industrial ministries, associations, and production enterprises were to be granted trading rights and allowed to set up their own FTCs (*ZGBKNJ 1980*: 304, 306).

In accordance with these principles, trading commodities were divided into three categories (*WMJJGJMY*, 1990, 3: 42). The first-category commodities were defined as goods of vital importance to the peoples' livelihood and which were imported and exported in large quantities. These goods would remain subject to centralized control by national FTCs. The second-category commodities included imported goods with sensitive prices and marked price differences between domestic and foreign markets as well as export goods subject to quota restrictions imposed by foreign countries. Trade in these goods would be jointly controlled by provincial and national FTCs. The third category covered all other goods, in which provincial FTCs and various approved foreign trade enterprises were allowed to trade.

After more than 15 years of implementation, this policy of decentralizing trading rights has achieved impressive results. The number of FTCs increased sharply from 12 in 1978 to over 7,000 in mid-1994 (*CDBW*, 15–18 May 1994) and the number of first-category commodities has been drastically reduced. By the end of 1992 only a few export commodities and 12 import commodities remained under the control of national FTCs (World Bank, 1994: 28).

Despite the significant decentralization of trading rights China's foreign trade system in the early 1990s was, however, still essentially a state trading system, for the following reasons. First, the participation of production enterprises in foreign trade was still rather limited. This is evident from the fact that out of the 4,000 FTCs in 1990 most were national and local FTCs run by either the central or local government. The number of FTCs set up by production enterprises themselves amounted to only about 1,000 by the end of the 1980s (Xie and Luo, 1990: 124). As of 1992, only half of the 10,000 large and medium-sized state enterprises had been given trading rights (*CD*, 1 Aug. 1992).

Second, although the number of trading commodities under the control of national FTCs was significantly reduced, the share of national FTCs in China's foreign trade was still quite dominant as most of the commodities under their control were China's major import and export items. Third, though the national FTCs' monopoly of trading rights was broken by a growing number of other FTCs the competition among them was limited. This was because most FTCs could not deal in all commodities and their transactions were confined to their respective approved area of import/export business.

LOOSENING OF FOREIGN TRADE CONTROL

In the past China's trade system was a command state trading system under which the operations of trading enterprises were tightly controlled by the government through foreign trade planning. The foreign trade plan was drawn up by the central bureaucracy and trading enterprises were issued with mandatory targets. Very often their targets were worked out in great detail with respect to the type and number of commodities to be traded. Hence, the decision-making autonomy of trading enterprises was severely limited. Since 1978 the command state trading system has been loosened.

To give trading enterprises more initiative and autonomy the scope of foreign trade planning was significantly reduced. For example, on the eve of the reforms in 1978 the foreign trade plan in respect of exports covered some 3,000 commodities. By the early 1990s, however, all mandatory export planning was abolished in principle (World Bank, 1994: 28). There was a similar change in the regulation of imports, for the number of commodities under the foreign trade plan was cut by 1992 to only 11 items and their share in Chinese imports had by then declined to 18.5 per cent (World Bank, 1994: 28).

With the increased decentralization of trading rights in China, accompanied by the declining importance of foreign trade planning, the methods of state control over trade decisions changed from plan control to direct and indirect trade control. Direct trade control is executed through direct administrative interventions in the form of a quota, licensing, canalization (monopoly or limited export and import rights), and other quantitative controls. Indirect trade control makes use of indirect price-based instruments such as tariffs, taxes, and subsidies to control trade decisions.

In recent years China has made use of both direct and indirect trade control methods to restrict its imports. Direct import controls (excluding mandatory import plan controls) covered 32.9 per cent of Chinese imports in 1992. The major instruments used were import canalization and licensing (World Bank, 1994: 67). Indirect import controls consisted mainly of tariffs. The average (unweighted) tariff rate for imports increased from 38.4 per cent in 1986 to 43 per cent in 1992 (World Bank, 1988b: 154; 1994: 48). Compared with other large developing countries, China's average tariff rate was the third highest after India and Pakistan (World Bank, 1994: 55).

With respect to exports the major indirect control methods were export taxes and subsidies. Export subsidies were phased out in early 1990. The use of export taxes, however, expanded as the product categories subject to export taxes rose from 19 in 1987 to 54 in 1992 (World Bank, 1994: 69). The main direct export controls were export quotas and licences and the foreign trade CRS which will be discussed in more detail in the latter part of this chapter. Export quotas and licences accounted for about 15 per cent of Chinese exports in 1992.

China's trade control system entered a new phase of development in the early 1990s, for in an attempt to regain its membership in GATT China stepped up the pace of import liberalization. As from 1991 tariffs were reduced for 45 imported items (*CM*, 1992, 6: 10). In January 1992 tariffs on another 225 imported items were cut and in December 1992 tariffs were cut further by an average of 7 per cent for 3,371 imported items (World Bank, 1994: 105). In addition, import adjustment taxes for 16 imported items were abolished in 1992. In

1994 tariffs were again reduced by an average 8.8 per cent for 2,898 imported items. It is anticipated that by the time of China's entry into GATT it would have reduced overall tariffs by 50 per cent compared to 1992 (*CD*, 10 June 1994).

Apart from cutting import tariffs China in 1992 also announced its intention to cut the number of items subject to import licences by three-quarters within a span of three years (*CM*, 1992, 6: 10). Finally, under a memorandum of understanding with the United States concluded in 1992, China committed itself to eliminate almost all import controls by 1997 (World Bank, 1994: 106).

REALIGNMENT OF DOMESTIC PRICES WITH FOREIGN PRICES

In the past Chinese domestic prices were completely divorced from world market prices through an arbitrary internal pricing system for importables and exportables which aimed at insulating domestic enterprises from the influence of foreign prices (Chai, 1983; World Bank, 1988*b*: 256). For exports the method used was that FTCs procured export commodities from domestic producers at internal prices set by the government. For agricultural products the internal prices of exportables were agricultural purchase prices and for industrial products they were ex-factory prices. The FTCs sold the export commodities at foreign prices on the world market. Any discrepancy between converted foreign prices at the official exchange rate and internal prices constituted profits or losses for FTCs which were then absorbed by the state budget as either profit delivery or subsidies.

On the import side FTCs procured import commodities at foreign prices and sold them to domestic end users at the internal prices of domestically produced equivalents. Again, any profit or loss by FTCs due to the discrepancy between converted foreign prices at the official exchange rate and internal prices was absorbed by the state budget as either profit delivery or subsidy.

Domestic prices were first tenuously connected to foreign prices through the calculation of the export efficiency index (the E-index) in the first phase of the reforms. The E-index simply established the ratio between the foreign and domestic prices of exportables, which represented the average domestic cost of earning a unit of foreign exchange.

The index was a 'second-best' solution to the comparative cost measurement problems under distorted domestic prices and a distorted exchange rate as it bypassed the arbitrary exchange rate by comparing domestic prices directly with foreign prices. The idea was to rank export commodities in terms of their average costs of earning a unit of foreign exchange. Attempts were also made to maximize the exports of those commodities with a low E-index and to minimize exports of those with a high one (*GJMY*, 1982, Feb.: 43–4).

Although the E-index avoided the distortion in the measurement of China's comparative advantage in trade caused by the arbitrary exchange rate it did not eliminate the distortion caused by the arbitrary domestic price system. During the second phase of reforms attempts were made to link a greater number of domestic prices directly to world market prices, with the widespread adoption of the 'agency system' in 1984. Under this system FTCs acted as agents in importing and exporting commodities on behalf of domestic enterprises on commission. Hence, domestic end users were charged at and domestic producers received the foreign price equivalent. Thus the domestic prices of a growing number of importables and exportables were directly linked to world market prices.

On the eve of the reforms only 20 per cent of all importables and exportables had their domestic prices based on world market prices (*CP*, 1991, 4: 12). By the early 1990s the percentage share of import and export commodities that had their domestic prices based on world market prices had already risen to 90 and 80 per cent respectively (*CP*, 1992, 2: 19).

FOREIGN EXCHANGE REFORM

In the past China had maintained an inconvertible RMB together with an artificial exchange rate system. Foreign exchange reforms since 1978 have aimed to achieve a more realistic exchange rate for the RMB through successive devaluation of its rate and the greater use of market forces to determine its rate.

The devaluation of the RMB occurred in two stages. In the first stage the official exchange rate was not affected. Instead, a shadow exchange rate, known as the internal settlement rate, was introduced on 1 January 1981. The internal rate was calculated from the average cost of earning a dollar through exports and was set at RMB 2.8 to the US dollar. At this time, the official rate was 1.5 RMB to the dollar. The internal rate constituted a *de facto* devaluation of the RMB by almost 50 per cent against the US dollar for trading enterprises.

Since the mid-1980s the RMB has been devalued on several fronts. First, the official exchange rate of the RMB was devalued. In 1985, the dual exchange rate was abolished and the official exchange rate was realigned with the internal settlement rate of that time, namely 3.71 *yuan* per dollar. Since then the official exchange rate of the RMB has experienced a continuous depreciation and the official RMB–dollar exchange rate saw a decline from 1.56 in 1978 to 5.76 in 1993 (*ZGTJZW 1994*: 107).

Second, the effective exchange rate of the RMB was further devalued by the opening of the formal parallel exchange market or swap centres. These existed as early as 1985, and by 1994, 110 swap centres had been established in China's major cities (*SCMPIW*, 2–3 April 1994). Initially access to swap centres was limited to enterprises that sold their surplus retained foreign exchange to other enterprises at the market rate. From 1991 all citizens were allowed to sell foreign exchange at swap centres. However, their access to purchases of foreign exchange at the centres was still restricted. The swap rate of foreign exchange was determined by market forces at the centres and was usually higher than the official rate. For example, in 1993 the swap rate was 8.7 *yuan* per dollar which was 33 per cent below the official rate. As the proportion of foreign exchange retained and traded by enterprises soared during the second phase of the reforms the importance of the swap rate of foreign exchange also grew. By the late 1980s approximately half of all foreign exchange was already traded and, hence, priced at the market rate. By 1992 this share had risen to 80 per cent (World Bank, 1994: xix).

Third, to meet the requirement of China's re-entry into GATT and in preparation for RMB convertibility the official exchange rate was abolished in early 1994 and unified with the depreciated swap market rate. Thus China's exchange rate system became a managed floating one whereby the *yuan* exchange rate is determined by market forces at swap centres. To keep the rate stable the PBC uses monetary and interest rate policies. In 1994 the foreign exchange market was also segmented into two parts, namely one for domestic firms and one for foreign-invested firms. The former may purchase foreign exchange through the new interbank market for foreign exchange whereas foreign-invested firms must use the existing swap centres.

FOREIGN EXCHANGE RETENTION SYSTEM

In the past, domestic enterprises had little interest in foreign trade as the foreign exchange they earned had to be surrendered to the central authority at the artificially low official exchange rate and any profits or losses incurred were absorbed in the state budget. To restore the material interest of domestic enterprises in trade a foreign exchange retention system was introduced in 1979 (*FS*, 1990, 9: 1). Under this system domestic economic units contributing to foreign exchange earnings were allocated a foreign exchange use quota in proportion to the foreign exchange earned. This proportion varied among localities. On average only 25 per cent of foreign exchange earned was allocated, of which 12.5 per cent was provided to the enterprise that supplied the export products and the other 12.5 per cent went to the respective local authorities (*GJMY*, 1990, 3: 43). However, in coastal regions the foreign exchange retention ratio was allowed to reach 50 per cent. In the Special Economic Zones (SEZs) the foreign exchange retention ratio before 1989 even reached 100 per cent. In order to use the foreign exchange quota enterprises had to use RMB to buy back the foreign exchange from state banks at the official exchange rate. The foreign exchange purchased, subject to approval by higher authorities, could then be used to import goods or could be sold for domestic currency at swap centres. As the swap rate was higher than the official rate enterprises provided with a foreign exchange use quota were able to receive a quota rent.

The system of foreign exchange retention was expanded and rationalized in 1991. The average foreign exchange retention was raised to 80 per cent (*HKTDC*, 1990: 17). Out of this 80 per cent 10 per cent was assigned to the enterprise that supplied the export products, 10 per cent accrued to the local authorities, and 60 per cent was for the FTCs. However, to ensure that its access to foreign exchange was sufficient to meet its own requirements the central government reserved the right to purchase at the prevailing swap rates an additional 30 per cent of the foreign exchange initially earned, e.g. an additional 20 per cent from the FTCs and 10 per cent from the export producers. Thus, in effect, 50 per cent of the overall foreign exchange earnings was still appropriated by the central government (World Bank, 1994: 31). Furthermore, the previous practice of differential retention rates in different regions was abolished and a uniform retention rate was introduced for all regions (*GJMY*, 1990, 3: 42–4).

In 1993 China started the phased implementation of the cash retention system which allowed enterprises to retain foreign exchange earnings in cash instead of quota. However, China still has a long way to go to achieve full convertibility of the RMB.

FOREIGN TRADE CONTRACT RESPONSIBILITY SYSTEM

The main weakness of the foreign exchange retention system is that as long as enterprise budget constraints remained soft it tended to induce local authorities and enterprises to maximize foreign exchange earnings regardless of domestic currency costs. Thus, to harden enterprise budget constraints a contract responsibility system (CRS), similar to the one adopted in the industrial sector, was introduced in 1988.

The aim of the CRS was to encourage FTCs to earn more foreign exchange and to minimize their domestic currency costs. The predominant form of the system was for a local government to contract with the central government to fulfil the targets for export receipts, foreign exchange remittance, and possible RMB subsidies for the targeted export receipts. The local governments then decomposed these targets and sub-contracted them out to their local FTCs (for a sample copy of this contract see Appendix 1). The entire system can be seen as a bonding contract between the principal (the government) and the agents (FTCs) to reduce agency costs. The FTCs undertook to attain the specified export targets in return for ownership of part of the surplus income produced. Both the local government and the FTCs aimed to maximize foreign exchange retention while hoping to minimize the amount of RMB subsidies.

Thus, as the analysis in Appendix 2 shows, if the target to increase export receipts and the target to reduce export earning costs are of equal importance to FTCs, the CRS in theory should induce FTCs to maximize foreign exchange earnings and minimize their costs. In practice, however, the target of maximizing export receipts was of paramount importance to all FTCs, simply because it was mandatory to fulfil their target of foreign exchange remittance to the state. This is evident from the incentive schemes specified in the sample contract between the local government and local FTCs in Appendix 1.

As the sample contract shows, bonuses were directly proportional to export earnings. In addition, the target of export receipts had to be met and the sub-contractor was required to use his own retention (or use his own RMB funds to purchase foreign exchange at swap centres) to cover any shortfall. Although bonuses might not be granted if the sub-contractor failed to meet the export earnings cost targets, much heavier penalties, such as a cut in the enterprise manager's basic salary by 10 to 50 per cent, were normally imposed for failure to fulfil the given export earning targets. Furthermore, while the target of export earnings was a 'hard' one, that of export earning costs was a 'soft' one, subject to frequent re-negotiations and revisions between the contractor and sub-contractor. For instance, although it was stated that the targets, once set, should remain unchanged for three years export earning costs have sometimes been revised within a period of less than 12 months because of dramatic increases in export procurement prices.

Thus, to further harden the budget constraints of FTCs, the content of the CRS was significantly modified in the early 1990s. For example, financial subsidies for targeted export receipts were abolished (*GJMY*, 1991, 3: 28). The three new targets contracted out to both the local authorities and FTCs became export receipts, foreign exchange submission to the centre, and the amount of exports (*HKTDC*, 1990: 8).

Though the CRS was meant to harden the FTCs' budget constraints it had the side effect of limiting their export autonomy, for the export targets specified in the contract were compulsory in nature; and, hence, enterprises were constrained in their choice of what goods they could export in order to maximize profits (World Bank, 1994: 39).

PRELIMINARY RESULTS

Trade participation ratio

The liberalization of trade has resulted in the rapid expansion of China's trade. In the period 1979–93 trade grew at an annual average rate of 16 per cent, i.e. at almost twice the economic growth rate (9.3) (*ZGTJNJ 1994*: 3). As a result, the aggregate trade participation ratio rose from 11 to 38 per cent, and by 1994 it reached 45 per cent (*TKP*, 13 Jan. 1995). Concomitantly, China's share in world exports also rose from 0.8 per cent in 1978 to 2 per cent in 1992. And in 1991 China had become the thirteenth-biggest exporter in the world (*SCMP*, 30 March 1992).

However, part of the increase in China's foreign trade appears to be exaggerated. To begin with, a substantial proportion of China's trade was in fact re-export trade which inflated China's trade participation ratio. The re-export trade stemmed from increased imports of materials for export processing which has become one of the major sources of China's export growth in recent years.

Furthermore, in recent years the trade participation ratio has also been boosted by the devaluation of the RMB. The trade participation ratio is simply a ratio between trade volume and GDP, both measured in domestic currency. Hence the rate of its growth is the sum of the rate of growth of the trade volume in foreign currency and the rate of appreciation of foreign currency minus the rate of growth of GDP. In the decade under discussion the RMB depreciated by 82 per cent; and, hence, the sharp increase in China's trade participation ratio can partly be explained by the sharp increase in the US dollar exchange rate of China's domestic currency.

Integration with the world economy

One of the objectives of China's open door policy was the greater integration of its domestic economy with that of the world. In general, the increased integration of two economies as a result of trade liberalization is accompanied by the convergence of prices between them (Lloyd, 1993: 4). Hence, the extent to which the Chinese economy was integrated with the world economy as a result of its trade liberalization can be assessed in terms of the convergence of its domestic prices with world market prices. Table 8.1 shows that even though China's domestic prices were increasingly linked to world market prices a considerable disparity between the two still prevails, due to the limited convertibility of the RMB and other trade barriers.

Table 8.1 shows the estimated nominal rate of protection (NRP) for selected goods for which the relevant price data are available. For most farm products, energy, and industrial producer goods NRPs were found to be negative, indicating that in the early 1990s China's domestic prices for these goods were still significantly lower than international prices. For most industrial consumer goods, however, domestic prices were significantly higher than international prices, indicating that these products were still very much protected on the domestic market.

TABLE 8.1. *Nominal Rates of Protection (NRP) for Selected Products, 1992*

Product	Free market price (*yuan*/t)	World market price (*yuan*/t)	NRP[a] (%)
A. *Agricultural products*			
Rice	996.9	1,678.5	−42.4
Wheat	789.1	748.2	0.5
Maize	354.1	628.2	−43.6
Tea	25,051.5	10,830.8	131.3
Pork (frozen)	4,641.3	6,289.2	−26.2
Beef (frozen)	6,990.8	15,547.7	−55.0
Soy beans	1,888.4	1,400.5	34.8
B. *Energy*			
Coal	64.5	232.1	−72.2
Crude oil	109.2	759.9	−85.6
Refined petroleum	1,050.9	1,306.4	−19.6
C. *Industrial producer goods*			
Steel in ingots	1,057.4	3,150.5	−66.4
Semi-finished steel	1,168.5	2,741.3	−57.4
Flat-rolled products of steel	1,622.0	2,741.3	-40.8
Bars and rods of iron and steel	1,493.7	2,238.6	−33.3
Wire cables of steel	2,581.9	2,238.6	15.3
Refined copper	15,893.4	13,671.5	16.3
Wood logs, oak	555.8	1,291.8	−57.0
Lumber, oak	549.9	2,753.0	−80.0
Polystyrene	7168.2	3,343.4	114.4
Rubber tyres for cars	1,640.0	1,753.5	−6.5
Petrol engines, 50 c.c.	860.6	584.5	47.2
D. *Industrial consumer goods*			
Refrigerators	1,623.8	1,753.5	−7.4
Washing machines	454.5	876.8	−48.2
PC-XT computers	14,240.0	5,845.0	143.6
Cassette recorders	455.9	350.0	30.0
VCRs	3,000.0	1,169.0	156.6
Colour TVs	1,903.6	1,153.7	65.0
Petrol automobiles	101,314.8	70,140.0	44.5

[a] Defined as the percentage by which the domestic (free market) price exceeds the international price (converted into *yuan* using the average swap market rate of 5.845).

Source: World Bank, 1994, Table A 3.7.

Contribution to economic growth

The contribution of trade to economic growth can be evaluated from either the demand or the supply side. On the demand side an increase in exports stimulates economic growth by increasing effective demand. Total effective demand consists of personal consumption, C, investment, I, government expenditures, G, and exports, X, less imports, M, and net factor income from abroad, Y_f. The relative contribution of the various components of effective demand to economic growth measured in terms of the ratios of their real increase to the increase in real GNP is presented in Table 8.2. As this table shows, the relative contribution of exports to economic growth rose from 2.3 per cent in the pre-reform period to 19.4 per cent in the reform period. However, in both periods it was smaller than the relative contribution of personal consumption and investment. Thus Chinese economic growth was mainly domestic demand led rather than export led.

The limited contribution of exports to economic growth is also confirmed by the fact that while the correlations between economic

TABLE 8.2. *Relative Contribution to Economic Growth of the Components of Effective Demand, 1967–1991 (%)*

	C	G	I	X	–M	Y_f
Pre-reform						
1967–70	40.3	13.2	49.1	–2.0	0.6	0
1971–75	56.5	10.6	34.8	13.0	15.0	0
1976–78	38.8	14.6	58.8	0.4	12.5	0
TOTAL 1967–78	42.0	14.7	47.3	2.3	6.3	0
Reform						
1979–84	62.2	9.4	27.1	18.2	17.7	0.9
1985–91	42.0	10.4	29.1	21.6	4.2	1.0
TOTAL 1979–91	49.1	9.3	36.9	19.4	15.3	0.6

	1967–78	1979–91
Correlation between G(Y) and:		
G(C)	0.919	0.455
G(I)	0.850	0.779
G(X)	0.010	–0.105
G(M)	0.208	0.403

Notes: G(Y), G(C), G(I), G(X), and G(M) are growth rates of GNP, private consumption, investment, exports, and imports respectively. Exports and imports include non-factor services.

Sources: *World Tables, 1988/89*: 192–3; *1993*: 184–5.

growth and growth of personal consumption as well as investment are statistically significant, that between export growth and economic growth is not (see Table 8.2).

Efficiency implications

In general, the growing linkage between domestic and foreign prices should improve the efficiency of foreign trade. However, in contrast to a market economy the budget constraints of China's trading enterprises were still rather soft and Chinese domestic prices were still distorted in this period. Hence, the reduction in the rate of divergence between domestic and foreign prices does not necessarily imply an improvement in trade efficiency. On the contrary, trade efficiency might have worsened, as occurred in the Hungarian reforms (Brada, 1973). A closer examination of some of China's trade efficiency indicators during this period suggests that China may have encountered the same problem as its Hungarian counterparts.

One of the trade efficiency indicators is the domestic currency cost of earning one unit of foreign exchange or US dollar through exports. A rising domestic currency cost of foreign exchange earning indicates a worsening of export efficiency. For China the cost of foreign exchange earning rose rapidly during the reform period. The average domestic currency cost of earning one US dollar through exports rose from 2.53 to 4.00 during the period 1978–84 (Chan, 1987: 435). By 1994 it had soared to between 8 and 9.

One of the main reasons for the soaring domestic currency cost of export earning was the rise in domestic prices due to inflation. Another major reason stemmed from the improper timing of the trade liberalization process. For the decentralization of export rights and the relaxation of foreign exchange controls were not accompanied by a significant hardening of the budget constraints of trading enterprises. This encouraged them to export regardless of domestic costs. As a result both the local authorities and the FTCs, in their attempts to maximize foreign exchange retention, engaged in fierce price competition between themselves. In export procurement on the domestic market they tended to overbid each other in terms of purchase prices. In export sales on overseas markets they tended to undercut each other in selling prices. Thus, domestic purchase prices were pushed up and export prices were depressed.

Another trade efficiency indicator is cost effectiveness in the use of foreign exchange for imports. Import efficiency is maximized if scarce foreign exchange is used to import goods which command the highest value to society. In China, however, due to the distorted price system, goods commanding the highest value to society, such as basic necessities or scarce raw materials, intermediate goods, and equipment vital for industrial and/or agricultural production, usually commanded a relatively low domestic price. This was because they qualified for government subsidies. On the other hand, luxury consumer goods, such as automobiles, colour television sets, refrigerators, cigarettes, liquor, and canned beverages, usually commanded relatively high domestic prices. The decentralization of foreign exchange and import rights discouraged imports of the former and encouraged imports of the latter, with the result that there was a general reduction of cost effectiveness in the use of foreign exchange or import efficiency (*CP*, 1992, 2: 20).

Stability implications

Trade liberalization in other developing countries has usually been accompanied by an improvement in their balance of payments (Michaely *et al.*, 1991: 274). Specifically, both exports and imports tend to increase following the launching of a trade liberalization policy. But in most cases the growth of imports was smaller than that of exports, and, hence, resulted in an improvement in the balance of payment. In China, prior to 1978, due to the centralized control of imports and exports, the country was able to balance imports with exports and achieve a small trade balance surplus. Since 1978, however, imports have constantly outstripped exports, causing a widening trade gap. Thus, for instance, between 1978 and 1994 trade deficits were recorded for 11 out of 17 years (*ZGTJZY 1994*: 105 and *TKP*, 13 Jan. 1995). To control the growing trade deficit the government had to rely from time to time on the centralization of import rights.

SUMMARY AND CONCLUSION

Attempts to open the Chinese economy to more and efficient international trade during the past 15 years have led to significant progress. The complete isolation of the domestic market from the foreign market is now a thing of the past. Various links between the two markets have been restored. The decision-making structure in the foreign trade sector has been decentralized. Domestic economic units have gained more rights to participate directly in foreign trade. The information structure has been improved. And there is also a growing interdependence between external and internal prices as a result of the reform of the exchange rate and of the internal pricing mechanism for traded commodities. The motivation structure has been modified and domestic economic units are now more interested in greater participation in foreign trade.

The preliminary results of the above reforms are impressive. Both China's exports and its aggregate trade participation ratio have risen sharply. Exports have become an increasingly important contributor to Chinese economic growth.

In spite of the above achievements a certain inertia stemming from China's traditional foreign trade system remained in the early 1990s. The trade system was still essentially a state trading system since the state had not only owned most of the trading enterprises but also maintained various links with them. The RMB was still not fully convertible. Access to the Chinese market for foreigners was still rather limited because of the limited convertibility of the RMB and other trade barriers. A closer examination of the growth, efficiency, and stability implications of China's trade liberalization also reveals that its preliminary achievements were less spectacular than prevailing or popular opinions hold them to be.

The rise in the trade participation ratio is partly inflated by the sharp devaluation of the RMB in the period of investigation. The efficiency implication of China's trade liberalization is at best uncertain. In view of the fact that China allowed the decentralization of foreign trade to run ahead of its domestic economic reforms there is no reason, a priori, to predict that the elimination of some of the distortions would necessarily improve China's trade efficiency, as has been suggested by Lardy (1994). According to the theory of second best, the removal of some restrictions in the presence of other restrictions and in a non-competitive environment does not necessarily improve efficiency (Gondolfo, 1994: 142–3). The available empirical data are not good enough to judge whether or not Chinese trade efficiency has increased. However, the surging average domestic currency cost of foreign exchange earnings and the reduction of the cost effectiveness in their utilization indicate that China's trade efficiency might not have improved much in the period under investigation. Finally, the persistent trade deficit during the same period also suggests that trade liberalization might have adversely affected China's trade balance.

The implications of the above findings for other socialist countries attempting trade liberalization are clear. Trade liberalization should be preceded, or at least accompanied by, a fundamental reform of the domestic pricing system and of the incentive system of trading and production enterprises. Otherwise the success of trade liberalization is likely to be limited.

9 The Open Door Policy II: Foreign Direct Investment

The liberalization of China's foreign direct investment (FDI) regime went through three distinct phases. In the first phase (1979–86) FDIs were welcome but highly regulated (Chai, 1986: 141–50; World Bank, 1988b: 259–74). The screening and approval of FDIs was highly centralized in this period and involved numerous government bureaucracies. Though formally no upper limit was imposed on foreign ownership, joint ventures (JVs) were definitely preferred and wholly owned foreign enterprises (WOFEs) were discouraged. Moreover, both the management and the transactions of FDI ventures were subject to many restrictions during this period. Thus, for instance, Chinese JV legislation required that the chairman of the board of directors, the highest decision-making authority in a JV, was to be a Chinese citizen irrespective of the relative equity contribution of the foreign partner.

An FDI venture's authority in input, output, pricing, and financial decisions was also severely circumscribed. On the input side the managerial prerogatives of FDI ventures to hire, fire, and set wages of workers were limited. With respect to output the domestic sale of output was severely restricted. In the area of pricing, FDI ventures were not free to determine the prices of products falling under state-determined price categories, i.e. the fixed and floating price categories. With respect to financial decisions FDI ventures were not allowed to raise loans on the domestic capital market. Neither could they convert their RMB earnings into foreign currencies. In fact, FDI ventures were required to balance their foreign exchange expenditures with their foreign exchange earnings.

The second phase began in 1986. Because of the growing dissatisfaction of foreign investors with China's investment environment there had been a sharp decline in the number of approved FDIs in that year. Consequently the government was forced to introduce new FDI regulations which significantly reduced government intervention in FDIs. The screening and approval of FDIs was decentralized and the procedure was simplified. In addition, informal restrictions on foreign ownership were abandoned and the setting up of WOFEs in China was encouraged. The project duration of FDI ventures was extended and the requirement that the chairman of the board be a Chinese citizen was lifted. FDI management was also granted more autonomy in decision making on input, output, and finance. Thus, for instance, they were given increased access to the domestic raw material and labour markets and were gradually granted more autonomy in the hiring and firing of workers and in wage setting. They were also allowed to increase the sales volume of their output on the domestic market if their products were those which China had to import. Foreign investors in export-oriented (EO) and technologically advanced (TA) projects were allowed to raise loans on local financial markets. Finally, the foreign exchange balance requirement was relaxed. To cover their foreign exchange shortfall FDI ventures were allowed to use their RMB earnings to procure local products for exports or to convert them into foreign exchange at the newly opened swap centres.

The new policies not only made life for overseas investors in China easier but also offered more incentives. FDI incentives in developing countries can be either product or factor based (Guisinger, 1989). Product-based incentives aim to protect the products of FDI ventures on the domestic market through tariffs or non-tariff barriers. Factor-based incentives attempt to reduce the factor costs of FDI ventures through tax holidays, accelerated depreciation, subsidized infrastructure, etc. As is evident from Table 9.1, FDI incentives in China were mainly factor based. They usually took the form of tax holidays, investment allowances, reductions or exemptions of imported raw materials and equipment from sales tax and custom duties, as well as reduced fees for land use, labour services, and other public utilities. Special incentives were provided for foreign investors in preferential treatment areas, i.e. the SEZs as well as the open coastal cities and provinces (Grub and Lin, 1991: 45–53).

The FDI incentives in the second phase were significantly enhanced compared with those in the first phase (see Table 9.1). Preferential treatment areas were also significantly enlarged. During the first phase these had been confined to four SEZs, Guangdong and Fujian provinces, Hainan Island and the 14 open coastal cities, thus covering a total of about 117 cities and *xians* (*YHJJKFQJJYJHTJZL*, 1989: 147–9). In the second phase these were extended to cover 11 open coastal provinces which comprised 288 cities and *xians*. Moreover, foreign investors were provided with more generous tax incentives.

TABLE 9.1. *Summary of Investment Incentive Changes, 1979–1990*

	1979–85	1986–90
I. Nationwide		
1. Enterprise income tax[a]	33%	33%
2. Tax holiday	5 years, first 2 years 100% exception and for 3rd to 5th year 50% exception	Extended beyond 5 years for EO and TA projects
3. Remittance tax	10%	Exempt for EO and TA projects
4. Tax refund for re-invested profit	40%	100% refund for EO and TA projects
5. Sales tax and customs imports	Exempt for (a) equipment and materials imported as part of investment and (b) materials, parts, components imported for export production	For items (a) and (b) import licence exempted
6. Sales tax and customs duty on exports	No exemption	Exempt (except on export-restricted items)
7. Land-use fees	Rates varied with proximity to city centre	Reduced rate for EO and TA projects
8. Wage surcharge	Compulsory social security contribution and compensation for state subsidies[b] for workers averaging 25% of total wage bill	Payment of some of the state subsidies for workers exempted for EO and TA projects
9. Other fees	Site development and connection fees for sewage disposal and treatment, public utilities,[c] public utilities construction fees, etc.	No reduction but granted priority in obtaining utilities, transport, and communications facilities for EO and TA projects
II. Preferential incentives area	4 SEZs plus 14 open coastal cities, Hainan Island, Guangdong and Fujian provinces	4 SEZs, 14 open coastal cities, and 11 open coastal provinces

[a] Including local income tax.

[b] On food, housing, medical care, and education.

[c] For water, gas, and heating.

Sources: World Bank, 1988a: 264–7; *ACFERT 1991/2*: 114–15, 120–1, 123–30; Grub and Lin, 1991: 45–59.

The third phase began in 1992 following Deng Xiaoping's tour of the southern provinces and his call for more reform and the further opening of the Chinese economy. Since then the terms for foreign investors have been further improved, with more preferential areas opened to foreign investors. In 1992, another 28 cities and eight prefectures along the Yangtze River and 13 border cities in the country's northeastern, southeastern, and northwestern regions were declared preferential treatment or open areas (*CD*, 1 Aug. 1992). Furthermore, in its bid to re-enter GATT, China opened its formerly closed service sectors, such as banking, retailing, and telecommunications, as well as major infrastructural facilities to foreign investors (*SCMPIW*, 17–18 Sept. 1994). Last, the government also relaxed the existing sale restrictions for foreign ventures on the domestic market (*HSEM*, December 1994).

TREND AND PATTERN OF FDIS

The number of FDI approvals grew slowly during the initial years (see Table 9.2). The growth of FDIs picked up momentum in 1984 and reached its peak in 1985 when the number of approved FDIs more than doubled. There was a setback in 1986 when the total fell by

TABLE 9.2. *Annual FDI Intake in China, 1979–1994 (in billion US$)*

	Contracted FDI	Realized FDI
1979–82	7.0	1.7
1983	2.0	0.9
1984	2.9	1.5
1985	6.3	2.0
1986	3.3	2.3
1987	4.3	2.7
1988	6.2	3.7
1989	6.3	3.8
1990	7.0	3.8
1991	12.4	4.7
1992	58.7	11.3
1993	111.4	26.0
1994[a]	62.6	25.2

[a] The first 10 months only.

Sources: *ZGTJZY 1994*: 110; *SCMPIW*, 3–4 Dec. 1994.

nearly 50 per cent. But the change in FDI policies in 1986 improved the climate for foreign investment in China. This, together with the loss of the comparative advantage of the four Asian newly industrialized countries (NICs) in labour-intensive industries and the resulting relocation of their production bases to neighbouring countries with a labour surplus, stimulated a large increase in FDI inflow into China during the second half of the 1980s. The credit squeeze in the late 1980s, introduced by the government to combat inflation, coupled with the political uncertainty in the aftermath of the Tiananmen Square incident in June 1989, however, caused another setback in the growth of FDIs in China. The number of newly approved FDIs remained constant in 1989, indicating a 'wait-and-see' attitude on the part of foreign investors. With the slow but steady restoration of investors' confidence and the official sanctioning of indirect trade and investment with mainland China by the Taiwanese government in the early 1990s, the FDI inflow into China picked up momentum again.

In 1992, the number of newly approved FDIs jumped by more than 377 per cent after the southern tour of Deng Xiaoping. This robust growth continued in 1993, with the value of newly approved FDI rising to $111.4 billion. This was equivalent to the accumulated value of all FDI over the previous 13 years. Actual FDI in 1993 stood at $26 billion, making China the world's second largest recipient of FDI after the United States. Contracted FDI suffered another setback in 1994 as a result of a credit squeeze introduced to cool the overheated economy and the clampdown on real estate investment projects. However, actual FDI continued to soar at a rate of 44 per cent in the first 10 months of 1994. By October 1994 the accumulated value of approved FDI in China stood at $290.4 billion, of which $89.9 billion had actually been invested. Altogether 22,700 foreign-invested enterprises (FIEs) were established, employing over 23 million workers (*TKP*, 10 Jan. 1995). These enterprises accounted for 37 per cent of China's foreign trade.

Most FDI projects in China are relatively small in scale. The average planned investment per project was only $1.7 million in the period from 1979 to 1993 (*ZGTJZY 1994*: 110). In the early years FDIs were dominated by a few large projects engaged in raw materials extraction (coal and oil) and real estate (mainly hotels) invested in by MNCs from industrialized countries. Hence, the average size of FDI projects initially was relatively large. In recent years FDI projects tended to be dominated by small- and medium-scale EO projects by MNCs from

Hong Kong and Taiwan (Shapiro, 1991: 29). Hence the average investment size declined from $7.6 million in the early 1980s to $1.3 million in 1993.

In the early 1980s foreign investors generally preferred the 'lower' forms of FDI. The most popular were the contractual joint venture (JV) and joint exploration, neither of which involved foreign equity capital. Other popular forms of FDI in this period were equity JVs, compensation trade, and processing trade. In recent years the improved investment environment and the changed attitude of the Chinese government towards foreign ownership stimulated an increase of FDI in the higher forms. Thus equity JVs and WOFEs grew in importance. By 1994 these two forms accounted for 40.8 and 37.9 per cent respectively of actual investments by Hong Kong or Macau and Taiwan investors (*TKP*, 14 Jan. 1995). For other foreign investors the equity JV was the most popular form, accounting for 71.5 per cent of their actual investment.

Table 9.3 shows the major foreign investors in China. In 1985 most of them came from Hong Kong or Macau, followed by those from the United States and Japan. In 1993 Hong Kong and Macau investors still ranked first but by then investments from Taiwan and Japan had overtaken those from the United States. In recent years, with the normalization of diplomatic relations between China and South Korea, the latter has emerged as another major investor in China. As of May 1994 South Korea had about 1,400 investment projects in China and had invested about $1.2 billion (*TKP*, 4 Jan. 1995).

Initially, most FDIs were located in the coastal regions and within these they were concentrated in the four SEZs in Guangdong and Fujian provinces, and particularly in Shenzhen. Later on FDIs tended

TABLE 9.3. *Realized FDI by Country, 1985, 1989, and 1993 (%)*

Country	1985	1989	1993
Hong Kong/Macau	49.9	62.1	64.9
Taiwan		11.4	11.3
USA	18.3	7.6	7.4
Japan	16.1	10.8	4.9
Others	15.7	8.1	11.5
TOTAL	100.0	100.0	100.0

Sources: ZGSYWJTJZL 1952–1988: 548; HSEM, Dec. 1994.

to be more geographically dispersed. In 1994 the coastal region still accounted for 83.5 per cent of total actual FDI (*TKP*, 14 Jan. 1995). Within the coastal regions there was, however, a significant shift of FDIs from Guangdong in the south to the coastal provinces in the northeast. Thus the share of Guangdong in actual FDI intake fell between 1991 and 1993 from 42 to 27 per cent whereas that of Shanghai and Jiangsu increased from 3 and 5 to 11 and 10 per cent respectively (*HSEM*, 1994, December).

Initially FDIs were concentrated in the service sector, especially in real estate, hotels, and other tourism-related projects which guaranteed foreign exchange earnings (Pomfret, 1991: 102). But in the second phase there was a significant shift of FDIs towards the industrial sector (see Table 9.4). This was primarily due to the growing tendency of Asia's NICs and Japan to relocate the production bases of their labour-intensive manufactured exports to China, following the Plaza Accord of 1985 in which the G-5 (group of five major industrial countries) forced Japan and the Asian NICs to appreciate their currencies. In 1990 FDIs in industry accounted for 88 per cent of China's contracted FDIs. In the third phase, with the opening of the service sector to FDI, the share of industry declined whereas that of real estate and other services increased once again.

Most FDIs in China were export oriented. The shortage of foreign exchange required FDI ventures in general to export an overwhelming proportion of their output. Hence domestic-market-oriented FDIs were rare. Despite the relaxation of foreign exchange controls in the

TABLE 9.4. *Contracted FDI Inflow by Sector, 1985, 1990, and 1993 (% share)*

	1985	1990	1993
Industry[a]	39.7	87.7	49.5
Agriculture	2.0	2.0	1.1
Real estate	36.0	6.5 ⎫	
			44.7
Other service sector	22.3	3.8 ⎭	
TOTAL	100.0	100.0	100.0

[a] Including construction.

Source: *ACFERT*, 1991, 2: 659; *ZGSYWJTJZL 1952–1988*: 530; *HSEM*, Dec. 1994.

second phase there is no evidence that FDIs have become more domestic market oriented (*CBR*, Nov.–Dec. 1990: 30). The reason for this is that even with the relaxation of foreign exchange balance requirements FDI ventures still encountered great difficulties in balancing their foreign exchange receipts and expenditures. Specifically, they found it difficult in practice to use their RMB earnings from domestic market sales to purchase local goods for export in order to earn enough foreign exchange to meet their foreign exchange expenditures (Grub and Lin, 1991: 55; Shapiro, 1991: 204).

THE REAL IMPACT OF FDIS

There are both real and financial effects of FDI on the host country's economy. Real effects include measurable static effects on income, productivity, employment, and export growth as well as hard-to-measure dynamic qualitative effects, such as technology transfer, linkage, structural change, etc. (Lim and Fong, 1991: 86). Some early studies focusing on the first phase of FDI in China found that FDI contributed positively to capital formation, income, employment, and export growth in China (Chai, 1983; World Bank, 1988*b*; Hiemenz, 1990). However, the extent of the contribution was limited because most FDIs were concentrated in the real estate and tourism-related sectors and the environmental and government policies facing FDI ventures were very restrictive in this period. Hiemenz also found that the distorted factor prices, coupled with the protection of domestic industries against competition from abroad in this period, led foreign ventures to adopt more capital-intensive techniques of production than those used by domestic firms (Hiemenz, 1990: 90, 96). Recent studies focusing on the second phase of FDI in China, however, found that the impact of FDI on income and export growth was much more positive (Kueh, 1992; Chi, 1994).

Empirical studies of the real impact of FDI on the host country's economy focus on the link between foreign ownership and firms' behaviour. The objective of such studies is to test whether the behaviour of foreign-owned enterprises is systematically different from that of locally owned ones. The ideal test would be to select a number of foreign and local firms, matched in pairs in terms of their size and product line, compare their behaviour, and assess the implications for economic efficiency (Jenkins, 1991: 113). Unfortunately, this approach is not feasible in China as micro-data on foreign-owned enterprises are not readily available. Fortunately, however, regional data on foreign ownership and economic performance abound in China. So the impact of FDI can be inferred from a comparison of the relative share of foreign ownership in a region and the region's respective performance indicators.

Table 9.5 compares the FDI component of fixed-asset investment and the macro-economic performance of selected regions in China for 1985–90. The selection of the regions was non-random, influenced by data availability. The regions selected include the four SEZs, the two special provinces, and the five northeastern cities which are grouped according to the share of FDI in their domestic fixed-asset investment. The performance indicators under observation are economic growth, incremental capital productivity, and export growth.

TABLE 9.5. *Economic Performance of Regions Grouped by Size of their FDI Intake*

	(1)	(2)	(3)	(4)	(5)	(6)	(7)
SEZ average	21.1	16.1	0.31	23.7	33.5	1.36	1.31
Shenzhen	30.5	20.8	0.27	16.5	44.5	1.97	1.05
Zhuhai	19.4	18.9	0.29	27.0	45.9	1.13	1.69
Shantou	11.5	9.5	0.35	16.2	16.3	1.61	1.15
Xiamen	22.8	15.2	0.31	35.1	27.3	0.72	1.34
Special provinces average	11.4	11.0	0.32	26.4	14.2	0.42	1.34
Guangdong	14.1	11.2	0.30	22.2	17.6	0.61	1.26
Fujian	8.6	10.7	0.35	30.6	10.7	0.22	1.42
Other localities average	5.9	4.4	0.12	13.0	6.9	0.15	3.50
Shanghai	4.2	1.1	0.03	7.7	4.4	0.21	2.93
Tianjin	2.6	2.5	0.06	0.8	5.7	0.13	2.10
Beijing	6.6	5.8	0.12	10.2	7.7	0.10	7.40
Dalian	10.1	8.3	0.28	33.3	9.6	0.14	1.56

Notes:
(1) % share of FDI in fixed investment, 1985–90.
(2) Average annual growth of real NMP, 1985–90.
(3) Incremental output–capital ratio, 1985–90.
(4) Average annual growth of exports (including non-locally produced exports), 1988–91.
(5) Average annual growth (%) of industrial output, 1985-90.
(6) Import share in GDP, 1988–91.
(7) Ratio of import and export share of FIEs, 1988–91.

Sources: Kueh, 1992: 656, 660, 662, 682, 684, 688–90; *ZGTJNJ 1991*: 658–67; 674–83.

As Table 9.5 shows, in the period from 1985 to 1990 those regions more exposed to foreign ownership, such as the four SEZs and the two special provinces, generally experienced faster export growth. Their efficiency in capital utilization was on average also higher than that of other regions. Higher export growth and capital productivity contributed directly to higher economic growth in these regions. Thus, in general, one can hardly reject the hypothesis that FDI contributed significantly to China's economic growth during this period.

Turning to the dynamic and qualitative effects of FDI, FDI has undoubtedly made an enormous contribution to regional industrialization in China. As is evident from Table 9.5, on average the regions which experienced higher FDI intake also recorded higher industrial output growth. The local linkage effect, however, remained rather limited. The forward linkage effect of FDIs was limited because most FDIs were export oriented. The backward linkage effect was poor as well because most of the raw materials required by FDI ventures were in fact imported. This is evident from Table 9.5 (column 6) which shows that the propensity to import is relatively high in regions with a relatively large share of FDIs. Apparently FDI ventures had little motivation to purchase their materials on the domestic market because materials of the required quality at reasonable prices and with reliable delivery schedules were usually not available locally (Shapiro, 1991: 171–5). Finally, the geographical concentration of FDI ventures in the SEZs and other areas with preferential treatment also tended to limit the points of contact between foreign ventures and local firms and hindered the establishment of local linkages.

There are no quantitative estimates of the extent of the technology transfer effected by FDIs in China. FDIs undoubtedly transferred a significant amount of technology to China as they brought in machinery and equipment and trained Chinese managers and workers (Pomfret, 1991: 135–6). However, available evidence suggests that both the level and effectiveness of the technology transfer should not be overrated. First, most FDIs were initiated by small and medium-sized firms from Hong Kong and Taiwan which relocated their labour-intensive 'sunset' industries into China. Hence most of the machinery and equipment transferred to China was unlikely to be of the high-technology type. Second, Chinese partners in JVs were mainly engaged in the production process rather than in marketing, research, and development (Chai, 1983: 134). Hence the range of software technology transferred into China was also limited. Finally, the effectiveness of technology transfer depends on the technology absorption and diffusion capability of Chinese indigenous firms. Their record in this respect, unfortunately, has so far not been impressive (Chai, 1983: 134–8; Shapiro, 1991: 208–13).

FINANCIAL EFFECTS OF FDI

The financial effects of FDI on the host country include the impact on the balance of payments and on domestic savings. These effects may be positive or negative depending on whether an FDI improves or worsens the balance of payments of the host country and on whether an FDI complements or displaces domestic savings. In view of the chronic shortage of foreign exchange and capital in China the financial effects of FDI are of equal importance to their real effects.

The balance of payments impacts of FDI in China have so far been largely negative as the import intensity (imports deflated by total output) of FDI ventures was consistently higher than their export intensity. This is evident from Table 9.5 which shows that the ratio of FDI ventures' regional import share and export share was consistently larger than one. The relatively higher ratio of their share in imports in the northern cities suggests that the negative contribution of FDI to the trade balance was greater in this region where FDI ventures tended to be of the domestic market-oriented type.

One study of the impact of foreign capital on domestic savings in Asian developing countries in the period 1965–82 found that while foreign aid displaced domestic savings FDIs complemented it (Rana and Dowling, 1988). The Chinese experience is in line with the experience of other Asian developing countries. To attract FDI China not only had to spend a great deal on infrastructural investments but also had to match the foreign equity contribution. According to one Chinese estimate, for each US dollar of FDI attracted an average of 3 RMB had to be spent (Kueh, 1992: 658). Thus the fact that FDI complements China's domestic savings is to be expected.

CONCLUDING REMARKS

Despite the sizeable benefits of FDI in China, its role should not be exaggerated. In view of the size of China's economy FDIs accounted for only 6 per cent of China's total fixed-asset investment between 1980 and 1993. Furthermore, FDI also led to some social problems, for example the abuse of domestic workers by FIEs (*SCMPIW*, 26–7 Feb. 1994). Industrial safety was found to be worst in Hong Kong and Taiwan FIEs, with more than 10 per cent of the 206 large-scale industrial fires in 1993 involving FIEs. Workers in FIEs were reportedly underpaid and forced to work long hours. Some workers were even beaten and some female staff were denied maternity leave. Foreign investors were also accused of cheating by inflating the value of their assets invested in joint ventures. There is also evidence that FIEs in Shenzhen used transfer pricing to evade taxes.

Another problem is that the concentration of FDIs in the coastal belt partly contributed to the increase in the interregional income gap. For example, on the eve of the reforms the income gap between the coastal and western regions of China was moderate, with the coastal region's average income only about 50 per cent higher than that of the western region. By the end of the 1980s, however, the average income of the former was almost twice that of the latter (Chai, 1995).

10 The Role of the Non-State Sector

China's non-state sector consists of the collective and private sectors. The collective sector includes urban collectives and township and village enterprises (TVEs). The private sector comprises individual and private enterprises (IEs and PEs). China's non-state sector was the most important contributor to the country's economic growth over the last 15 years. In the early 1990s its output share exceeded that of the state sector and by 1994 it accounted for more than half of China's industrial output, retail sales, and exports. This chapter identifies the composition and significance of the non-state sector and explores the trend of its development. Since foreign-invested private enterprises have already been discussed in the previous chapter this chapter focuses mainly on domestic collective and private enterprises, namely, TVEs, IEs, and PEs.

TOWNSHIP AND VILLAGE ENTERPRISES

TVEs were created in the late 1950s as commune- and brigade-run enterprises under Mao's 'walking on two legs' policy which envisioned the coexistence of labour-intensive small-scale rural industrial enterprises beside medium- and large-scale modern urban industrial enterprises. They were established to mobilize surplus labour and other local resources in the countryside to achieve local self-reliance and rural industrialization (Riskin, 1987: 213–18). With the collapse of the commune system they were renamed TVEs.

The growth of TVEs, as can be seen from Table 10.1, can be divided into four phases. In phase one (1978–83) their growth was slow, and their number actually declined. During this period the development of TVEs was adversely affected by the lack of government support as government officials were still sceptical about the efficiency of TVEs and not sure whether their growth would be compatible with socialism (Byrd and Lin, 1990: 47). Moreover, during this period a national economic readjustment programme was carried out to restructure China's industry (Howe and Walker, 1984) and a significant number of high-cost and high-energy-consumption TVEs producing heavy industrial products were closed down.

TABLE 10.1. *Development of Township and Village Enterprises, 1978–1993*

	Number (10,000) (1)	Employment (million) (2)	Output (billion *yuan*) (3)
1978	152.4	28.3	49.3
1979	148.0	29.1	54.8
1980	142.5	30.0	65.7
1981	133.8	29.7	74.5
1982	136.2	31.1	85.3
1983	134.6	32.3	101.7
1984	186.4	39.8	146.6
1985	185.0	43.3	205.0
1986	172.8	45.5	251.7
1987	158.3	47.2	323.8
1988	159.1	48.9	436.3
1989	153.6	47.2	485.6
1990	145.4	45.9	542.9
1991	144.2	47.7	772.0
1992	152.0	51.5	1,210.0
1993	168.5	57.7	2,036.0
Annual average growth rates (%)			
1978–1983	−2.4	2.6	15.6
1983–1984	38.5	23.2	44.2
1984–1991	−3.6	2.6	26.8
1991–1993	8.1	10.0	62.4

Sources: *ZGTJNJ 1994*: 32, 361–3; *ZGNCJJTJDQ 1949–1986*: 286–7.

The growth of TVEs experienced a sharp acceleration in phase two (1983–4) with their number jumping by 39 per cent and their nominal output by 44 per cent in 1984. The main factor behind this sudden spurt had been the call by the Central Committee of the CCP to support the development of TVEs and other types of rural enterprise. Such enterprises were required in order to provide employment for the growing number of surplus rural labourers released from the agricultural sector as a result of the rapid increase in agricultural productivity under the HRS. Restrictions on bank loans to TVEs were also relaxed after this call (Byrd and Lin, 1990: 58).

The growth of TVEs slowed down significantly in phase three (1985–91). Their numbers declined though output continued to soar. The tight monetary policy introduced by the government to control inflation in 1985 and again in 1988/9 severely affected the supply of credit to TVEs. Furthermore, under the rectification programme of 1988–91 three million rural enterprises were closed down and the planned establishment of another 20,000 was either abandoned or postponed (*ZGNYNJ 1990*: 43). The development of TVEs entered a new phase in 1992 after Deng Xiaoping's tour of the southern provinces and the Party's commitment to the establishment of a socialist market economy. Since then both the number and the output of TVEs have grown rapidly.

The size of TVEs was relatively small. In 1993 an average township enterprise (TE) employed about 66 workers and the average village enterprise (VE) was only one-third as large (*ZGTJNJ 1994*: 361–2). Industrial TEs were generally less than half the size of the average state-owned enterprise (SOE). TVEs were mainly concentrated in the industrial sector. The share of industrial TVEs in total TVEs' output rose from 78.1 per cent in 1978 to 84.5 per cent in 1991 (*ZGNYNJ 1992*: 365).

The industrial composition of TVEs was similar to that of SOEs and covered both light and heavy industries (Table 10.2). One of the notable differences is that SOEs tended to be engaged more in upstream products, especially petroleum extraction, processing, and coking, the supply of electricity, gas, and water, metal smelting, and machine building. TVEs, on the other hand, tended to produce more building materials, textiles, garments, and leather, as well as metal products.

The regional distribution of TVEs was rather uneven (see Table 10.3). In 1993 TVEs accounted on average for about 28 per cent of rural employment, ranging from a low 10 per cent in Guizhou to 71 per cent in Beijing. Most TVEs were located in the more developed coastal regions, where their share in the employment of the rural work-force averaged 45 per cent. In contrast, only 17 per cent of the rural work-force were engaged in TVEs in the least developed western region in the same year. The concentration of TVEs in the coastal regions can largely be explained by their relatively abundant supply of industrial resources (capital, skilled labour, and agricultural raw materials), their larger domestic markets, and their better accessibility to FDIs and foreign markets.

The concentration of TVEs in the eastern coastal region meant that the shift of the population away from the low-productivity agricultural sector to the high-productivity industrial sector occurred in this region at a much faster rate than elsewhere in China. This contributed

TABLE 10.2. *Industrial Structure of Township and Village Enterprises, 1993 (%)*

	SOEs (1)	TVEs (2)	(1)–(2) (3)
Coal mining	2.1	1.6	0.5
Petroleum extraction	2.5	neg.[a]	2.5
Metals and non-metal mineral mining	1.4	3.5	−2.1
Logging	0.4	0.1	0.3
Food, beverages, and tobacco	9.9	8.1	1.8
Textiles, garments, and leather	12.9	17.9	−5.0
Timber processing and furniture	1.1	2.5	−1.4
Paper and printing	2.4	3.1	−0.7
Culture and sports articles	0.5	0.8	−0.3
Petroleum processing and coking products	3.7	0.6	3.1
Chemical industry	6.0	5.1	0.9
Pharmaceutical goods	1.8	0.6	1.2
Chemical fibres	1.2	0.6	0.6
Rubber and plastic goods	2.9	4.1	−1.2
Building materials	5.9	12.2	−6.3
Ferrous and non-ferrous metal smelting	12.4	6.9	5.5
Metal products	3.3	7.0	−3.7
Machine building	23.3	18.2	5.1
Intruments and meters	0.9	0.5	0.4
Electric power, gas, and water supply	4.1	0.4	3.9
Others	1.5	6.2	-4.7
TOTAL		100.0	100.0

[a] Negligible.

Note: Enterprises under an independent accounting system only.
Sources: *ZGTJNJ 1994*: 378–9.

to the widening east–west regional income gap which has developed in recent years. To reduce this regional imbalance the government has intensified its efforts to promote TVEs in the less developed regions. As a result TVEs' output in these regions has jumped significantly in the last few years. For example, in the first half of 1994 overall TVEs' industrial output grew by 44 per cent nation-wide. However, TVEs in central China increased their output by 50 per cent and those in western China by 70 per cent (*SCMPIW*, 29–30 Oct. 1994).

TABLE 10.3 *Regional Perspectives of Township and Village Enterprises, Individual Enterprises, and Private Enterprises, 1993*

	Share of TVEs in rural employment (%) (1)	Share in non-agric. employment (%)		GDP per capita (*yuan*) (4)
		IEs (2)	PEs (3)	
Eastern region	44.7[a]	10.0[a]	1.8[a]	3,909[a]
Beijing	71.3	5.7	1.0	6,805
Tianjin	55.7	4.9	1.8	4,696
Shanghai	62.6	2.7	1.7	8,652
Liaoning	50.9	8.1	1.7	3,254
Shandong	37.9	16.9	1.5	2,307
Jiangsu	34.0	8.3	0.8	2,858
Zhejian	31.7	14.0	2.1	2,850
Fujian	35.9	12.1	3.0	2,264
Guangdong	37.3	11.1	3.2	3,575
Hebei	29.6	15.7	1.2	1,827
Central region	27.9[a]	11.0[a]	1.0[a]	1,645[a]
Heilongjiang	36.4	8.8	0.5	2,433
Jilin	30.0	9.3	0.9	2,071
Henan	31.6	10.2	1.0	1,377
Shanxi	37.4	11.4	2.0	1,744
Anhui	25.5	12.2	0.7	1,253
Hubei	28.5	10.2	0.7	1,827
Hunan	21.9	13.6	1.1	1,487
Jiangxi	23.6	13.7	0.9	1,439
Sichuan	20.0	9.6	0.8	1,356
Shaanxi	24.5	10.8	1.4	1,458
Western region	17.1[a]	13.3[a]	1.2[a]	1,565[a]
Guangxi	19.4	14.1	1.0	1,318
Ningxia	21.0	10.1	1.5	1,635
Xizang	n.a	25.7	0.4	1,486
Xingjiang	19.8	15.9	1.8	2,458
Neimenggu	25.3	10.0	1.1	1,712
Yunnan	11.0	13.6	0.7	1,334
Guizhou	10.1	10.7	1.8	1,009
Gansu	19.4	10.9	1.2	1,314
Qinghai	10.8	8.8	1.3	1,821

[a] Unweighted average.

Sources: *ZGTJNJ 1994*: 36–7, 84–6, 103.

In contrast to SOEs the TVEs operated in a semi-market environment and were subject to fewer government controls. They also faced a much harder budget constraint as they had limited access to subsidized energy, raw materials, and bank loans (Byrd and Lin, 1990: 89). In addition, their product market was less protected. Moreover, township and village governments, the TVEs' owners, unlike the central government, could not print money or force the state banking system to print money to bail out loss-making enterprises (Perkins, 1994: 37). Thus, TVEs were able to outperform SOEs in terms of both efficiency and output growth. In terms of efficiency, during the years 1980–92, while the industrial SOEs' total factor productivity (TFP) grew at an annual average of 2 to 3 per cent, that of industrial TVEs grew at a rate of 7 per cent (Jefferson and Rawski, 1994: 56). Similarly, during the same period, while the industrial output of SOEs grew at an annual average of 7.8 per cent, that of TVEs grew at a rate of 18.4 per cent (Jefferson and Rawski, 1994: 48). The higher growth of TVEs' industrial output contributed partly to the declining share of SOEs in China's total industrial output. By 1994 this share had fallen from 76 per cent in 1980 to only 38.7 per cent and the non-state sector now accounts for the lion's share of China's industrial output.

Compared with PEs, however, the property rights of TVEs are still rather ambiguous (Byrd and Lin, 1990: 89, 125). TVEs are in fact mini-SOEs owned by local governments. They enjoy less autonomy than PEs as they are under the supervision of the industrial corporation of the local government. A significant proportion of their after-tax profits is siphoned off for community expenditures or the development of other TVEs. Investments made by workers in TVEs cannot be inherited or returned as dividend to the workers. Finally, workers in TVEs are more protected than their counterparts in PEs which tend to be over-staffed and pay inflated wages.

According to one study the TVEs' performance is not significantly different from that of PEs (Byrd and Lin, 1990: 243–54). However, the sample on which this study is based is too small to arrive at a firm conclusion. Furthermore, some of the TVEs included in the sample may be fake TVEs or PEs disguised as TVEs to avoid political persecution and gain access to preferential tax treatment. In fact, some provinces reportedly gave at least 83 per cent of PEs the title of TVEs (*CDBW*, 22–8 May 1994).

Partly because of soaring material and labour costs and partly because of the loss of preferential tax treatment as a result of the unification of the enterprise income tax rate, the proportion of loss-making TVEs increased from 4 per cent in 1993 to 7 per cent in the first nine months of 1994 (*CD*, 15 Nov. 1994). To strengthen their financial discipline a growing number of TVEs were converted into co-operative shareholding enterprises (*ZGJJTZGGNJ 1993*: 426), in which collective assets are divided into communal government and worker shares. The former cannot be bought or sold whereas the latter are equally divided among workers and used to determine their dividend entitlement. However, workers are not allowed to transfer their shares or take them out when they leave the enterprise. In addition to the above two types of share, investment shares were also introduced to allow individuals to invest in enterprises. These shares, however, are transferable. By 1993, 10 per cent of the country's TVEs had been converted into co-operative shareholding enterprises (*CD*, 6 June 1994).

INDIVIDUAL ENTERPRISES

An IE is officially defined as an individual proprietorship and as a household firm employing not more than seven workers. IEs constitute the largest component of China's private sector in terms of employment. Their average size is of course very small. Most are individual proprietorships without employees. Quite a few of them hire one worker while the number of those with two employees or more is insignificant (Heberer, 1989: 367). Over the years, however, the average size of IEs has risen steadily from 1.1 persons in 1978 to 1.7 persons in 1993 (see Table 10.4).

The growth of IEs was highly uneven as can be seen from Table 10.4. During the first phase of the reforms the growth of IEs was rapid, with their number rising on average by 77 per cent a year. In the second phase of the reforms, however, their growth slowed to an average of only 6.1 per cent a year. Between 1989 and 1991 the number of IEs actually declined, reflecting the negative impact of the Tiananmen Square incident. The growth of IEs accelerated once again during the third phase of the reforms.

For the entire period between 1978 and 1993, however, the growth of IEs was significantly higher than that of non-IE enterprises. Whereas non-agricultural employment in China grew overall at an average annual rate of only 5.5 per cent, that of IEs experienced a spectacular average annual growth rate of more than 35 per cent from

TABLE 10.4. *Development of Individual Enterprises, 1978–1994 (000)*

	Urban		Rural		Total	
	No.	Employment	No.	Employment	No.	Employment
1978	140	146	160	184	300	330
1979	250	320	310	356	560	676
1980	400	806	497	748	897	1,554
1981	869	1,057	961	1,218	1,830	2,275
1982	1,132	1,359	1,504	1,840	2,636	3,199
1983	1,705	2,087	4,195	5,378	5,900	7,465
1984	2,222	2,917	7,082	10,120	9,304	13,031
1985	2,798	3,839	8,916	13,823	11,714	17,662
1986	2,910	4,076	9,201	14,383	12,111	18,459
1987	3,383	4,924	10,342	16,660	13,725	21,583
1988	3,823	5,784	10,704	17,265	14,527	23,049
1989		6,480			12,471	19,414
1990		6,140		14,910	13,283	20,928
1991		6,920		16,160	14,168	22,580
1992	4,766	7,402	10,574	17,275	15,339	24,677
1993	5,757	9,295	11,912	20,098	17,669	29,393
1994					21,470	

Sources: GTJJDCYYJ, 1986: 296; Heberer, 1989: 83; *ZGGTSYJJ*, 1990: 2, 4; *ZGTJNJ 1991*: 16; *1992*: 16, 110; *1994*: 114, 858; *TKP*, 10 Jan. 1995.

1978 to 1993. As a result the IEs' share in non-agricultural employment rose sharply from less than 1 per cent in 1978 to more than 11 per cent in 1993 (*ZGTJNJ 1994*: 85–6).

In the early stage of their development IEs were spread more or less evenly between town and countryside. However, by the mid-1980s they had become more concentrated in rural areas; then in the late 1980s the trend reversed and the share of urban IEs in employment was on the rise again. But in 1993 rural IEs still accounted for the lion's share of total IEs. Most IEs were concentrated in the service sector in general and in trade in particular (see Table 10.5). Only 12 per cent of IEs were engaged in industry.

The geographic distribution of IEs is also uneven. Most are found in the eastern coastal region where, in 1992, 71 per cent of them were located (*ZGJJTZGGNJ 1993*: 347). Measured in terms of their share in non-agricultural employment, however, they were more important in provinces like Xizang, Xingjiang, and Guangxi and least important in Shanghai, Beijing, and Tianjin (see Table 10.3). As with the informal sector (IS) in developing countries, the significance of IEs in each

TABLE 10.5. *Distribution of Individual Enterprises by Economic Sectors, 1981–1992*

	Industry	Trade	Services
1981	10.9	45.4	43.7
1985	12.9	53.1	34.0
1990	12.3	54.2	33.5
1992	12.0	55.1	32.9

Sources: *GTJJDCYYJ*, 1986: 296; *ZGGTSYJJ*, 1990: 2; *ZGTJNJ 1990*: 17; 1991: 16; *ZGJJTZGGNJ 1993*: 347.

province appears to be inversely correlated with its per capita income (Turnham *et al.*, 1990: 20). In other words, IEs were of greatest importance in backward, less industrialized regions as an alternative employment provider.

What were the factors which initially triggered and then sustained the development of IEs in China since 1978? At the beginning of the reforms IEs were allowed in urban areas, in order to create jobs for the returned educated youths who had been sent to the countryside during the Cultural Revolution (1966–76). In rural areas the immediate stimulus to the development of IEs was the policy objective of the government to soak up the rural surplus labour which had been generated by the improved labour productivity in agriculture under the HRS.

IE growth was later sustained by the continued growth of rural–urban and socialist system–private sector migration. Prior to 1979, rural–urban migration was strictly controlled. For example, under the household registration scheme farmers were not allowed to reside in cities or take up urban employment. Neither were they able to obtain foodstuffs in cities as these were strictly rationed on the basis of residential status. By the mid-1980s, however, with the introduction of the two-track price system, rural migrants in the cities were able to purchase foods on the market. As a result, their numbers soared. According to an official estimate the number of farmers who left their rural homes for seasonal work in other areas rose from less than one million in 1982 to over 24 million in 1993 (*CD*, 20 June 1994). In early 1994 this figure increased to between 50 and 60 million and at least half of them had moved to cities (*CD*, 7 May 1994). Those who had moved to the cities, however, were not acknowledged as urban residents by the urban authorities, and this is why they are known as the floating population. This expanding floating population provided the major source of supply of workers for urban IEs.

With the lifting of price controls on food and edible oils in 1993 residence-based household registration cards no longer served as certificates for the purchase of these items. Consequently the household registration system was reportedly scrapped in June 1994 and farmers were allowed to move to county and smaller towns (*CD*, 17 May 1994). With the increased legalization of rural–urban migration the number of urban IEs is expected to grow even more in the future.

Another factor which has sustained the growth of IEs in recent years has been the increase in migration from the socialist to the private sector. A nation-wide survey of urban IEs revealed that the average earnings of self-employed (IE) workers were two to three times those of the average worker in the socialist sector (*ZGGTSYJJ*, 1990: 5–6, 23). Thus, by all indications, China's IE sector does not simply constitute the transposition of rural under-employment. It is also the result of socialist system–private sector migration which has occurred in response to the increased income differential between the two in the transition from a centrally planned to a market-oriented economy.

PRIVATE ENTERPRISES

According to the official definition PEs in China are private firms with more than seven hired workers (*ZGGTSYJJ*, 1990: 309). Available data on PEs are patchy and most PEs are disguised as collective enterprises in order to avoid social prejudice and government restrictions, as well as to gain access to the benefits of the 'collective title' in the form of tax reductions and tax exemptions.

PEs first appeared in 1980 (*GYJJGLCK*, 1989, 5: 60) and in 1984 official sanctions against private firms hiring more than seven workers were lifted (Byrd, 1990: 81). However, it was not until 1987 that PEs were formally recognized as a legitimate part of China's economy by the 13th Party Congress. As a consequence national laws and regulations for PEs were promulgated in 1988 (*ZGGTSYJJ*, 1990: 309–24).

In spite of formal recognition the growth of PEs in the late 1980s was slow because of social prejudice against PEs and numerous restrictions. The latter included complicated registration procedures, their banning from foreign trade and JVs with foreign firms, the imposition of various administrative fees on them, such as compulsory donations, and the denial of credit to them by state banks.

Since the early 1990s, however, the growth of PEs has experienced a sharp acceleration as a result of strong government support and the easing of restrictions on them (see Table 10.6). Most PEs were registered either as sole proprietorships or as partnerships. In 1992 the former accounted for about 55 per cent and the latter for 32 per cent of China's total PEs (*ZGJJTZGGNJ 1993*: 347). The rest were joint stock companies which were still in their infancy in China.

TABLE 10.6. *Development of Private Enterprises, 1988–1994*

	No. (000)	Employment (000)	Reg. capital (billion *yuan*)	Output (billion *yuan*)
1988	41			
1989	91	1,640	8.45	9.74
1990	98	1,702	9.52	12.18
1991	108	1,839	12.32	14.66
1992	140	2,320	22.12	20.51
1993	239	3,730	103.63	
1994	420		140.00	

Sources: 1988–92: *ZGJJTZGGNJ 1993*: 347. 1993–4: TKP, 10 Jan. 1995; *CDBW*, 22–8 May 1994; *ZGTJNJ 1994*: 85.

A combination of factors, such as scarcity of land, strict labour hiring rules, and stiff competition from strong state and collective enterprises in the cities meant that most PEs in the past were located in rural areas. In the early 1990s, however, the number of urban PEs rose and by 1993 they accounted for half of total employment in PEs (*ZGTJNJ 1994*: 85). In 1992 over 62 per cent of PEs were engaged in industry, and another 24 per cent in commerce.

A 1988 survey of PE entrepreneurs in Liaoning's Yingkuo city found that 57 per cent of them were either former employees of TVEs or former production brigade or team cadres. Another 41 per cent were successful IE entrepreneurs who had upgraded their business (*GYJJGLCK*, 1989, 5: 60). The earnings of PE entrepreneurs were significantly higher than those of IEs and some had achieved Chinese millionaire status.

The importance of PEs in terms of their share in total non-agricultural employment varies across provinces. In 1993 it ranged from 0.4 per cent in Xizang to a high of 3.2 per cent in Guangdong (see Table 10.3). In general, local government policies played an important role in determining the pace of PE development in each province (Byrd, 1990: 93).

SIGNIFICANCE AND IMPACT

After more than 15 years of development the non-state sector has become an important component of the Chinese economy. Estimates of its real importance in the economy depend very much on the statistical measures used. As Table 10.7 shows, the non-state sector has already achieved dominance in most non-agricultural activities. In the early 1990s it accounted for an overwhelming proportion of output, sales, and employment in industry, construction, retail trade, catering, and other services.

TABLE 10.7. *Share of Non-State Sector in the Chinese Economy, 1980–1994 (%)*

Sector	1980	1985	1992	1993	1994
Industry (output)					
State	76.0	64.9	48.1	43.1	38.7
Collective	23.5	32.1	38.0	38.4 ⎫	61.3
Private	0.5	3.0	13.9	18.5 ⎭	
Retail trade (volume)					
State	51.4	40.4	41.3	39.7	
Collective	44.6	37.2	27.9	26.3	
Private	neg.[a]	22.4	30.8	34.0	
Catering (employment)					
State	30.9	13.9	12.0		
Collective	55.0	30.9	20.0		
Private	14.1	55.2	68.0		
Service trade (employment)					
State	35.5	16.5	19.1		
Collective	48.5	31.9	25.6		
Private	16.0	51.6	55.3		
Construction (output)					
State	63.7	48.2	43.4	37.4	
Collective and private	36.3	51.8	56.6	62.6	

[a] Negligible.

Sources: ZGTJNJ 1993: 414, 561, 590; *ZGTJNJ 1994*: 373, 425, 429, 497; *SCMPIW*, 21–2 Jan. 1995.

Overall, the non-state sector accounted for 60 per cent of China's GNP in 1991 (*CD*, 20 Oct. 1992). In 1994 the share of the non-state sector surged further ahead, with the private sector alone reportedly accounting for about one-third of Chinese GNP (*SCMPIW*, 21–2 Jan. 1995). It should be noted that the significance of the private sector in China is usually underestimated because of the widespread underreporting of output and sales, a frequent practice by IEs and PEs to evade taxes. Furthermore, a significant proportion of IEs and PEs remained unregistered.

The role of the non-state sector *vis-à-vis* the state sector can be either complementary or depletive. In China, the non-state sector performs several vital complementary roles for the state economy. First, it fills the gap in the production of goods and services which the state sector obviously cannot adequately cover. This is of particular importance in retail, catering, and personal services where individual needs and service requirements are so diverse that the state sector is unable to satisfy them. For instance, the curbing of the private sector's activities in the past drastically reduced provision of these services. From 1957 to 1978 the number of retail, catering, and personal service establishments per 10,000 population dropped from 41.8 in 1957 to 13 in 1978 (*ZGTJNJ 1983*: 339, 103). Since 1979, thanks to the development of the private sector, the situation was reversed and by 1992 this ratio had risen to 116 (*ZGTJNJ 1993*: 81, 590).

Second, the non-state sector provides employment opportunities for surplus labour. The rate of unemployment in urban areas rose sharply in the late 1970s with the return of educated youths who had been sent to the countryside and rose further in the 1980s with the growing numbers of the floating population. The non-state sector accounted for 56 per cent of urban job creation in 1993 and contributed significantly to the reduction of the official rate of urban unemployed to 2.6 per cent in 1993 (*ZGTJNJ 1994*: 106). In the countryside the non-state sector was even more important in generating employment: it was responsible for almost 100 per cent of rural non-agricultural employment creation in the period under investigation.

Third, the non-state sector provides investment opportunities for private savings which otherwise would have fuelled consumer demand and inflationary pressures. Over the last 15 years it has become a significant contributor to the nation's fixed capital formation. Its share in the latter rose from a negligible level in 1978 to 38.5 per cent in 1993 (*ZGTJNJ 1994*: 139).

Fourth, the non-state sector also provides a healthy source of competition for state enterprises. It has, for example, often been reported that both the number and quality of services provided by state-run retail shops and food catering units improved markedly after IEs and PEs were allowed to compete with them. Similarly, in the industrial sector competitive pressure exerted by non-state enterprises motivated greater efficiency in the state sector, as is confirmed by the finding that large provincial shares of non-state industrial output are associated with high levels of total factor productivity in state industry (Jefferson and Rawski, 1994: 60).

However, many non-state economic activities are also depletive for the state sector. The non-state sector often competes with the state sector in input and in product markets. Since income earned in the non-state sector has been significantly higher than that in the state sector skilled labour has tended to be diverted from the latter to the former. Similarly, scarce raw materials have also tended to be diverted to non-state enterprises as these could afford to bid at a higher price because their selling prices were subject to fewer government controls and, hence, they were able to pass higher input costs on to consumers (*CP*, 1992, 9: 13). In the product market non-state enterprises, because of their superior efficiency in production and marketing, have driven some state enterprises out of the market altogether.

The operation of the non-state sector has also exacerbated income disparity. Survey results of the private sector reveal that a considerable income gap has existed between the private entrepreneur and the average worker in the state sector, on the one hand, and between private entrepreneurs and their employees on the other. A sample survey in Beijing in 1987 shows that earnings of entrepreneurs in IEs were about two to three times those of the average worker in the state sector (*BJCZDSRGG*, 1989: 81, 87). A sample survey of PEs in Guangdong, Zhejiang, Jiangsu, and Henan provinces in 1987 further reveals that the average earnings of PE entrepreneurs were almost 20 times those of their employees (*JJYJZL*, 1988, 17: 59).

Finally, the rise of non-state economic activities was accompanied by a rise in illegal economic activities. This happened because in an economy where most resources are state-owned and most economic activities are subject to government regulation it is almost impossible for the non-state sector to expand without violating some law or regulation. One of the most prevalent forms of illegal economic activity in the non-state sector was tax evasion by IEs and PEs, the rate of which was very high in some localities. For example, it reached 53, 90, and 90 per cent respectively in Jiangsu, Liaoning's Haicheng county, and Shanghai in 1988 (*ZGGTSYJJ*, 1990: 7). The cause of tax evasion was of course the high tax rate imposed on private-sector earnings in the past (*ZGGTSYJJ*, 1990: 23, 309–16, 334, 336). The marginal tax rate of IEs for annual gross income exceeding 30,000 *yuan* was as high as 60 per cent and jumped to 84 per cent for annual gross earnings over 50,000 *yuan*. The profits of PEs were subject first to 35 per cent corporate income tax and the distributed after-tax profits were subject to another 40 per cent income tax.

To evade taxes a large proportion of IEs remained unregistered. According to a nation-wide sample survey in 1988 the unregistered proportion was one-third in large and medium-sized cities and one-fifth in small ones (*ZGGTSYJJ*, 1990: 6). To evade tax as well as to gain preferential access to scarce inputs PEs tended to disguise themselves as collective enterprises. As mentioned earlier, in some localities 83 per cent of PEs were registered as collective enterprises.

Another widely publicized illegal activity connected with the non-state sector was bribery. Non-state enterprises tended to offer bribes to state enterprise managers in order to gain access to rationed goods such as energy, raw materials, credits, foreign exchange, etc. Very often the market prices for these goods were significantly higher than the controlled prices. Hence bribes were offered to capture the rental income created by these price differentials.

Though illegal activities in the non-state sector have risen in recent years there is no reason to assume that they will escalate or even continue in future. The increased liberalization and marketization of China's economy can be expected eventually to eradicate most of the root causes of irregular economic activities and corruption. For instance, to the extent that the gap between market and controlled prices is successfully closed and to the extent that the planned distribution of goods is increasingly replaced by market distribution the incentive to bribe is diminished.

OUTLOOK

Judging from past growth trends the non-state sector will continue to increase its share in output, sales, and employment at the cost of the state sector in China's economy. However, whether this trend of 'creeping privatization' will be allowed to continue unchecked in the future depends very much on the government's policy towards this sector and the ability of this sector to compete successfully for inputs and a greater market share with the state sector. Looking ahead, a clampdown on non-state economic activities appears very unlikely. One of the main reasons for optimism is the growing labour absorption problem which the government faces. For China's official rate of urban unemployment of only 3 per cent in 1994 was grossly under-estimated. Moreover, 20 per cent of all SOEs' employees are considered surplus labour (*CD*, 26 Aug. 1994). In rural areas unemployment was estimated at more than 100 million in 1994 (*SCMPIW*, 20–1 Aug. 1994). By the year 2000, according to the projection by the Ministry of Labour, there will be 68 million unemployed in cities and 200 million unemployed in the countryside and the rate of unemployment nation-wide is expected to reach 22.3 per cent. The major constraint preventing the state sector from absorbing the unemployed is the high capital intensity of its job creation. Thus, to avoid a massive increase in the budgetary deficit it seems that the government has no choice but to allow non-state sector activities to grow significantly, in order to absorb the growing surplus labour.

Another reason why the government is likely to pursue a more liberal policy towards non-state and especially private economic activities is the need to develop the service sector. This is one of the major consumer areas likely to experience rapid expansion in the 1990s (Chai, 1992: 748). Services are currently 'under-consumed' because they are in limited supply, especially in rural areas. In 1990, for example, services made up less than 10 per cent of Chinese urban and rural families' budget spending. Judging from the Japanese experience, as China's income per capita increases in the near future the share of service expenditures in the family budget is likely to expand significantly.

To satisfy the greater need of the population for service consumption the share of services in China's GNP will have to be increased. Some services are highly labour intensive, such as the retail trade, catering, and personal services. Therefore, the growth in these sectors is unlikely to encounter severe resource constraints. Other services, such as transport, health, and education are relatively capital intensive and their growth is likely to face severe resource constraints. To fill the gap between the growing capital demand of the service sector and the meagre supply of state capital the government again has no choice but to allow a significant increase in the volume of non-state activities in this area.

Apart from government policy the future development of the non-state sector also depends on its competitive relationship with the state sector. In this respect, three types of non-state enterprise can be identified. The first is non-state enterprises in the industrial sector. They are likely to remain subordinated to the state sector because of their limited economies of scale, and their low capital intensity and technological level. Since they operate in residual markets their future development depends on factors affecting the expansion of the state enterprises which dominate the market. Specifically, it depends very much on whether the corporatization of SOEs can be carried out smoothly so that their budget constraint can be hardened and their management and marketing efficiency and, hence, their competitiveness *vis-à-vis* the non-state enterprises can be increased. To the extent that this is possible the rapid expansion of the non-state enterprises may be checked eventually, even though they may still perform a useful and complementary role for the state sector in the form of a subcontracting relationship.

The second type is non-state enterprises in the service sector. Because of the characteristics of the services they provide, economies of scale are not important for them, their technological change is slow, they can compete with the state sector, and, hence, there seems to be ample room for their expansion. The third type is non-state enterprises in trade activities in which market imperfections ensure their capacity to compete efficiently with modern state trading establishments and, hence, there is also room for their further expansion.

It is envisaged that in future the distinction between state and non-state enterprises is going to be blurred. To increase the ability of state enterprises to compete with non-state enterprises new systems of management are likely to be developed. When these are put in place state enterprises are likely to operate on principles that are not very different from those of non-state enterprises.

11 China's Transition: Overview and General Assessment

China's strategy of transition to a market economy is often held up as superior to the one adopted by the Central and Eastern European countries (Gordon, 1992). For it seems that China, in contrast to the latter, was able not only to improve the standard of living of its population while it was undergoing reforms but to achieve rapid economic growth as well as a reasonable degree of political and social stability. This chapter assesses China's relative success up to the early 1990s in its transition from a centrally planned to a market economy. An objective evaluation of the relative success of China's transition would ideally require a point by point comparison of the strategies adopted by the Central and Eastern European countries and China. However, such a detailed comparison is beyond the scope of this book. Instead this chapter will focus only on the differing initial conditions of the Central and Eastern European countries and China and their short-run transition costs. It will attempt to explain why China was able to avoid some of the short-run transition costs that the Central and Eastern European countries have incurred.

The success of a transition programme depends largely on the criteria chosen to measure success. In the following discussion we apply the criteria used by the OECD (1991, Vol. I, chapter 4), according to which the success of a transition programme is measured in terms of (a) the progress of the transition itself, (b) the short-run transition costs incurred, and (c) the success of the country in attaining the long-term goal of transition—sustainable growth.

PROGRESS OF TRANSITION

The progress of transition can be measured in terms of the degree of success achieved in economic liberalization, structural reforms, and macro-economic stabilization. China's progress in each of these areas will be reviewed briefly in the light of the more detailed analysis of the preceding chapters.

Economic liberalization

Economic liberalization of a socialist economy involves deregulation and the freeing of prices of both products and production factors, as well as the liberalization of foreign economic relations, including currency convertibility.

Deregulation. Deregulation involves the elimination of mandatory planning and direct administrative controls over enterprise activities. While China has made considerable progress in dispensing with mandatory planning, progress in the elimination of administrative controls over enterprises is less impressive. Mandatory production planning has been completely eliminated in agriculture, while its significance in industry has been drastically reduced. The share of mandatory planning in total industrial output has fallen from 95 per cent in 1979 to a mere 7 per cent in 1993.

In the agricultural sector farm enterprises have become autonomous producers with the abolition of the compulsory procurement system and of the central rationing of basic agricultural inputs in 1985. Large and medium-sized industrial enterprises in the state sector have also gained increased autonomy with respect to output, marketing, pricing, materials acquisition, and investment decisions. However, the authorities still intervene heavily in their other decisions. For example, the hiring, firing, and promotion of enterprise managers is still in the hands of the state bureaucracy. Enterprises are also restricted in the hiring and firing of their workers. Moreover, some key inputs, such as certain materials, energy, bank credits, and foreign exchange remain rationed by the bureaucracy. These controls give the supervising authorities considerable room for intervention in enterprise decisions. Moreover, under the CRS the supervising authority tends to incorporate numerous plan targets into its contracts with enterprises and thereby it effectively limits their autonomy.

Price liberalization. China's overall progress in the liberalization of prices is mixed. On the one hand, the country has made substantial strides in increasing price flexibility. For example, by 1992, 80 per cent of industrial producer goods and 90 per cent of industrial consumer goods were sold at market and floating prices. The situation is similar with respect to agricultural purchase and retail prices where around 90 per cent of sales were concluded at market and floating prices. Thus the relative domestic prices approximate relative scarcities much more closely now than they did in 1979. Moreover, thanks to the introduction of the two-track system under which controlled and market prices are allowed to coexist for the same good, most producer and consumer marginal decisions are now made at the uncontrolled market prices.

On the other hand, the inertia of the price system remains. In 1992 about one-fifth of producer and 15 per cent of agricultural raw materials were still sold at administered prices. But more important is the fact that China has failed so far to develop an effective indirect instrument for macro-economic control. Therefore periodic outbursts of inflation have led to the subsequent tightening of controls and the renewed distortion of relative prices; and repressed inflation has been significantly reduced but not completely eliminated.

Liberalizing foreign economic relations. The liberalization of foreign economic relations refers to the opening of the economy through the reduction or elimination of barriers to trade and foreign investment, the objective of which is to integrate the domestic economy with that of the world. A key to this is the establishment of full convertibility of the currency.

China has achieved significant progress in trade liberalization. Direct administrative controls of foreign trade have been drastically reduced. For example, by the early 1990s mandatory export planning had been abolished and only 19 per cent of imports were still subject to foreign trade planning. Moreover, the notorious monopoly of foreign trade by a handful of national FTCs is now a thing of the past. The number of trading enterprises soared from 12 in 1978 to more than 7,000 by mid-1994. In addition, a better linkage between external and internal prices was achieved through the devaluation of the RMB and the reform of the internal pricing mechanism of traded commodities.

In spite of these developments China's foreign trade is still heavily controlled by the government, for not only do national FTCs still control the major import and export commodities but the competition between trading enterprises is still very limited because each of them remains confined to trade in only one area of imports and exports approved by the government. The FTCs' export autonomy is also constrained by the foreign trade CRS which sets specified mandatory export targets for FTCs. And even though China's domestic prices are now increasingly linked to world market prices a complete realignment has not yet occurred. This is because of the limited internal convertibility of the RMB.

China has achieved good progress in the relaxation of its foreign exchange controls. By 1994 more than 110 swap centres existed and about 80 per cent of the foreign exchange used by Chinese trading firms and enterprises was bought in these centres in 1993. The official exchange rate has been unified with the parallel exchange rate. Nevertheless China still has a long way to go in achieving full internal convertibility of its currency. Furthermore, to be meaningful, currency convertibility must be accompanied by commodity convertibility (Williamson, 1991: 252). Commodity convertibility means that an enterprise is allowed to use its cash balance for imports without needing the permission of a bureaucrat. Imports in China, however, are still heavily regulated by the government through a whole range of administrative and trade control instruments, such as quotas; licensing, etc.

China has made most progress in the liberalization of foreign direct investment (FDI). The number of open areas, where foreign invested enterprises (FIEs) are subject to fewer restrictions and enjoy preferential treatment, increased significantly during the second phase of reforms and by 1989 included 288 cities and *xians* in the coastal provinces. By 1992 another 28 cities and eight prefectures along the Yangtze River and 13 border cities in the counties of the northeast, southwest, and northwest regions were added. Furthermore, since 1985 many of the restrictions on FIEs have been relaxed. By October 1994 22,700 FIEs had been established in China and they accounted for 34 per cent of China's foreign trade.

None the less, China's domestic market still remains basically closed to FIEs. And despite the relaxation of the foreign exchange balance requirements FIEs still encounter great difficulties in balancing their foreign exchange receipts with expenditures.

Structural reforms

Structural reforms aim at the establishment and strengthening of the market mechanism and economic institutions. This usually involves three steps:

(1) The establishment of framework policies and specifically of 'laws and regulations that define rights and obligations and set the basic

parameters within which market relations can develop' (Koromzay and Zecchini, 1991: 34–5). Among the various laws and regulations those which specify and enforce property rights and accountability are the most important ones in ensuring economic efficiency (Blommestein and Marrese, 1991: 50).

(2) The creation of market institutions and specifically of product and factor markets.

(3) Motivating enterprise managers to behave in accordance with the rules of the market.

Property rights. In the agricultural sector China has made excellent progress in the clarification of property rights. During the reforms farm households acquired most of the income and control rights of farm land from the collectives. However, their transfer rights are still very restricted so that no real market for farm land has yet developed.

In the non-agricultural sector China has made substantial strides in removing entry barriers for new private enterprises. By 1994 420,000 PEs and 21.5 million IEs had been established and the share of the private sector in GNP had risen from 2 per cent in 1978 to about 33 per cent in 1994. Private-sector activities are mainly confined to the tertiary sector, namely to retail trade, catering, and services. However, the privatization of SOEs so far has made little progress. Some small SOEs were leased to individuals but the generally rather short lease period does not encourage the lessee to invest in the enterprise. Furthermore, the income and transfer rights of the lessee are very much attenuated. Privatization of large- and medium-sized SOEs is still unheard of. Moreover, the shareholding system is still in the experimental stage. By 1992 3,200 large- and medium-sized SOEs had issued shares (*CD*, 1 Aug. 1992) but 85 per cent of these had been sold to their own employees and only 3 per cent were acquired by the general public (*CD*, 17 June 1992). Two stock markets have been established, one in Shanghai and one in Shenzhen, where bonds and shares can be traded. In addition, 700 securities transaction facilities have been set up in more than 100 cities (*CD*, 29 Aug. 1992).

Enterprise accountability. Enterprise accountability is related to the relative hardness of the enterprise budget constraint. In rural areas farm enterprises' budget constraint was hardened significantly by the de facto privatization of farm land. Moreover, the budget constraint of rural TVEs is much harder than that of state enterprises.

Nevertheless, because of their proprietary links with the local government (Granick, 1990) and the availability of bank credits and grants from the latter, their budget constraints remain relatively soft compared with the private sector.

In the urban industrial sector the budget constraint of small SOEs remains soft. Although these enterprises are under lease and the lessee has to deposit part of his/her personal assets as security the deposit is generally too small in relation to the average asset value of the leased enterprise. Hence, it is difficult to make lessees fully accountable for any loss.

With regard to large- and medium-sized SOEs the introduction of the CRS constituted a limited ownership reform because it separated ownership from control. However, the sum of profit and tax to be delivered to the government under the CRS is still subject to bargaining. This, together with the lack of enforcement of the existing bankruptcy law and the indiscriminate availability of bank credits, contributes to the continued softness of the budget constraint of these enterprises.

Input and output markets. China has achieved good progress in the creation of product markets, especially in the agricultural sector. By 1992 there were 9,111 markets for farm products which sold three-quarters of all farm products (*CD*, 3 Aug. 1992). However, one-quarter of all farm products and 20 per cent of agricultural producer goods were then still purchased and sold by the government (*CD*, 30 May 1992). Moreover, the input and output markets faced by farm households were not competitive since state commercial agencies still possess significant monopoly power in these markets.

Compared with agricultural product markets those for industrial products are less developed. 'Small' industrial products were relatively free of controls and in 1992 were sold in over 3,000 markets (*CD*, 13 Aug. 1992). 'Large' industrial products, i.e. materials and equipment, remained controlled by the government. In 1992 22 items were still subject to central allocation by the SPC and the rest were sold at the 400 material and equipment trading centres set up and controlled by the State Material Bureau.

Factor markets are even less developed in China than product markets (Tisdell, 1992: 147–8). Labour markets remain underdeveloped, especially in the urban industrial sector. The mobility of labour is still highly restricted due to a combination of the high proportion of workers enjoying tenure, the dependence of workers on the social services of their employing enterprises, and the rigidity of the housing market. So far the capital market in China has been limited to interbank loans and security markets. The security markets in turn are mainly confined to government bonds. The issue, pricing, and transfer of enterprise shares and bonds are heavily regulated as the government is apprehensive that in the absence of enterprise accountability and scarcity prices the free issue of bonds and shares would encourage enterprises to borrow beyond the limits of their debt-servicing capacity. It also fears, not without reason, that the financial resources mobilized would be used for wasteful purposes.

Enterprise behaviour. Some progress has been made in motivating enterprise managers to behave in accordance with the rules of the market in the urban industrial sector. A survey of 300 large- and medium-sized state industrial enterprises in the late 1980s shows that their managers were increasingly profit oriented and that they responded to input and output price changes in the same manner as the typical neo-classical firm. However, their supply and demand response to price changes remained rather weak (Chai and Tisdell, 1992: 14–23).

Macro-economic stabilization

Macro-economic stabilization policies involve four steps, namely (a) the eradication of the 'monetary overhang', i.e. the involuntary accumulation of financial claims or repressed inflation; (b) the removal of the flow causes of the chronic excess demand; (c) the development of a set of indirect instruments for effective macro-economic control; and (d) the minimization of price instability (Blommestein *et. al.*, 1991: 18–19). China has achieved some success in eradicating the 'monetary overhang'. The booming private sector and the introduction of the two-track system in the state sector have caused a significant reduction in repressed inflation or involuntary held liquid assets.

   Progress in removing the flow causes of chronic excess demand in the state sector and the creation of indirect macro-economic control mechanisms has, however, been limited. Since financial discipline at the enterprise level has not yet been restored economic liberalization has tended to be accompanied by an explosion in investment and wage expenditures (Tisdell, 1992: 148–9). At the same time the supply responses of enterprises have remained weak. Consequently, the growth of aggregate demand has constantly outstripped that of aggregate supply, causing periodic outbursts of inflation which could only be stemmed by the reassertion of administrative controls.

The discussion shows that progress in China's transition has been mixed. China has made substantial strides in economic liberalization but its progress in structural reforms and in macro-economic stabilization is much slower. Also, the pace of progress in the rural sector is much faster than that in the urban sector. Table 11.1 compares the progress of China's transition with that of five Central and Eastern European countries in terms of a few major progress indicators. It shows that by 1992 China's progress in respect of two of the indicators, namely price liberalization and the output share of the private sector, was comparable to that of the five European countries. However, with respect to the other four indicators China still lagged very much behind, even though its reforms started more than 14 years ago while the Central and Eastern European countries were kick-started only in the late 1980s. Thus China's transition must be judged to be less advanced than that of its Eastern European counterparts.

SHORT-RUN TRANSITION COSTS

The transition in the Central and Eastern European countries has been accompanied specifically by development in output and the standard of living. These can be represented by a j-curve in output and real wages with a dip where both fall first and then start to rise (Siebert, 1991: 14–15). Their transition is also marked by an increase in economic insecurity which can be shown as an inverted u-curve where unemployment and inflation initially rise sharply and fall thereafter. As shown in Tables 11.2–11.5, China has been largely able to avoid most of these short-run transition costs. Chinese output not only did not suffer a dip (Table 11.2) but actually increased at an annual rate of 9.3 per cent which was 55 per cent faster than its growth rate in the pre-reform period from 1952 to 1978. Similarly, China not only did not experience a dip in its real wages (see Table 11.3) but saw a doubling of its living standard between 1978 and 1990 (Chai, 1992: 722–3). China's unemployment and inflation rates during the transition period were significantly higher than those in the pre-reform

TABLE 11.1. *Selected Market Economy Indicators in Central and Eastern European Countries and China, 1992*

Country	Privatization laws	Progress in privatization	Output share of private sector	Price liberalization	Quantitative restrictions on trade	Internal convertibility
Bulgaria	Passed in April 1992	Small-scale: several through leasing and restitution Large-scale:18–20 enterprises by 1992	Agriculture: 70% Industry: 5%	80–90% in CPI	Export licensing for a few agricultural products and industrial raw materials	Introduced
Czech and Slovak Republics	Passed in stages, 1990–1	Small-scale: auctions and restitutions in progress Large-scale: first wave of vouchers 1992	9% of GDP	95% in total turnover	Restrictions only on imports of gas, oil, narcotics, and arms Export licensing for a few items	Introduced
Hungary	Passed in stages; started 1988	Small-scale: over 4,000 firms sold Medium-scale: substantial progress Large-scale: started 1990	33% of GDP	More than 90% in CPI	90% of imports free from control	Introduced
Poland	Passed in July 1990	Small-scale: almost entirely privatized Large-scale: 15% of state assets sold	Agriculture: most Non-agriculture: 41%	89% in CPI	Restrictions only on imports of most radioactive and military materials	Introduced
Romania	Enacted in Aug. 1991	Small-scale: 580 commercial units sold Large-scale: started in 1992	Agriculture: 80% Industry: 6%	83% in CPI	Virtually no restrictions	Introduced
China	Not yet	Small-scale: several through leasing Medium- and large-scale: no progress	Agriculture: de facto privatization Industry: 6%	94% in CPI	33% of imports still subject to quantitative restrictions	Not yet introduced

Note: CPI = consumer price index.

Sources: East European countries: Husan and Sahay, 1992: 802. China: see text.

TABLE 11.2. *Output in Central and Eastern Europe and China (% change)*

Country	Net material product					Industrial output			
	1989	1990	1991[a]	1992[a]	1993[a]	1989	1990	1991	1992
Former USSR		-2.2	-9.0	-18.5	-12.0	1.5	-0.8	-8.1	
Bulgaria	-0.4	-13.6	-23.0			2.2	16.8	-11.2	-15.6
Czechoslovakia	1.0	-3.1	-16.0	-8.5	-2.0	0.8	-3.7	-24.7	-12.2
Hungary	-0.2	-5.9	-8.0	-5.0	-1.0	-2.5	-4.5	-21.9	-9.8
Poland	-0.2	-13.0	-8.0	1.0	4.0	-0.5	-23.3	-19.6	2.9
Romania	-7.9	-10.5	-12.0	-10.0		-2.1	-10.8	-21.7	
China 1979–1993 (annual average)					9.3				14.2

[a] GDP

Sources: Central and Eastern European countries: Koeves, 1992: 21; Bruno, 1992: 754–5; Lipton and Sachs, 1992: 245. China: *ZGTJNJ 1994*: 21, 23, 743, 755.

TABLE 11.3. *Real Wages in Central and Eastern Europe and China (% change)*

	1990	1991
Bulgaria	-32	-197
Czechoslovakia	-10	-40
Hungary	-10	-12
Poland	-89	-6
Romania	6	-99
China: 1979–1991 (annual average): 4.0		

Sources: Central and Eastern European countries: Bruno, 1992: 754–5. China: *ZGTJNJ 1992*: 63.

period. However, both were much lower than those experienced by its Eastern European counterparts (see Tables 11.4–11.5).

Why have China's short-run transition costs been much lower? One of the main reasons was undoubtedly China's gradual approach to transition. The sharp fall in output and employment and the consequent sharp rise in inflation in the initial transition stage in the Central and Eastern European countries is partly attributable to their 'big bang' approach to transition. This was imposed on them because of these countries' desire to join the European Union (EU) as soon as possible. In order to qualify for membership in the EU most of them, with the exception of Hungary, decided to shorten their transition periods as far as possible by following the IMF shock therapy method, whereby price and trade systems were liberalized at one stroke and the internal convertibility of their currencies was restored through a sharp currency devaluation under very restrictive fiscal, monetary, and income policies (Bruno, 1992: 750). The overall liberalization of prices, together with the currency devaluation, led to a sharp rise in inflation. At the same time the withdrawal of subsidies and the immediate trade liberalization exposed enterprises to brutal market forces and foreign competition. This, together with the credit squeeze under tight monetary policies, led to a sharp fall in output and employment in the state sector (Bruno, 1992: 762). (See Table 11.4.)

TABLE 11.4. *Unemployment Rates in Central and Eastern Europe and China (% change)*

	December		June	December
	1989	1990	1991	1991
Bulgaria	0.0	1.4	6.0	10.0
Czechoslovakia	0.0	1.0	3.8	6.8
Hungary	0.5	1.6	3.9	8.3
Poland	0.3	6.1	8.7	11.1
Romania			2–3	5–6
China 1978–1991 (annual average): 2.8[a]				

[a] Urban only.

Sources: Central and Eastern European countries: Koeves, 1992: 23; China: *ZGTJNJ 1992*: 118.

In contrast, China followed a gradual approach to transition which incurred lower short-run transition costs in various ways. To begin with, the absence of significant progress in structural reforms in the state sector meant that enterprise managers in this sector were spared the supply-side shock as not only did their market remain sheltered from foreign competition but also they continued to receive subsidies and soft bank loans from the state. Hence, a large fall in output and employment was prevented. This is most evident from the over 10,000 large- and medium-sized SOEs which accounted for almost 50 per cent of China's national industrial output. In 1992 two-thirds of these enterprises were reportedly suffering a loss and yet they were allowed to keep their production up. As a result, stockpiles of 400 billion *yuan* of industrial output, equivalent to 14 per cent of China's industrial output in 1991, were accumulated (*CD*, 24 June and 5 Aug. 1992). Moreover, even though one-quarter of their work-force was regarded as redundant these enterprises were not allowed to shed surplus workers.

Second, the gradual approach in China's price reform contributed to the moderation of the rate of inflation in China (see Table 11.5). Up to 1991 almost one-third of all retail prices were still controlled by the government and one-third of China's state budget was still used to subsidize food, housing, transport, and other sectors of the economy (*CD*, 17 May 1991).

TABLE 11.5. *Inflation Rates in Central and Eastern Europe and China (% change)*

	1989	1990	1991
Bulgaria	9.8	64.0	339.0
Czechoslovakia	1.4	18.0	54.0
Hungary	17.0	33.0	32.0
Poland	640.0	249.0	60.0
Romania		5.0	223.0
China 1978–1991 (annual average): 6.0			

Sources: Central and East European countries: Koeves, 1992: 21 and Bruno, 1992: 754–5. China: *ZGTJNJ 1992*: 235.

Third, the postponement of political reforms enabled China not only to avoid political disintegration but also to maintain relative political and social stability. Empirical studies of the determinants of FDI flow across countries reveal that political stability is the most decisive factor in attracting FDI (Schneider and Frey, 1985). Hence the stable political environment—even with the rupture of the Tiananmen Square incident—enabled China to attract a large number of FDIs which contributed significantly to its exports and thereby to its output and employment growth.

Apart from this gradual approach another reason why China was able to lower its transition costs was the distinctiveness of conditions there at the beginning of the reforms. One of the major differences between China's initial conditions and those of its European counterparts was the absence in China of an external shock which catapulted the country into a reform programme. In the Central and Eastern European countries the collapse of Comecon trade in the late 1980s generated two external shocks.

One was the loss of the Comecon export market on which they had been highly dependent prior to the transition. For example, in 1989 the Comecon share of export trade amounted to 43, 41, 60, and 69 per cent respectively for Hungary, Poland, the former Czechoslovakia, and Bulgaria (Bruno, 1992: table 1). The loss of such an important export market was a major contributory factor to the subsequent fall in output of the economy of these countries. IMF estimates show that the percentage contribution of the fall in exports to the fall in GDP in 1991 amounted to 8, 4, 9, 16, and 10 per cent respectively for Hungary, Poland, the former Czechoslovakia, Bulgaria, and Romania (Bruno, 1992: table 3).

Another external shock was caused by the former USSR's termination of its subsidies to exports of energy and raw materials for the Central and Eastern European countries. Overall, the resulting loss in the terms of trade for the five countries is estimated at about $3.5 billion per year or half the value of their expected trade deficit for 1991 (Zecchini, 1991: 32). Estimates of the impact of the terms of trade loss on the drop in output in these countries are not available but it is likely to be substantial in view of the high degree of import dependence of these countries on their USSR supply sources.

In contrast, China was much less dependent on the external environment in its economic transition and the world economy proved much more accommodating for China. Thanks to the Sino-Soviet dispute in the late 1950s China's trade had long since been diversified into western markets and its dependence on Comecon was almost nil when China started its transition. Moreover, when China opened the country to foreign investments its neighbouring Asian countries, especially the Asian NICs and Japan, were in the process of relocating the production bases of their labour-intensive industries to other Asian labour-surplus countries. These industries had lost their comparative advantage owing to the forced appreciation of their currencies under the Plaza Accord and the increased shortage of labour in these countries. Hence China was able to attract a substantial inflow of FDI during its transition.

Another major difference in the conditions existing at the start of the economic reforms was the shorter period of existence of the Communist system in China. China had experimented with the Soviet-type economy for only about thirty years when it started its transition to the market economy in 1979. Because of this relatively short period much of the software of the market mechanism still remained relatively intact in China. Economic agents in China at the start of the reform programme were still familiar with markets and knew how to respond to market signals. In fact, some of the successful capitalist entrepreneurs during the Kuomintang era were still very much alive in 1979. Hence, the transition to the market mechanism could be effected much more smoothly in China than in the Central and East European countries.

The relative weight of agriculture in China's economy was also much greater than in its Central and East European counterparts. Agricultural output accounted for almost one-third of China's GDP in 1979 (World Bank, 1980: 139). In contrast, on average, agriculture accounted for only 10 per cent of the GDP of Bulgaria, Hungary, and the former Czechoslovakia in 1989 (World Bank, 1981: 209). Countries with a substantial agricultural base start the transition to a market economy with some notable advantages. First, agriculture can be relied on to absorb laid-off employees. Second, privatization can be implemented much more quickly in agriculture than in industry. Land is easily divisible and can be returned to the peasants whereas productive assets in a corporation like machines, brand names, and know-how are not physically divisible or owned by any specific member of the corporation. Hence, the rights over these assets cannot be delineated in the way that land can be divided (Cheung, 1989: 3). Last but not least, the production process in agriculture is generally far simpler than that in industry, and has limited specialization and inter-sectoral linkage. Hence partial reform or liberalization in the agricultural sector is not constrained by the lack of progress of reforms in other sectors.

The initial level of income per capita in China was also much lower than that in its Eastern European counterparts. China's GNP per capita at the time of the start of its reform process in 1979 was only one-tenth the average of Bulgaria, Poland, Hungary, and the former Czechoslovakia in 1989 (World Bank, 1980: 125 and 1991: 205). The theory of technological gap predicts that a country's rate of growth in general is inversely correlated to its initial level of income per capita (Baumol, 1986). Thus China could be expected to benefit from its relative backwardness and achieve a relatively higher growth rate than its Eastern European counterparts during the transition to a market economy.

Finally, another difference between China and the European countries in terms of their initial conditions was the existence of large and thriving rural collective enterprises in China, namely the so-called TVEs. They operated in a semi-market environment and were subject to relatively few government controls. As a result they became the most important contributor to China's rapid industrial growth in recent years. For instance, in 1994 when gross output of state industrial enterprises grew at a rate of 5 per cent the output of rural and urban TVEs grew at 21.4 per cent (*SCMPIW*, 21–2 Jan. 1995). Consequently, TVEs combined with urban collectives, private enterprises, and FIEs accounted for 84.8 per cent of China's industrial growth in 1994. In addition, TVEs were also the major absorber of the rural surplus labour released as a result of greater productivity under the HRS.

SUSTAINABLE GROWTH

Transition to a market economy is not an end in itself but a means to achieve long-term sustainable growth. Thus the ultimate test of transition is success in creating an economic system that generates self-sustaining growth under the condition of stable prices (Brainard, 1991: 95). Apart from price stability another important condition for sustainable growth is an improvement in the standard of living. This is especially important for China, as for any low-income country, since any decline in the transition period would undermine popular support for the government, no matter how rapid the growth.

To achieve a simultaneous increment in economic growth and consumption, growth has to be intensive rather than extensive. This is achieved if the growth of GDP is largely due to productivity growth. If, however, the GDP rises mainly because of a sizeable influx of labour and capital it is extensive growth. As the expansion of the labour supply requires a sacrifice of leisure and the expansion of capital stock requires a sacrifice of current consumption in order to accumulate capital, extensive growth necessarily entails economic growth being achieved at the expense of living standards.

Yet another important condition for sustainable growth is equity. Rapid growth is not sustainable if the benefits of growth are not distributed equitably (Perkins, 1988: 636).

Finally, sustainable growth also implies ecological sustainability. Rapid growth cannot be accompanied by unacceptable environmental damage so that the improvement in the living standard of the current generation is at the cost of that of future generations (World Bank, 1992: 34). To ensure ecological sustainablility two criteria in natural resource use need to be met (Brookfield and Byron, 1993: viii), namely, first, natural resources that are renewable need to be maintained or improved; and second, the rate of depletion of non-renewable resources needs to be optimized with due regard to possibilities for substitution of such resources.

As mentioned above, China was able to achieve an impressive growth during the reform era. However, it is far from certain that this high rate of growth is sustainable over the long term, for there are some indications that China has not yet met any of the above-mentioned four conditions for sustainable growth to a sufficient degree.

Price stability

To begin with, China's achievement with regard to price stability is mixed, as mentioned earlier. Though China's rate of inflation is much lower than those experienced by the Central and Eastern European countries it is definitely accelerating. Thus, for instance, the official retail price index increased at an average rate of only 2.8 per cent during the first phase of the reforms from 1978 to 1984. But in the period from 1985 to 1989 it shot up to 9 per cent. In 1994 China's rate of inflation hit 21 per cent, the highest rate of inflation since 1949.

Productivity growth

Productivity growth in China was impressive during the reform period from 1979 to 1990, averaging 2–3 per cent per annum (Yeh, 1992: 514). In contrast, productivity growth during the pre-reform period from 1949 to 1975 was close to zero (*CD*, July 1992). However, the fact that productivity growth declined in recent years is not a good sign. As Table 11.6 shows, productivity growth averaged 3.8 per cent and contributed 43 per cent of China's net material product (NMP) growth in the first phase of reforms. In the second phase, however, it

TABLE 11.6. *Sources of Growth of Net Material Product in China (annual % change)*

	1976–1985	1985–1990
Growth of NMP	8.8	7.5
Contribution to NMP growth		
Capital	3.3	4.4
Labour	1.7	1.6
Productivity	3.8	1.5

Source: Yeh, 1992: 514.

slipped to only 1.5 per cent per annum and contributed only 20 per cent of China's NMP growth. Hence, China's economic growth in the second stage was extensive rather than intensive. This also explains why the growth rate of China's consumption standard in the second stage of reforms was only half of that achieved in the first stage (Chai, 1992: 749).

Equity

Income differentials in a country are primarily determined by the income disparity within urban and rural households and by the urban–rural income gap. They are also determined by the share of the urban population. With a given urban–rural income gap, the shift of the population from rural areas with a relatively low level of income to urban areas with a higher level of income will increase income inequality up to the point where half the population are in the urban areas (Perkins, 1988: 639).

China was rather successful in constraining the rise of income differences during the first phase of the reforms. Income inequality appears to have remained relatively stable or even to have declined slightly during this period. This was due to the fact that in this period urban and rural income differentials showed countervailing trends which balanced each other: rural income inequality increased while urban income inequality declined and at the same time the urban–rural income and consumption differentials narrowed significantly (Chai, 1992: tables 10–12). However, with the second phase of the reforms the urban–rural income gap widened again and income disparity in both rural and urban sectors rose again. These trends, together with the rising share of the urban population, contributed to the increased income disparity in this period (Chai, 1992: 737–41).

Ecological sustainability

Finally, China's record of environmental degradation is appalling. This is richly documented in studies by Smil (1984 and 1993) and Tisdell (1994). The following paragraphs summarize briefly the extent of degradation of China's major natural resources under the reforms.

Land and habitat. During the years 1978–93 Chinese farm land disappeared at a rate of 0.3 per cent a year owing to increased diversion of cultivated land for rural housing construction as well as industrial use. The cumulative loss in this period was 4.3 million hectares, an amount equal to all farm land in Japan (*ZGTJNJ 1994*: 329). Soil erosion caused by intensive cultivation through the increased use of chemical fertilizers and plastic sheeting to meet the food requirements of the growing population affected more than 10 million hectares of farm land and reduced the volume of the grain harvest by 12 million kilograms a year (*CD*, 4 June 1994). The area of mature forest also decreased by one-third between 1982 and 1989 (Smil, 1993: 191).

Water. In the early 1990s 50 cities in China faced acute water shortages as groundwater levels dropped by 1 to 2 metres a year (World Bank, 1992: 36). The sanitation in the cities was so poor that in the late 1980s less than 40 per cent of city dwellings had their own toilet facilities (Chai, 1992: 736). Moreover, sewage contamination of seafood was thought to be responsible for a serious outbreak of hepatitis A in Shanghai in the late 1980s. In rural areas, 800 million rural residents were still without safe drinking water in 1994 (*CD*, 7 June 1994).

Air. According to China's National Environmental Protection Agency China has the world's highest growth rate in the emission of carbon dioxide and it emits more acid rain and produces more sulphur dioxide than any other country in the world (*CD*, 6 June 1994). The main culprit is the misuse of coal, for less than 30 per cent of coal in China is used for generating electricity while the rest is burnt directly and more than 81 per cent of the coal consumed was not washed. Polluted air has been the major cause of spreading respiratory disease during the period 1988–94.

Atmospheric change. China's generation of greenhouse gases rose rapidly in the late 1980s as the coverage rate of consumer durables, such as refrigerators and air conditioners in households increased (Chai, 1992: 747). It is expected that with the increase in car ownership China will become the world's largest emitter of greenhouse gases sometime in the second decade of the next century (Smil, 1993: 191).

All in all, the total economic loss caused by environmental pollution was estimated at $11.5 billion each year in the early 1990s (*CD*, 16 March 1994). The indirect causes of China's environmental degradation were undoubtedly the increased population and the accelerating rate of economic growth, industrialization, urbanization, and the associated increased rate of energy consumption. However, the direct cause was the government's failure to cut the links between growth and pollution. The government's initiatives to adopt cleaner and more efficient technologies have been slow. So far, it has spent less than 1 per cent of its GNP on environmental protection. The fines for enterprises breaking anti-pollution laws are minimal and amount to only 0.1 per cent of China's annual industrial output (*CD*, 16 March 1994).

Furthermore, the inadequate specification of ownership rights under the reforms actually encourages the overuse of natural resources. Under the responsibility system most resources in China, including land, are contracted out to individuals but they are formally still publicly owned and their transferability is normally restricted. The responsibility and rights of the sub-contractor over resource use are not clearly delineated, and the contracts are not long or secure enough to encourage private investment and conservation.

The reforms have shifted the level of decision making from the centre to local and individual levels, which increasingly rely on price signals as the basis for their decisions. Yet most of the common resources, such as air and water, either have no price or are underpriced because of the absence or under-development of markets for them. Insecurity of ownership induces individuals to maximize short-term rather than long-term profit. This behaviour, together with the under-valuation of most resources, has led to their overuse as well as to the lack of maintenance and conservation.

CONCLUDING REMARKS

In summary, the success of China's transition is mixed. It would be premature to assert that China's transition model is superior to those of its Central and Eastern European counterparts because, in spite of a longer transition time, a much smoother development, and a more favourable external environment, the Chinese transition by the early 1990s was less advanced than those of the European countries. The Chinese leadership has so far failed to establish indirect macroeconomic control measures compatible with a market economy. Instead it periodically resorts to a reassertion of administrative controls which stop the reform measures dead in their tracks. Neither has it started comprehensive structural reforms in the key economic sector of large- and medium-sized state industrial enterprises. So far it has also failed to tighten the budget constraint for enterprise managers and to secure adequate demand and supply responses from enterprises. Moreover, its domestic market is still relatively closed to external competition.

The cautious approach that has been adopted to structural reforms has partly contributed to China's relatively low short-run transition costs. But it can be argued that since China's reforms have not yet substantially affected the key economic sector of large- and medium-sized state industrial enterprises some of the transition costs have only been postponed. This hesitant approach to structural reforms in industry, together with rising inflationary pressure and income inequality and increased environmental degradation, have undermined the conditions for China to achieve sustainable growth in the long run. Moreover, China's relatively lower transition costs can be partly explained by the distinctiveness of China's initial conditions and by a more accommodating international environment. These factors limit the transferability of China's transition model to other former socialist countries.

APPENDIX 1

Contract Responsibility System in Foreign Trade: Abstract of a Sample Contract

(1) Contractual Parties: The Local Foreign Economic Relations and Trade Commission and the Local Finance Bureau are jointly referred to as Party A and the local FTC is Party B.

(2) Objective of the Contract:

    (a) To attain the target of export receipts foreign exchange to be submitted to the central government and total RMB subsidy for export receipts targets contracted out by the state to the local government.

    (b) To encourage local FTCs' export initiative.

    (c) To develop the external trade of the locality.

(3) Responsibilities of Party B are specified under the targets of export plan, export receipts, foreign exchange to be submitted, export earning costs, export subsidy or profit, and export procurement plan.

(4) Rights and obligations:

    (a) In accordance with the relevant state regulations Party B can enjoy independent operational rights. Party B should provide periodic reports regarding its business operation, financial accounts, use of capital, etc. The profitable FTC should submit to the Local Finance Bureau its profits every month and the accompanying accounts should be sent to the Local Foreign Economic Relations and Trade Commission.

    (b) The Local Finance Bureau, upon receipt of subsidies from the state, should allocate an export subsidy to the FTC as well as bonus for export receipts and bonus for exports. The allocation is based on progress made on the target of the foreign exchange submitted to the central government.

(5) (a) If the FTC fails to attain the target for export receipts the shortfall will have to be covered by Party B's foreign exchange retention or purchased in the adjustment centre using its own RMB funds. In addition, the basic salary of the FTC manager (who signed the contract) will be cut by 10–50 per cent in the following year.

    (b) If the FTC fails to attain other targets its bonus will be eliminated. However, the FTC will retain its rights regarding how much bonus will be paid to its employees.

    (c) The target for export procurement is for reference only and is subject to negotiation and adjustment.

(6) Other:

    (a) The retained profit by the FTC should be used to establish a 'Risk Reserve Fund' for future shortfall and to supplement the circulation capital.

    (b) Upon guarantee that the target for export receipts and foreign exchange submitted to the centre will be attained, the FTC can apply for foreign exchange 'for importing to help exports' (*yijin yangchu*).

    (c) Other terms not covered in this contract will be in accordance with other relevant stipulations or supplemental mutual agreements.

Source: Kamm-Chan, 1989.

APPENDIX 2

Profit Maximizing Behaviour of Foreign Trade Corporations under the Contract Responsibility System

Under the CRS the FTC aims to maximize foreign exchange retention and to minimize the RMB subsidies incurred. Their objective function is as follows:

$$\text{Maxi.} P = P_1 + P_2 \tag{1}$$

$$P_1 = \{a(Q - Q^*) + (Q^* - F^*)\}(r - r^*), \tag{2}$$

$$P_2 = (E^* - r^*)Q^* - (E - r^*)Q, \tag{3}$$

where: Q^* = target export receipts, in US\$;
  Q = actual export receipts, in US\$;
  F^* = target foreign exchange to be submitted;
  E^* = target export earning cost (RMB/US\$);
  E = actual export earning cost (RMB/US\$);
  r^* = official RMB/US\$ exchange rate;
  r = RMB/US\$ exchange rate in foreign exchange adjustment centres;
  a = foreign exchange retention rate for export earnings above target ($1 > a > 0$);
  P = profits of FTC.

Independent variables are Q and E, whereas Q^*, F^*, E^*, r^*, and r are parameters. The conditions for profit maximization are:

$$\frac{dP}{dQ} = 0. \tag{4}$$

Since export earning costs (E) increase as the value of exports rises due to an increase in procurement prices for exports,

$$\frac{dP_2}{dQ} < 0,$$

hence to maximize profits, an FTC would endeavour to increase exports, Q, until the marginal gain in P_1 equals the marginal loss in P_2, i.e.

$$\frac{dP_1}{dQ} = \frac{dP_2}{dQ}.$$

Abbreviations of Sources

ACBF	*Almanac of China's Banking and Finance*
ACFERT	*Almanac of China's Foreign Economic Relations and Trade*
ASDXB	*Anhui Shida Xuebao (Anhui Normal University Academic Journal)*
CBR	*China Business Review*
CD	*China Daily*
CM	*China Market*
CMJJ	*Caimao Jingji (Finance and Trade Economy)*
CN	*China Newsletter*
CP	*China Price*
CSJJ	*Chengshi Jingji (Urban Economy)*
CZJR	*Caizheng Jinrong (Finance and Banking)*
FS	*Financial Studies*
GHDSSWN	*Guanghui di Sansiwu Nian (The Glorious 35 Years)*
GJMY	*Guoji Maoyi (International Trade)*
GJMYWT	*Guoji Maoyi Wenti (International Trade Problems)*
GMJHGL	*Guomin Jihua Yu Guanli (National Economic Planning and Management)*
GWYGB	*Guowuyuan Gongbao (State Council Bulletin)*
GYJJ	*Gongye Jingji (Industrial Economy)*
GYJJGLCK	*Gongye Jingji Guanli Congkan (Industrial Economic Management Journal)*
GYQYGL	*Gongye Qiye Guanli (Industrial Enterprise Management)*
HSEM	*Hang Seng Economic Monthly*
JFRB	*Jiefang Ribao (Liberation Daily)*
JJCK	*Jingji Cenkao (Economic Reference)*
JJGL	*Jingji Guanli (Economic Management)*
JJYJ	*Jingji Yanjiu (Economic Research)*
JYJZL	*Jingji Yanjiu Ziliao (Economic Research Data)*
KDJDS	*Kan De Jian De Shou (Visible Hand)*
NCGZTX	*Nongcun Gongzuo Tongxun (Rural Work Communication)*
NYJJ	*Nongye Jingji (Agricultural Economy)*
NYJJCK	*Nongye Jingji Congkan (Agricultural Economic Journal)*

NYJJWT	*Nongye Jingli Wenti (Agricultural Economic Problems)*
RMRB	*Renmin Ribao (People's Daily)*
SCMP	*South China Morning Post*
SCMPIW	*South China Morning Post International Weekly*
SDJJXXB	*Shoudu Jingji Xinxi Bao (Capital City Newspaper)*
SHKXZX	*Shehui Kexue Zhanxian (Social Science Frontier)*
SLJJJSJJYJ	*Shuliang Jingji Jishu Jingji Yanjiu (Quantitative and Technical Economic Research)*
SYC	*Statistical Yearbook of China*
TKP	*Ta Kung Pao (Ta Kung Daily)*
WMJJGJMY	*Waimao Jingji Guoji Maoyi (International Economy and Trade)*
WWP	*Wen Wei Pao (Wen Wei Daily)*
WZGL	*Wuzi Guanli (Material Management)*
WZJJYJ	*Wuzi Jingji Yanjiu (Material Economic Research)*
YHJJKFQJJYJHTJZL	*Yanhai Jingji Kaifangqu Jingji Yanjiu He Tongji Ziliao (Economic Research and Statistical Materials on Open Coastal Economic Regions)*
ZGBKNJ	*Zhongguo Baike Nianjian (China's Encyclopaedic Yearbook)*
ZGFZYGG	*Zhongguo: Fazhan Yu Gaige (China: Development and Reform)*
ZGGDZCTZTJZL	*Zhongguo Guding Zichan Touzi Tongji Ziliao (Statistical Materials on China's Fixed Asset Investments)*
ZGGTNJ	*Zhongguo Gangtie Nianjian (China's Iron and Steel Yearbook)*
ZGGYJJFQHB	*Zhongguo Gongye Jingji Faqui Huibian (A Collection of China's Industrial Economic Legislation)*
ZGGYJJGL	*Zhongguo Gongye Jingji Guanli (China's Industrial Economic Management)*
ZGGYJJTJNJ	*Zhongguo Gongye Jingi Tongji Nianjian (China's Industrial Economic Statistical Yearbook)*
ZGGYJJXB	*Zhongguo Gongye Jingji Xuebao (China's Industrial Economic Journal)*
ZGJJNJ	*Zhongguo Jingji Nianjian (Yearbook of China's Economy)*

ZGJJTZGG	*Zhongguo Jingji Tizhi Gaige (China's Economic System Reform)*
ZGJJTZGGNJ	*Zhongguo Jingji Tizhi Gaige Nianjian (China's Economic System Reform Yearbook)*
ZGJXDJNJ	*Zhongguo Jixie Dianji Nianjian (China's Machinery and Electronics Yearbook)*
ZGLDGZTJZL	*Zhongguo Laodong Gongzi Tongji Zilia (Statistical Materials on China's Labour and Wages)*
ZGNCJJTJDQ	*Zhongguo Nongcun Jingji Tongji Daquan (Comprehensive Statistics on China's Rural Economy)*
ZGNCTJNJ	*Zhongguo Nongcun Tongji Nianjian (China's Rural Statistical Yearbook)*
ZGNYNJ	*Zhongguo Nonye Nianjian (China's Agricultural Yearbook)*
ZGQYGL	*Zhongguo Qiye Guanli (China's Enterprise Management)*
ZGSYWJTJZL	*Zhongguo Shangye Wujia Tongji Ziliao (Statistical Materials on China's Commerce and Prices)*
ZGTJNJ	*Zhongguo Tongji Nianjian (China's Statistical Yearbook)*
ZGTJZY	*Zhongguo Tongji Zhaiyao (A Statistical Survey of China)*
ZGWJNJ	*Zhongguo Wujia Nianjian (China's Price Yearbook)*
ZGWZLT	*Zhongguo Wuzi Liutong (China's Material Circulation)*
ZGXZQHJC	*Zhongguo Xingzheng Qihua Jiance (A Simple Guide to China's Administrative Regions)*

Bibliography

Ash, R. F. (1993), 'Agricultural Policy Under the Impact of Reforms', in Y. Y. Kueh and R. F. Ash (eds.), *Economic Trends in Chinese Agriculture*, Oxford: Clarendon Press, 11–45.

—— (1992), 'The Agricultural Sector in China: Performance and Policy Dilemmas During the 1990s', *China Quarterly*, 131: 545–76.

Balasubramanyan, V. N. (1984), 'Incentives and Disincentives for Foreign Direct Investment in Less Developed Countries', *Weltwirtschaftliches Archiv:* 720–35.

Baumol, W. J. (1986), 'Productivity Growth, Convergence and Welfare: What the Long-Run Data Show', *American Economic Review*, 76 (5): 1072–85.

Bei, Duoguang, (1989), *Zhonguo Zijin Liudong Fenshe* (A Study of China's Financial Flow), Shanghai: Joint Publishing Co.

Beijing Chengzhen di Siren Gugong (*BJCZDSRGG*) (The Private Hiring of Labour in Beijing City) (1989), Beijing: Beijing Economic College Publishing House.

Bell, M. W., Khor, H. E., and Kochhar, K. (1993), *China: At the Threshold of a Market Economy*, Washington, DC: IMF.

Blejer, M., Burton, D., Dunaway, S., and Szapary, G. (1991), *China: Economic Reform and Macroeconomic Management*, Washington, DC: IMF.

Blommestein, H., Marrese, M., and Zecchini, S. (1991), 'Centrally Planned Economies in Transition: An Introductory Review of Selected Issues and Strategies', in H. Blommestein and M. Marrese (eds.), *Transformation of Planned Economies*, Paris: OECD: 11–28.

—— and Marrese, M. (1991), 'Developing Competitive Markets', in OECD, *The Transition to a Market Economy*, Paris: OECD, Vol. II: 44–62.

Brada, J. (1973), 'The Microallocative Impact of the Hungarian Economic Reform of 1968: Some Evidence from the Export Sector', *Economics of Planning*, Vol. 134, No. 1–2: 3–14.

Brainard, L. (1991), 'Strategies for Economic Transformation in Central and Eastern Europe: Role of Financial Market Reform', in Blommestein and Marrese (eds.) (1991): 95–108.

Brookfield, H. and Byron, Y. (eds.) (1993), *South-East Asia's Environmental Future: The Search For Sustainability*, Tokyo: UN University Press.

Bruno, M. (1992), 'Stabilization and Reform in Eastern Europe: A Preliminary Evaluation', *IMF Staff Papers*, Vol. 39, No. 4: 741–77.

Buck, J. L. (1930), *Chinese Farm Economy*, Chicago: University of Chicago Press.

Byrd, W. (1983), 'Enterprise Level Reforms in Chinese State-owned Industry', *American Economic Review*, Vol. 73: 29–32.

—— (1987), 'The Impact of the Two-Tier Plan/Market System in Chinese Industry', *Journal of Comparative Economics*, Sept.: 295–308.

—— (1990), 'Rural Industrialization and Ownership in China', *Comparative Economic Studies*, Vol. 32: 73–107.

—— (1991), *The Market Mechanism and Economic Reforms in China*, Armonk: M. E. Sharpe.

—— and Lin, Qingsong (1990), *China's Rural Industry: Structure, Development and Reform*, New York: Oxford University Press.

Chai, J. C. H. (1981), 'Domestic Money and Banking Reform in China', *Hong Kong Economic Papers*, No. 14: 37–52.

—— (1983), 'China's Open-door Strategy: A Preliminary Assessment with Special Reference to the Foreign Trade Sector', in Se-Hee Yoo (ed.), *Political Leadership and Economic Development: Korea and China*, Seoul: The Institute for Sino-Soviet Studies, Hanyang University: 104–32.

—— (1985), 'Property Rights and Income Distribution under China's Agricultural Household Responsibility System', in C. K. Leung and J. C. H. Chai (eds.), *Development and Distribution in China*, Hong Kong: Centre of Asian Studies, University of Hong Kong: 75–100.

—— (1986) 'The Economic System of a Special Economic Zone under Socialism', in Y. C. Jao and C. K. Leung (eds.), *China's Special Economic Zones*, Hong Kong: Oxford University Press: 141–59.

—— (1989) 'Recent Development in China and its Implications for Asia-Pacific Region', in Fu-Chen Lo and N. Akrasanee (eds.), *The Future of Asian-Pacific Economies: Emerging Role of Asian NICs and ASEAN*, Kuala Lumpur: Asian and Pacific Development Centre: 246–68.

—— (1991), 'Agricultural Development in China', in E. K. Y. Chen and T. Maruya (eds.), *A Decade of 'Open Door' Economic Development in China, 1979–1989*, Tokyo: Institute for Developing Economies: 4–28.

—— (1992), 'Consumption and Living Standards in China', *China Quarterly*, No. 131, Sept.: 721–49.

—— (1994), 'Saving and Investment in China', *Saving and Development*, Vol. XVIII, No. 4: 497–516.

—— (1995), 'East–West Regional Income Gap: Problems of Divergent Development in China', in D. Cassel and C. Hermann-Pillath (eds.), *China: A New Growth Center in the World Economy*, Baden-Baden: Nomos Press: 93–108.

—— and Tisdell, C. (1992), 'The Two-Track System and China's Macro-Instability', Discussion paper No. 85, Department of Economics, University of Queensland.

—— and Chain, B. K. (1994), 'Economic Reforms and Inequality in China', *Rivista Internazionale di Scienze Economiche e Commerciale*, Vol. XLI, No. 8: 675–96.

Chan, T. M. H. (1987), 'Reform in China's Foreign Trade System', in J. C. H.

Chai and C. K. Leung (eds.), *China's Economic Reforms*, Hong Kong: Centre of Asian Studies, University of Hong Kong: 427–43.

Chen, K., Jefferson, G. H., Rawski, G. R., Wang, H., and Zheng, Y. (1988), 'Productivity Changes in Chinese Industry: 1953–1985', *Journal of Comparative Economics*, Vol. 12: 570–91.

Chen, Xiaohong *et al.* (1991), 'Preliminary Overview and Analysis of Concentration in Chinese Industry', in Wang Huijiong and Chen Xiaohong (eds.), *Chanye Zuzhi Ji Youxiao Jingzheng: Zhongguo Chanye Zuzhi de Chubu Yanjiu* (Industrial Organization and Effective Competition: A Preliminary Study of Chinese Industrial Organization), Beijing: Chinese Economic Publisher: 191–209.

Cheung, S. N. S. (1969), 'Transaction Costs, Risk Aversion and the Choice of Contractual Arrangements', *Journal of Law and Economics*, April: 23–42.

—— (1989), 'Privatization versus Special Interest: The Experience of China's Economic Reforms', *Hong Kong Economic Papers*, 19: 1–8.

Chi, P. S. K. (1994), 'Hong Kong and Taiwan Enterprises in Mainland China: Acceleration of Economic Transformation and Development?', Paper presented to International Symposium, 'China: A New Growth Centre in the World Economy', July, Duisburg, Germany.

China's Economic System Reform Research Institute (CESRRI) (1987), *Reform in China: Challenges and Choices*, Armonk: M. E. Sharpe.

Crook, F., and Crook, E. F. (1976), 'Payment Systems Used in Collective Farms in the Soviet Union and China', *Studies in Comparative Communism*, Vol. 9: 257–69.

Dai, Yuanchen (1983), 'Compensation Value and Cost Price', *Price: Theory and Practice*, 1983, No. 4: 4–10.

Dandai Zhongguo de Jingji Guanli (DDZGDJJGL) (Contemporary China's Economic Management) (1985), Beijing: China's Social Science Publishing House.

Dandai Zhongguo de Jinrong Shiye (DDZGDJRSY) (Contemporary China's Financial Institutions) (1989), Beijing: China's Social Science Publishing House.

Dernberger, R. (1982), 'The Chinese Search for the Path of Self-sustained Growth in the 1980s', in US Congress, Joint Economic Committee, *China Under the Four Modernizations,* Part 1, Washington, DC: US Government Printing Office: 19–76.

Donnithorne, A. (1967), *China's Economic System,* London: Allen and Unwin.

Eckstein, A. (1977), *China's Economic Revolution*, Cambridge: Cambridge University Press.

Field, R. M. (1988), 'Trends in the Value of Agricultural Output, 1978–86', *China Quarterly*, No. 116: 556–91.

Gaige Mianlin Zhidu Chuangxin (GGMLZDCX) (Economic Reform Facing

Challenge of Institutional Innovation) (1988), Shanghai: Joint Publishing Co.

Gaige Zhong Di Hongguan Jingji (GGZDHGJJ) (Macro-Economy under Reform) (1988), Chengdu: Sichuan People's Publishing House.

Gao, Shangquan (1987), *Jiunian Lai Di Zhongguo Jingji Tizhi Gaige* (China's Economic System over the Past Nine Years), Beijing: People's Publishing House.

Gao, Xiang (1982), *Lun Wujia Gaige* (On Price Reform), Beijing: China's Social Science Publishing House.

Garnaut, R. (1990), *Australia and the Northeast Asian Ascendancy,* Canberra: Australian Government Publication Service.

Geti Jingji Diaocha Yu Yanjiu (GTJJDCYYJ) (Survey and Study of Individual Enterprises) (1986), Beijing: Economic Science Publishing House.

Gondolfo, G. (1994), *International Economics I: The Pure Theory of International Trade*, second rev. ed., Berlin: Springer Verlag.

Gong, Qifong and Chen Deyan (1984), *Ligai Shui Dier Bu Shishi Zhunze Jisuan Banfa* (Tax for Profits Phase II: Implementation Principles and Calculation Methods), Beijing: Economic Science Publishing House.

Gordon, M. J. (1992), 'China's Path to Market Socialism', *Challenge*, Jan.: 53–6.

Granick, David (1990), *Chinese State Enterprise: A Regional Property Rights Analysis,* Chicago: University of Chicago Press.

Groves, T., Hong, Y., McMillan, J., and Naughton, B. (1994), 'Autonomy and Incentives in Chinese State Enterprises', *Quarterly Journal of Economics,* Feb.: 183–209.

Grub, P., and Lin Jianhai (1991), *Foreign Direct Investment in China,* New York: Quorum Books.

Gu, Xiuyan (1987), *Jiagexue Yuanli* (Principles of Pricing), Tianjin: Nankai University Press.

Guisinger, S. (1989), 'Total Protection: A New Measure of the Impact of Government Interventions on Investment Profitability', *Journal of International Business,* Summer: 280–95.

Hall, C. (1984), *Topics in Micro-economics: Price Theory with Transaction Costs and Property Rights,* Hong Kong: Precise Publishing.

Harding, H. (1987), *China's Second Revolution: Reform after Mao,* Washington, DC: Brookings Institution.

Hare, P. (1976), 'Industrial Prices in Hungary', *Soviet Studies,* April: 189–206.

Harrod, P., Hua, E.C., and Lou, J. (eds.) (1993) *Macroeconomic Management in China*, Washington, DC: World Bank.

Heberer, T. (1989), *Die Rolle des Individualsektors für Arbeitsmarkt und Staatswirtschaft in der Volksrepublik China,* China Research Monograph No. 18, Bremen: University of Bremen.

Hei, Aitang (1988), 'Reform of Investment Administration', *Touzi Yu Jianshe*, No. 2: 10–15.

Hiemenz, U. (1990), 'Foreign Direct Investment and Capital Formation in China since 1979: Implications for Economic Development', in Cassel, D., and Heiduck, G. (eds.), *China's Contemporary Economic Reforms as a Development Strategy*, Baden-Baden: Nomos Publisher, 85–104.

Ho, Y. K. (1986), 'China's Stock Issues', Discussion Paper No. 80, Department of Economics, University of Hong Kong.

Hong Kong Trade Development Council (HKTDC) (1990), *China's Foreign Trade System*, Hong Kong: HKTDC.

Howe, C. (1978), *China's Economy: A Basic Guide*, London: Elek Books Ltd.

—— and Walker, K. (1984), 'Readjustment in the Chinese Industry: Introduction', *China Quarterly*, No.100: ii–v.

—— (1989), *The Foundations of the Chinese Planned Economy: A Documentary Survey, 1953–1965*, Basingstoke: Macmillan.

Hu, Changnuan (1982), *Jiage Xue* (Study of Prices), Beijing: People's University of China Press.

—— (1985), 'On the Regularity in the Movement of Price System', *Jingji Yanjiu*, No. 5: 24–9.

—— (1987) *Shengchan Lingyu Jiege Gailun* (General Introduction to Producer Good Pricing), Beijing: People's University of China Press.

Hu, Yongtai, Hai Wen and Jing Yibiao (1994), 'How Successful is Chinese Enterprise Reform?', *Jingji Yanjiu*, No. 6: 20–7.

Husan, A., and Sahay, R. (1992), 'Does Sequencing of Privatization Matter in Reforming Planned Economies?', *IMF Staff Papers*, Vol. 39, No. 4: 801–24.

James, W. E., Naya, S., and Meier, G. M. (eds.) (1989), *Asian Development: Economic Success and Policy Lessons*, Madison: University of Wisconsin Press.

Jao, Y. C. (1989), 'Financial Reform in China and Hong Kong 1987–88: A Comparative Overview', Paper presented to the Inaugural International Conference on Asian Pacific Financial Markets, Singapore, 16–18 Nov.

Jefferson, G. H., and Rawski, T. G. (1994), 'Enterprise Reform in Chinese Industry', *Journal of Economic Perspectives*, Vol. 8, No. 2: 47–70.

—— and Zheng, Y. X. (eds.) (1992), 'Growth, Efficiency and Convergence in China's State and Collective Industry', *Economic Development and Cultural Change*, Jan.: 239–66.

—— and Xu, Wenyi (1991), 'The Impact of Reform on Socialist Enterprises in Transition: Structure, Conduct, Performance in Chinese Industry', *Journal of Comparative Economics*: 45–64.

Jenkins, R. (1991), 'The Impact of Foreign Investment on Less Developed Countries: Cross Section Analysis vs. Industry Studies', in Buckley, P. J. and Clegg, J. (eds.), *Multinational Enterprises in Less Developed Countries*, New York: St. Martin's Press: 111–30.

Ji, Chongwei (1980), 'Industrial Specialization and Cooperation', in *Gongye Jingji Jiben Zhishi* (Basic Principles of Industrial Economics) Beijing: Economic Management Journal Publishing House.

Jing, Jiandong, Xiao, Z., and Xu, S. (1991), *Zhongguo Zhengquan Shichang* (China's Security Market), Beijing: China's Finance Publishing House.

Jingji Tizhi Gaige Shouce (JJTZGGSC) (Handbook of Economic System Reform) (1989), Beijing: Economic Daily Publishing House.

Kamm-Chan, I. (1989), 'Contract System in China's Foreign Trade', unpublished M. Soc. Sc. (Economics) thesis, University of Hong Kong.

Klaus, V. (1990), Address to Conference on Development Economics, World Bank.

Koeves, A. (1992) 'Shock Therapy versus Gradual Change: Economic Problems and Policies in Central and Eastern Europe, 1989–1991', *Acta Oeconomica*, Vol. 44 (1–2): 13–36.

Kojima, R. (1988*a*), 'Industry', in Sino-Japanese Economic Association, *Zhongguo Jingji De Zhong Changqi Zhanwan* (China's Mid-and Long-term Economic Prospect), Beijing: Economic Science Publishing House.

—— (1988*b*), 'Agricultural Organization: New Forms, New Contradictions', *China Quarterly*, No. 116: 706–35.

—— (1992), 'The Growing Fiscal Autonomy of Province-Level Governments in China', *The Developing Economies*, Vol. 30, No. 4: 315–46.

Kornai, J. (1980), *Economics of Shortage*, Amsterdam: North Holland.

Koromzay, V., and Zecchini, S. (1991), 'The Transformation Process: an OECD View', in OECD (1991), Vol. I, 33–7.

Kueh, Y. Y. (1984), 'China's New Agricultural Policy Program: Major Economic Consequences, 1979–1983', *Journal of Comparative Economics*, Vol. 8, No. 4: 353–75.

—— (1992), 'Foreign Investment and Economic Change in China', *China Quarterly*, No. 131: 637–90.

Lardy, N. R. (1983*a*), 'Agricultural Prices in China', World Bank Staff Working Papers, No. 606, World Bank.

—— (1983*b*) Agriculture in China's Modern Economic Development, New York: Cambridge University Press.

—— (1992), 'Chinese Foreign Trade', *China Quarterly*, No. 131: 691–720.

—— (1994), *Foreign Trade and Economic Reform in China 1978–1990*, New York: Cambridge University Press.

Lawler, E. E. (1973), *Motivation in Work Organization*, Monterey: Brooks/Cole Publ. Co.

Li, K. W. (1994), *Financial Repression and Economic Reform in China*, Westport: Praeger.

Li, Yuan (1993), 'Distribution System Reform in the Transition to Market Economy', in P. Harrod, E. C. Hua, and J. Lou (eds.), *Macroeconomic Management in China,* Washington, DC: World Bank: 103–6.

Liang, Wensen, and Tian, Jinghai (1979), 'On Payment for the Use of Fixed Capital Assets', *Jingji Yanjiu*, No. 4: 16–28.

Lim, L. Y. C., and Fong, P. E. (1991), *Foreign Direct Investment and Industrialization in Malaysia, Singapore, Taiwan and Thailand*, Paris: OECD.

Lin, Cyril (1988), 'China's Economic Reform 2: Western Perspective', *Asian Pacific Economic Literature*, Vol. 2, No. 1: 1–25.

Lin, Justin (1987), 'Rural Factor Markets in China after the Household Responsibility System Reform', Discussion Paper No. 535, Economic Growth Center, Yale University.

Lipton, D., and Sachs, J. D. (1992), 'Prospects for Russia's Economic Reforms', *Brookings Paper on Economic Activity*, No. 2: 213–84.

Liu, Guoguang (ed.) (1980), *Guomin Jingji Guanli Tizhi Gaige Di Ruo-guan Lilun Wenti* (Theoretical Issues in National Economic System Reform), Beijing: China's Social Science Publishing House.

—— (ed.) (1984), *Zhongguo Jingji Fazhang Zhanlue Wenti Yanjiu* (Research on China's Economic Development Strategy), Shanghai: People's Publishing House.

—— (ed.) (1988), *Zhongguo Jingji Tizhi Gaige Di Moshi Yanyiu* (Research on China's Economic System Reform Model), Beijing: China's Social Science Publishing House.

Liu, Hongru (1980), *Shehuizhuyi Huobi Yu Yinhang Wenti* (Issues in Socialist Money and Banking), Beijing: Finance and Economics Publishing House.

Liu, Jieshan, Wang, W., and He, P. (1988), *Qiye Gongzhi Gaige Shiyong Shouce* (Practical Handbook of Enterprise Wage Reform), Beijing: China's Municipal Economic and Social Publishing House.

Liu, T. C. (1968), 'Quantitative Trends in the Economy', in Eckstein, A., Galenson, W., and Liu, T.C. (eds.), *Economic Trends in Communist China*, Edinburgh: Edinburgh University Press: 87–182.

Lloyd, P. J. (1993), 'Global Integration', Mimeo.

Lyons, T. P. (1985), 'China's Cellular Economy: A Test of the Fragmentation Hypothesis', *Journal of Comparative Economics*, Vol. 9, No. 2: 125–44.

Ma, Hong (1982), *Xiandai Zhongguo Jingji Shidan* (Contemporary Chinese Economy: A Compendium), Beijing: China's Social Science Publishing House.

—— and Sun, Shangqing (eds.) (1981), *Zhongguo Jingji Jiego Wenti Yanjiu* (Research on Problems of China's Economic Structure), 2 Vols, Beijing: People's Publishing House.

Ma, Jiantang, and Lu Xiuli, 'Progress in the Marketization of Chinese Economy: a Review of 15 Years', *Jingji Yanjiu*, No. 7: 23–36.

Michaely, M., Pagageorgiou, D., and Choksi, A. (1991), *Liberalizing Foreign Trade: Lessons of Experience in the Developing World*, Oxford: Basil Blackwell.

Min, Yaoling, and Li Bingkun (1988), *Zhongguo Nongcun Jingji Gaige Yanjiu* (Research on China's Rural Economic Reform), Beijing: China's Prospect Publishing House.

Naughton, B. (1992), 'Implications of the State Monopoly over Industry and Its Relaxation', *Modern China*, 18 (1): 14–41.

Nongcun Jingji Gaige Yu Fazheng (NCJJGGYFZ) (Rural Economic Reform and Development) (1988), Beijing: China's Prospect Publishing House.

Nongcun Renmin Gongshe Shengchan Zerenzhi Leibe (NCRMGSSCZR-ZLB) (Cases in Production Responsibility System in Rural People's Communes) (1981), Beijing: Beijing Agricultural Publishing House.

Nongye Shengchan Zerenzhi Zhixing Banfa (NYSCZRZZXBF) (Methods of Experimental Implementation of Agricultural Production Responsibility System) (1981) Beijing: Agricultural Publishing House.

Nuti, D. M. (1989) 'Hidden and Repressed Inflation in Soviet-type Economies: Definitions, Measurement and Stabilization', in C. Davis and W. Charemza (eds.), *Models of Disequilibrium and Shortage in Centrally Planned Economies,* London, Chapman and Hall: 101–46.

OECD (1991), *The Transition to a Market Economy,* Vols. 1 and II, Paris, OECD.

Perkins, D. H. (1988), 'Reforming China's Economic System', *Journal of Economic Literature,* Vol, 26: 601–45.

—— (1994), 'Completing China's Move to the Market', *Journal of Economic Perspectives*, Spring: 23–46.

Pomfret, R. (1991), *Investing in China: Ten Years of Open-door Policy,* New York: Harvester Wheatsheaf.

Pryor, F. L. (1973), *Property and Industrial Organization in Communist and Capitalist Nations*, Bloomington: Indiana University Press.

Pun, Zhenmin, and Luo Shouchu (1988), *Shehuizhuyi Weiguan Jingji Junheng Lun* (Equilibrium of Socialist Micro-economy), Shanghai: Joint Publishing Co.

Putterman, L. (1985), 'Theoretical Considerations Regarding the Demise of Team Farming in China', Working Paper, No. 85–86, Department of Economics, Brown University, March.

Qiye Changbao Zhinan (QYCBZN), (A Guide to Enterprise Contract System), (1988), Beijing: Science Publishing House.

Qiye Neibu Fenpei Zhidu Gaige Di Zhengce Yu Shijian (QYNBFPZDGGDZ-CYSJ) (Policy and Implementation of Intra-enterprise Distribution System Reform), (1988), Beijing: Labour and Personnel Publishing House.

Rana, P. B., and Dowling, M. J. (1988), 'The Impact of Foreign Capital on Growth: Evidence from Asian Developing Countries', *The Developing Economies,* March: 3–11.

Rawski, T. G. (1976), 'Chinese Economic Planning', *Current Scene,* No. 14, April: 1–15.

Renmin Gongshe Sengchan Dui Caiwu Guanli (RMGSSCDCWGL), (Financial Management in People's Commune Production Teams), (1981), Hangzhou: Zhejiang People's Publishing House.

Reynolds, B. L. (1989), 'Agricultural Reform, Rural Savings and Growth in China', in Longworth, J. W. (ed.), *China's Development Miracle with International Comparisons*, St. Lucia: University of Queensland Press, 305–20.

Riskin, C. (1987), *China's Political Economy: The Quest for Development since 1949*, New York: Oxford University Press.

Schneider, F., and Frey, B. S. (1985), 'Economic and Political Determinants of Foreign Direct Investment', *World Development*, Vol. 13, No. 2: 161–75.

Shapiro, J. E. (1991), *Direct Investment and Joint Ventures in China: A Handbook for Corporate Negotiation*, New York: Quorum Books.

Shirk, S. L. (1981), 'Recent Chinese Labour Policies and the Transformation of Industrial Organization in China', *China Quarterly*, No. 88: 575–93.

Shuishou Yu Caiwu Shouce (SSYCWSC) (Handbook of Taxation and Finance) (1987), Beijing: Economic Management Publishing House.

Sicular, T. (1988), 'Agricultural Planning and Pricing in the Post-Mao Era', *China Quarterly*, No. 116: 671–705.

Siebert, H. (1991), 'The Transformation of Eastern Europe', Discussion Paper No. 163, Institut für Weltwirtschaft, Kiel, Germany.

Smil, V. (1984), *The Bad Earth: Environmental Degradation in China*, Armonk: M. E. Sharpe.

—— (1993), *China's Environmental Crisis*, Armonk: M. E. Sharpe.

Srinivasan, T. N. (1990), 'External Sector in Development: China and India, 1950–1989', *American Economic Review*, Vol. 80, No. 2: 113–17.

Stiglitz, J. E. (1974), 'Incentive and Risk Sharing in Sharecropping', *Review of Economic Studies*, April: 219–56.

Summer, R., and Heston, A. (1988), 'A New Set of International Comparisons of Real Product and Price Level Estimates for 130 Countries, 1950–1985', *Review of Income and Wealth*, Vol. 35: 1–25.

Sun, Shangqing (1984), *Lun Jingji Jieguo Duice* (On Counter Measures in Economic Structure) Beijing: China's Social Science Publishing House.

Sung, Y. W., and Chan, T. (1987), 'China's Economic Reforms 1: The Chinese Debate', *Asian-Pacific Economic Literature*, Vol. 1, No. 1: 1–24.

Tam, On-Kit (1991a), 'Prospects for Reforming China's Financial System', Working Paper No. 4, Department of Economics and Management, Australian Defence Force Academy, Canberra.

—— (1991b), 'Capital Market Development in China', *World Development*, Vol. 5, No.19: 511–32.

Tidrick, G., and Chen, Jiyuan (eds.) (1987), *China's Industrial Reforms*, Oxford: Oxford University Press.

Tisdell, C. A. (1992), *Economic Development in the Context of China: Policy Issues*, London: Macmillan.

—— (1994), 'Asian Development and Environmental Dilemmas', *Contemporary Economic Policy*, Vol. 13, No. 1: 38–49.

Tseng, W. and Corker, R. (1991), *Financial Liberalization, Money, Demand, and Monetary Policy in Asian Countries*, Washington, DC: IMF.

Turnham, D., Salome, B., and Schwarz, A. (1990), *The Informal Sector Revisited*, Paris: OECD.

Walder, A. G. (1987), 'Wage Reform and the Web of Factory Interest', *China Quarterly:* 23–4.

Walker, K. R. (1984), 'Chinese Agriculture During the Period of Readjustment 1978–83', *China Quarterly*, No. 100: 783–812.

Wang, Zhenzi and Qiao, Rongzhang (1988), *Zhongguo Jiage Gaige De Hui Gu Yu Zhang Wang* (China's Price Reforms: Review and Prospects), Beijing: China's Material Publishing House.

Williamson, J. (1991), 'Convertibility', in OECD (1991): 252–64.

World Bank (1980), *World Development Report 1980*, Washington DC: World Bank.

—— (1983), *China: Socialist Economic Development*, Vols I–III, Washington, DC: World Bank.

—— (1988*a*), *China: Finance and Investment* Washington, DC: World Bank.

—— (1988*b*), *China: External Trade and Capital*, Washington, DC: World Bank.

—— (1989), *World Development Report 1989*, Washington, DC: World Bank.

—— (1990), *China: Macro-economic Stability and Industrial Growth under Decentralised Socialism*, Washington, DC: World Bank.

—— (1991), *World Development Report 1991*, Washington, DC: World Bank.

—— (1992), *World Development Report 1992*, Washington, DC: World Bank.

—— (1994), *China: Foreign Trade Reform*, Washington, DC: World Bank.

Wu, Jinglian and Zhou, Xiaochuan (1988), *Zhonggou Jingji Gaige di Zhenti Sheji* (The Integrated Design of China's Economic Reform), Beijing: China's Prospect Publishing House.

Wu, Xiaoling, and Xie Ping (1993), 'Monetary Policies in China's Economy in Transition', in P. Harrod *et al.* (eds.) (1993): 35–46.

Wu, Xiaotang (1992), *Government Borrowing and Financial Reform in China*, unpublished M.A. thesis, Canberra: Australian Defence Force Academy.

Wyzan, M. L. (1985), 'Soviet Agricultural Procurement Pricing: A Study in Perversity', *Journal of Comparative Economics*, March: 24–45.

Xie, Mengan and Luo, Yuanmin (1990), *Zhongguo Jingji Fazheng Sishi Nian* (China's Economic Development During the Last 40 Years), Beijing: People's Publishing House.

Xu, Feiqing (1988), *Zhongguo Di Jingji Tizhi Gaige* (China's Economic System Reform), Beijing: China's Finance and Economics Publishing House.

Xu, Shanda, and Ma, Ling (1993), 'Market Economy and Tax Reform in China', in P. Harrod *et al.* (eds.) (1993): 69–80.

Yeh. K. C. (1984), 'Macroeconomic Changes in the Chinese Economy During the Readjustment', *China Quarterly*, No. 100: 691–716.

—— (1992), 'Macroeconomic Issues in China in the 1990s', *China Quarterly*, No. 131: 501–44.

Yu, Zhongyi, Zheng, C., and Wen, J. (1988), *Zhongxiao Qiye Zulin Yu Gufenzhi Jiben Zhishi Wenda* (Basic Information on Leasing and Shareholding System in Medium- and Small-sized Enterprises), Beijing: Light Industry Publishing House.

Yue, Guangzhao (1988), *Laodong Gongzi Gaige Wenti Yanjiu* (Research on Issues in Labour and Wage Reform), Beijing: Labour and Personnel Publishing House.

Yusuf, S. (1994), 'China's Macroeconomic Management and Performance during Transition', *Journal of Economic Perspectives*, Spring: 71–92.

Zecchini, S. (1991), 'Assimilating Central and Eastern Europe into the World Economy' in OECD (1991): 27–32.

Zielinski, J. (1973), *Economic Reforms in Polish Industry*, New York: Oxford University Press.

Zhang, Fengbo (1988), *Zhongguo Hongguan Jingji Jiegou Yu Zhengce* (China's Macro-economic Structure and Policy), Beijing: China's Finance and Economics Publishing House.

Zhang, Zhuoyuan, Li, X., Bian, Y. and Shi, X. (1988), *Zhongguo Jiage Jiegou Yanjiu*, (Research on China's Price Structure) Taiyuan: Shanxi People's Publishing House.

Zhao, Haikuan (1979), *Zhonghe Xindai Jihua* (Consolidated Credit Planning) Beijing: China's Finance and Economics Publishing House.

Zhong, Jiefu (1988), *Jihua Guanli Yuanli* (Principles of Planning), Shengyang: Liaoning University Press.

Zhongguo Di Geti He Siying Jingji (ZGGTSYJJ) (China's Individual and Private Enterprises) (1990), Beijing: Reform Publishing House.

Zhongguo Nongcun Zhengce Yanjiu Beiwang Lu (ZGNCZCYJBWL) (Memorandum on China's Rural Policy Research) (1989), Beijing: Agriculture Publishing House.

Zhou, Xiaochuan (1993), 'Reform Sequencing and State Asset Management in China', in P. Harrod *et al.* (eds.) (1993): 125–158.

Zuo, Zongshan (ed.) (1985), *Wujia Zue* (Studies in Commodity Prices), Hefei: Anhei Science and Technology Publishing House.

Index